GOD IS
A GRUNT

GOD IS A GRUNT

AND MORE GOOD NEWS FOR GIs

LOGAN M. ISAAC

New York • Nashville

Worthy Books
Hachette Book Group
1290 Avenue of the Americas
New York, NY 10104
worthybooks.com twitter.com/WorthyPub

First Edition: April 2022

Worthy Books is a division of Hachette Book Group, Inc.

The Worthy Books name and logo are trademarks of Hachette Book Group, Inc.

The publisher is not responsible for websites (or their content) that are not owned by the publisher.

The Hachette Speakers Bureau provides a wide range of authors for speaking events. To find out more, go to www.hachettespeakersbureau.com or call (866) 376-6591.

Library of Congress Cataloging-in-Publication Data has been applied for.

ISBNs: 9781546000501 (hardcover), 9781546000525 (ebook)

Printed in the United States of America

LSC-C

Printing 1, 2022

For the two little pieces of my heart running around,
with prayers that I might help divide their grief, multiply
their joy, and add to their holy mischief. And for
my tango partner, with gratitude for being the answer
to so many of my prayers and for being so much better
than I am at this dance we call life together.

CONTENTS

A NOTE TO READERS

FOR CERTAIN WORDS, YOU WILL SEE A PARENTHETICAL REFERENCE to either a Hebrew (H___) or Greek (G___) word. The number following the "H" or the "G" is its *Strong's Concordance* number, which you can use to look up on any number of online Bible study aids. My favorite is BlueLetterBible.org, but there are lots of options. All references to scripture are from the New Revised Standard Version (NRSV), unless otherwise noted.

When I reference prominent or historical figures by their first names, no disrespect or familiarity is intended. Young soldiers often know only their battle buddies' last names, which appear on uniforms and equipment. By referring to Martin (of Tours or Luther King Jr.), for example, I want to break down the barriers we set up between their holiness and our own. Saints are just as human as soldiers are. By using first names, I hope my readers will feel as I did when I discovered battle buddies for the first time through their unfiltered given names rather than their military rank and family names.

On the other hand, I have omitted the names of some people that I think have behaved in a way they would (or should) regret. In those cases, I refer to their professional titles in recognition of the great responsibility they bear. After all, people can't abuse power they don't possess, and I believe nobody is as bad as their worst mistakes. To be truly human, however, we must own and confess our mistakes. By withholding certain names as I am able, my intent is to point to their status and power rather than to their person. My hope is this will not make repenting of harm they are responsible for any harder. In some cases, as with people who have published books or articles I cite, I cannot avoid naming them.

WHISKEY TANGO FOXTROT
(A PROLOGUE)

WHAT IS A GRUNT?

According to Major H. Gene Duncan, a grunt is "that tired, filthy, thirsty, hungry, footsore, ripped-trouser, camouflage-painted, lean, mean, son a bitch who has kept the wolf away from the door for over two hundred years."[1] Dictionaries are more concise, with *Oxford* defining it as a "low-ranking or unskilled soldier or other worker" and *Merriam-Webster's* as simply "unglamorous." Unlike the latter two, Duncan intended the term to be one of affection and endearment rather than derogatory.

Why do grunts need good news?

If the military suicide rate is any indication, grunts could stand to be reminded that there is reason to live, reason to smile, reason to carry on. As I write this, one soldier and seventeen veterans will take their lives each day, or one every eighty minutes.[2] A lot of ink has been spilled about military suicide as a mental health emergency, but not much has changed. According to the Department of Veterans

Affairs (VA), in 2014 veterans made up 8.5 percent of the population but were responsible for 18 percent of all suicides.[3] The relative change over time has remained steady, from a low of 19 per day in 2001 to a high of 21 in 2011. Since then it has remained "stable" at about 20 per day.[4] "Stable," dependable, unchanging. Like how I get asked if I am thinking of killing myself *every single time* I interact with the VA. With suicide, stability is the problem, not a solution. If we make only minor adjustments to the way we think about military suicide, we celebrate the shit out of minor improvements and take for granted that shit sucks just because.

The United States uses the NATO phonetic alphabet, which assigns a phonetically unique word to each letter of the English alphabet. Alpha, Bravo, Charlie, et cetera. Grunts love their acronyms, and Whiskey Tango Foxtrot (or Fox for short) is WTF in milspeak. Whiskey Tango Fox is that thing in your head right before you do a double take, an unspoken *Am I crazy, or...?* It's more than just a saying; it's a gut feeling that conveys surprise and confusion as well as disgust and offense. I feel it every time I go to the VA, every time I get asked if I am having thoughts of suicide. I'd rather feel pissed off than feel numb; I'd rather feel a lot of something than nothing at all. It's a shitty choice, but it's one that veterans have to make every day.

We need to fundamentally change everything we know about military suicide. If anything, we've talked about it to death. I've got a dark sense of humor, a coping mechanism I acquired during my time in service. Just to see what happens, I've thought about answering in the affirmative when, during literally every interaction I have with the Department of Veterans Affairs, I get asked, "Are you having thoughts of suicide?" It feels like that color-changing DVD logo bouncing around on a blank television screen. You just want to see it hit the corner. Just once, I feel like I should say yes, just to see where that morbid Choose Your Own VA Adventure leads. (Mischief aside, if you're having suicidal thoughts, please call the National Suicide Prevention Lifeline at 800-273-8255 and ask for help.)

When it comes to mental health, my motto is *Illegitimi non carborundum* ("Don't let the bastards get you down"). It's not proper Latin, but neither is "de oppresso liber."[5] Grunts don't have time for propriety. Often they don't have time for emotions either.

SMAD, THE NEW HANGRY

I have cried in public exactly two times. The first was on March 16, 2007, at the National Cathedral in Washington, DC. Celeste Zappala, a cofounder of Gold Star Families for Peace, was speaking about losing her son, Guardsman Sherwood Baker, in April 2004. I had been invited to read a short reflection written by Sergeant Joshua Casteel, a Christian soldier I would later meet and befriend over our interest in theology and Scripture. I learned of Joshua's death, from cancer exacerbated by burn pit exposure, while on tour for my first book. The moment I lost it, when my eyes became firehoses and my face contorted beyond my control, was the moment Celeste said, "A young vet wraps a garden hose around his neck and leaps away from the nightmares that beset him."[6] She was referring to Marine Reservist Jeffrey Lucey, whose suicide was narrated in the first piece of investigative journalism that broke the military suicide story.[7]

The second time I cried in public was on June 15, 2016, in the Wilson Recreation Center at Duke University in front of a world-renowned theologian (along with everyone there just trying to get a workout in at the gym). I'll get to it in a moment, but first I need to explain a little about how I got there. My three years as a student veteran there had sucked, but I chalked it up to being older and more experienced than most students. What I once shrugged off as isolated incidents eventually proved to be systemic. My concerns weren't even the tip of the iceberg; I discovered that a string of vets had voiced their concerns and were ignored or got in trouble. One Duke student veteran, Alex Ney, had even served in the same battalion as me at Fort Bragg after 9/11. But two years before I got to Duke, in April 2008, Alex took his own life in the middle of a PhD program, leaving behind a spouse and two-year-old child.[8] Learning of Alex's death didn't make me cry; it made me angry.

Men, especially those of us in or from the military, are not taught the difference between sadness and anger, so we often conflate the two. We won't readily admit we're sad, because it's a sign of weakness. Being mad doesn't have the same stigma, but it can also be unwelcome. Just like "hangry" is a mix of hunger and anger, "smad" is when we're somewhere between sad and mad. It's the abbreviated version of "I'm not crying; you're crying."

Dr. Ryan Martin, a research psychologist at the University of Wisconsin-Green Bay, says that "anger is a natural reaction to unfairness."[9] When kids angrily bark out that something isn't fair, they are disappointed in not getting something they want. That disappointment is expressed as anger, but it might be sadness in disguise. Parents often tell their kids that "life's not fair," code for "Shut the fuck up and drive on." As I'll go over in the first chapter, God creates a world that is good, a universe that "bends toward justice," as Martin Luther King Jr. observed.[10] It would be more accurate to say that *people* are unfair, and life is whatever you make it. Some things are not fair, and some of the things we want are good, like justice. Sometimes the statement "It's not fair" issues not from a place of entitlement but from a place of oppression.

We might feel both sadness and anger in response to injustice, and when we do it can be hard to tell the two emotions apart. When one of my kids is in danger, I react hastily with what looks like anger. They see anger and think they have done something wrong, so I need to explain to them that I reacted out of *fear*: fear of the grief I would feel if they were seriously hurt or killed. They know that anger is related to justice, but we need to be able to tell the difference between entitled anger (I did not get the thing I want) and righteous anger (the thing I want is justice).

Before #MeToo propelled assault, harassment, and discrimination to national headlines, I had been trained to listen for and report behavior that might violate civil rights. As one of two codirectors of the Divinity School Women's Center at Duke University in 2013, I had a responsibility to be familiar with the institutional channels available for assault survivors to report crimes that deprived them of their civil rights. Using my privilege to advocate for others was second nature to me after my time in combat. In January 2005, I watched as an Iraqi soldier took a grenade to the chest while protecting a voting center in downtown Mosul. After the platoon medic and I patched him up as best we could, battalion medics arrived to take him to a US facility for treatment. As they lifted the stretcher to load him into the aid truck, he raised his thumb in the air. To this day, I still have no idea if he did it to signal that he was okay and to thank us for our help, or if he raised his right thumb because it was the one stained in ink, signifying he had already exercised the right that terrorists were trying to take away from him and others.

I'm not crying; you're crying!

I am ready to die for civil rights like voting, equal opportunity, and freedoms of expression and worship. But the same culture that taught me not to cry also taught me that I could take anything the world threw at me, that I *could* shut the fuck up and drive on. That's the double-edged sword of resilience—either too much or too little can kill you. I knew what bias, harassment, and discrimination looked like when it was being done to other people. It took years to name it when it was happening to me. God forbid I should have to protect myself, to stand up and do something when the dude in distress was me.

As a student veteran in seminary, I had dismissed bad experiences as misfortune, as though I and other veterans had a bad experience just by chance. It was common for student veterans to hear from classmates, a decade younger than them, that military service was evil or to get side-eyed when they mentioned their service.[11] It was only slightly less common to get the same treatment from professors.[12] It was not just a Christianity issue, it was an institution-wide problem.

For the last day of classes (LDOC) in April 2012, undergrads paraded around campus in T-shirts adorned with cartoon bombs that read "The End Is Near." The formal withdrawal of troops from Iraq had occurred just six months prior on December 18, 2011. My phone buzzed in my pocket all day from other vets expressing their smadness at the privilege of kids these days. Sometimes, however, the implicit bias was light on the implicit and heavy on the bias. Like when I got an official government email asking my help in getting qualified, high-speed enlisted Marines to apply to Duke through the Marine Leadership Scholar Program. The email dropped the names of three general-grade Marine officers and Duke alumni who supported the program and wanted to see it succeed, but for years the undergraduate dean of admissions never returned calls or replied to (usmc.mil) emails.[13] One month after my bringing this to the administration's attention, that same dean was reappointed to a second five-year term.[14] There is a lot more, but the worst was before even all that.

While I was still a student, I caught wind of a Duke student veteran who had died before I arrived. I approached the university president as he walked to his Jaguar one day on my way to the bus, asking if he could help me find support to improve resources for veterans, both students and staff. He absentmindedly gave me a name, the vice president for student affairs, after muttering, "So sad, that veteran a few years ago…" It took years to figure out whiskey tango fox he was talking about, and I think finding out was what broke me.

THIS IS DUKE

Alexander Ney was an artilleryman, like me, but an officer. From what I could find out through public records and a few emails from people he knew, we were also both paratroopers at Fort Bragg for a few overlapping months. We weren't in the same battery, the artillery equivalent to an infantry company, but we almost certainly crossed paths. I reenlisted to go to Schofield Barracks in December 2002, and he deployed to Kuwait for the invasion of Iraq in January 2003.

The guys I kept in touch with after I left didn't have many good things to say about the first year of combat operations in Iraq. They came home in early 2004, as my deployment began, and Alex was discharged as a captain in time to start a PhD program in molecular cancer biology at Duke by the fall semester of 2005. Late in the evening of Wednesday, April 16, 2008, during his third year of studies, he was found dead at his home in East Durham. Arlington National Cemetery is his final resting place, not far from his hometown of Washington, DC.

I'm not crying. *Are you?*

"This is Duke" used to be a central branding message for the university, emblazoned on everything from webpages to T-shirts. It's hard to find nowadays, maybe because it is ripe for appropriation by naysayers (and truth-speakers).[15] "This is Duke" is about perspective; whose Duke? My experience of Duke as a student veteran was filled with bias, harassment, and discrimination. It wasn't called that, not even by me, at least not until I reached my breaking point. Duke may have been a great experience for some, but for a lot of veterans it was anything but. We're just accustomed to keeping quiet and being kept quiet.

When a student died unexpectedly at Duke, on campus or off, undergrad or graduate, the senior vice president of student affairs would distribute campus-wide statements. In two weekday examples in 2007 and 2010, statements went out the same day. In a particularly tragic weekend in September 2014, two deaths occurred with a statement the following Monday. In Alex's case, the only statement I could find was published four days after his death, on April 20, giving students less than twenty-four hours' notice before a memorial service at Duke University Chapel and offering no resources for grieving students, veteran or otherwise, in need of counseling or psychiatric services.[16] Among the incidents I found, he was the only veteran. Military communities can take it, though, right? Shut the fuck up and drive on.

The way veterans are treated is not fair. It's not that we want something we should not expect; it's that we deserve human dignity and we are denied it. Don't mistake injustice for entitlement, especially with military families who give so much and ask so little.

I'm not crying anymore. What good does it do?

The week before I found myself at the Wilson Recreation Center, I had filed a complaint with Duke's Office for Institutional Equity (OIE). I had swallowed my pride and asked for help, something that felt foreign to me as a combat-hardened grunt. After the registrar had assigned me the only evening section with half the number of students as other teaching assistants, I felt like I was not trusted with students despite my two years of teaching experience at Methodist University. I might have shrugged it off, but I had a child on the way and I was not going to miss the bedtime routine as a new father. So I scheduled a meeting with the dean of the Divinity School as the OIE-designated equal employment opportunity (EEO) representative.

We met on February 29, 2016, one hour after OIE hosted an optional implicit bias workshop for Divinity staff and faculty. The dean seemed surprised there were evening sections at all, and agreed it was odd to not distribute the number of students equally among teaching assistants. Discussion also fell to veterans in academia, and I pointed out there were no veterans on faculty at the Divinity School despite it being a favored seminary for military chaplains. The dean suggested I speak with the only member of the Divinity School staff she knew had served. Not faculty, but rather a fund-raiser, the dean of external relations (DER).

Behind closed doors, he asked me to share with him what my experiences were, because his were so different. I told him about Alex and gave him a laundry list of grievances I'd compiled from several student veterans, most of whom asked to remain anonymous. He seemed surprised at the details I provided him, and to this day, I believe his suggestion that he only ever encountered puppies and sunshine. Hell, his whole raison d'être was to keep the money coming by making funders happy. Emotional malnourishment was written into the job description. So *of course* he filtered the exchange through his toxic positivity cheese grater. He acknowledged that the Divinity School was "not as positive as it should be" and later told a compliance officer of the Department of Labor that I was "unhappy with veteran treatment."[17] Smad, unhappy, what's the difference?

A couple of weeks later I got an email from the DER with the subject line "Veterans Issues," telling me he had convened a meeting "to discuss how we can improve the environment for veteran and active duty students."[18] When I asked if any students or employed veterans were at the meeting, he claimed he "met with" two people, who denied his account of events. But the kicker was that he "shared the affirmative action plan for veterans with our HR office." The closest thing to a Divinity School "HR office," to my knowledge, was the registrar who hired me.

Reporting workplace impropriety is hard because retaliation is always a possibility. I'll never know why I got fewer students than my peers or why I was chosen to lead an evening precept, but I would later learn the registrar was unaware I had teaching experience, meaning she never read my résumé. The DER's email suggested she had now been put on alert that someone was talking about affirmative action. That someone was probably a veteran... and an employee...Sure enough, contracts for the fall semester went out a month later and I wasn't offered one.

Between the DER, the registrar, and the bias I had documented, I finally sucked it up and filed a complaint. I was done playing by whatever rules I was expected to, fed up with the failures of either self-interested people or brand-loyal administrators to do the right thing. It started with Alex Ney, a battle buddy I had never met but whom I could have fought beside. He had fallen, and I couldn't leave his memory behind. I still can't. Back to my sob story.

The first time I met with OIE was the day after sending an email to a professor with a penchant for dehumanizing Christian soldiers. My first academic adviser at Duke was a prolific academic whose scholarship focused on virtue ethics until 9/11, when it veered in the direction of theological punch lines and punditry. I began working toward my first theology degree interested in thinking about character and military service. There's probably an alternate-reality version of me who got to pursue that path, but when I got to Duke what I *wanted* to do was overshadowed by what I felt I *needed* to do, which was to combat bad theology based on antimilitary bias in the church. When I noticed the adviser's habit of conflating political decisions with the cannon fodder of those who carried them out, I pointed out that his cavalier commentary "does not reflect the high standard expected of serious scholars and it demeans the morally complex perspective of Christians struggling with what it means to serve."[19]

The meeting at Wilson was a follow-up to this exchange. My memory is foggy, but I do recall that he was already there when I arrived, at a table by a smoothie vendor. I remember my chest was shivering, like the time I sat in the National Cathedral as my eyes leaked and my face convulsed. I've since recognized it as a symptom of combat stress; it happens when I am vulnerable, when I enter difficult spiritual territory. He let me start, so I explained how his comments were increasingly harmful and ignorant. The first words out of his mouth in reply were "Who are *you* to judge *me*?" I listened for a while, not because anything he said was worth hearing, but because I was frozen in place, tears slowly tumbling down my face.

I never would have met with OIE had I not reached my breaking point. The thing with my old adviser was one of a thousand paper cuts that were slowly killing me and my battle buddies.

FIRE, LITE

If you had asked me what emotion I was feeling that day in the rec center, I wouldn't have said I was crying because I was sad; I would have said it was because I was tired. Or, as Fannie Lou Hamer put it, "sick and tired of being sick and tired."[20] The truth is that I was mad, but I couldn't show it. Anger is a natural response to injustice, even if you are the one responsible for it. When that's the case, anger is easy to weaponize: "I haven't done anything wrong; he's just an angry veteran." But sadness can also put veterans in a box they don't deserve to be in, and it's a well-worn box. For some, it can become a coffin.

Not long after I got out of the military, I was attending an antiwar demonstration where a young man, a newly minted veteran, was surrounded by cameras as he bawled his eyes out. I had no idea what he was talking about, but I can guess it had something to do with unresolved combat stress. People love a sob story, especially when it comes from "the troops" everybody claims to support. The problem with soldier sob stories is that they feed a civilian savior complex, the hope we have of being able to save/help/fix/repair veterans. The widely held assumption that military families need saving affirms the widely held belief that grunts are broken, war-weary, damaged goods. It might show vulnerability for a veteran to cry, but it might also be a mask for other emotions he or she isn't allowed to express. Like anger.

That complaint I filed snowballed fast, and I got a lot of heat from administrators, faculty, even friends and fellow vets. Somewhere in there, someone told me I was "all heat, no light." What they meant was that I was making people angry, getting all "fire and brimstone," but not giving anyone any hope. Old Testament scholar Walter Brueggemann wrote that the prophetic task must balance criticism with hope, and from outside appearances I was all criticism and no hope. I think the inverse was true, that Christians expect all light and no heat. Why else do you think services for Easter are so much more well attended than those for Good Friday? We want rainbows and puppies, but we don't want the rain or to have to pick up dog poop. In prophetic literature there's a recurring theme of a refining fire that tests us "as gold is tested" (Zech. 13:9) and that "will smelt away [our] dross" (Isa. 1:25). What good is the light *without* heat?

It's easy to look at someone crying out on account of injustice, saying something isn't fair, and accuse them of being an entitled little shit. But what if, and hear me out on this, something is *actually* unfair? What if military suicide is not so much about the internal mental health of soldiers and veterans as the human dignity they are denied by civilian society? What if the responsibility to change or improve isn't on military families, what if soldiers and veterans aren't the ones who are entitled? I understand if sometimes we can't take the heat, if we need "fire, lite" instead of fire and light. I know it can be hard to see anger (I have kids, remember?). At some point we need to put an end to childish fragility and face the things we have done and failed to do.

WHO AM I (TO JUDGE)?

One of the things I think Christianity has failed to do for a long time is to treat grunts fairly, in Scripture and in tradition. I identify myself as an author because writers are artisans. It takes discipline and practice to "write." Authors, on the other hand, are made by chance, and my writing is a product of circumstance rather than design. I wrote my first book, *Reborn on the Fourth of July*, because I saw a crack that battle buddies were falling through. I wrote an autobiography because I couldn't find books that treated military service and Christian faith with intellectual and scriptural integrity. Autobiographies are easy; your story belongs to you, and nobody can tell you otherwise. My second book, *For God and Country (in That Order)*, was written shortly thereafter and profiles nearly fifty Christian soldiers who defied the false dichotomy between pacifist and patriot, Democrat and Republican, or Progressive and Conservative. I never wanted to write; I wanted to teach. But blowing the whistle on a powerful institution like Duke made that difficult.

The more people tried to fit me in their box, the more I stubbornly refused to suck it up and drive on with my humanity in tatters. Close friends questioned my well-being, asking, "How much longer will you fight this? When is enough enough?" When I went over to see the founding pastor of a house church my family had attended, a man who also worked in the Duke administration, he said he felt threatened because I came to his house with a six-pack of beer. His wife, a mental health professional, came to the door to say, "You're crazy...everything you touch turns bad." I won't lie, that one hit a nerve. So, I walked out of the gentrified part of the neighborhood to the Section 8 area, where my battle buddy for life, Jeremy Stainthorp-Berggren, lived. Before I got the whole story out, he started laughing. Maybe I would have cried, I don't know, but vets are fucking crazy like that. We laugh at weird shit. When we caught our breath he said, about my being crazy, "Well, she's not *wrong*." He was right. She wasn't.

God Is a Grunt was born in the fire-and-brimstone shower I got caught in leaving Duke. Eventually, I became a father and had a lot of time to read as I lay next to the crib waiting to low crawl away so the babies wouldn't freak out. As a stay-at-home dad I read voraciously. Combat taught me that nothing is a waste if you learn from it. I revisited my second master's thesis, "Theology in the Crosshairs: Toward a Martial Hermeneutic," in which I tried to map out my Christian faith with the human dignity of soldiers and veterans in mind. When I turned it in, one grader remarked that it was "too broad" and "too informal." That's precisely what happens when we overlook so much material for so long; the longer you hold your pee, the more you'll go and the messier it will be when you finally hit the head.

There is a gaping hole in theology and culture that my battle buddies are falling through. Eighteen lives a day is eighteen too many. This book is about ripping open packs of gauze and shoving them into the sucking chest wound that is military suicide. I don't try to hide the anger and sadness that birthed this book because time is a luxury my battle buddies don't have. Dr. Ryan Martin, the anger management psychologist, closes by saying, "We *should* be mad when we're truly treated unfairly…Were you treated unfairly? Then get mad and let's do something about it."

I'll drink to that.

INTRO:
MILITARY 101

I SUPPORT THE TROOPS" MAY BE POPULAR, BUT IT ISN'T HELPFUL. Before we get into the good news for grunts, we need to go over some basic terminology.[1]

"MILITARY"

In the widest sense, the military includes everyone currently or formerly obliged to public service as well as their families. Historically, military forces have protected the social order from internal threats like crime (police) and natural disasters (fire, medical), not from just external threats. It would be more historically coherent to think of the "military" as any service that maintains and protects a country, not just armies and navies. Besides, every able-bodied adult male could be called upon to serve in most societies, so there was not always the distinction between civilian and soldier that we have today. In the interest of brevity, however, I will use the term "military" to refer to servicemembers, veterans, and their dependents in this book. Not as inclusive as I think is prudent, but more inclusive than most Americans probably imagine.

Within even that more restrictive sense, of a military being armies and navies, there are still important distinctions that are needlessly flattened together. Since 1903, when state militias were federalized and removed from the exclusive command of state governors, thirteen armed service branches have been created, comprising the Total Force. There are the five main branches (by age: Army, Navy, Marine Corps, Coast Guard, and Air Force); their five reserve components; Space Force; and two National Guard branches (Army and Air). Although the word "active" gets thrown around a lot, Reservists and Guardsmen *are* "active" servicemembers, though they do not report for duty with the same frequency as the rest do. These distinctions are influential for those who serve, and there is a kind of hierarchy, both social and moral, that should not be overlooked.

"SOLDIER"

The different branches have their own unique cultures, even if they all are bound together by one mission: to defend the Constitution from foreign and domestic threats. As members of an armed force, they all are soldiers in the generic sense, and this is the definition I will use most frequently through this book. Military communities will recognize the need to point this out because all members of the Army, Army Reserves, and Army National Guard are referred to as Soldiers, a proper noun.[2] This can lead to some interesting paradoxes, like the fact that every servicemember is a soldier, but not every servicemember is a Soldier. You can count on me almost exclusively using the generic sense of the word "soldier" in this book.

The camaraderie between the many branches includes a kind of sibling rivalry in which each branch has their caricatured reputation: Airmen are intelligent but pampered; Sailors are squared away but slutty; Marines are loyal but stupid; Soldiers are down to earth but ineffective. But just like anything fun, there is a danger in overhyping the differences between branches, as though these caricatures are binding. Or as though the branches and their members are not all coequal.

Branch distinction fades after discharge, and veterans are often clumped together into one. Just like there is a distinction between soldier and Soldier, there is also a distinction between veteran and Veteran. The former is any prior member of an armed service branch, but the latter is a legal status withheld from former soldiers issued a dishonorable discharge. According to federal law, a Veteran is a soldier "who was discharged or released…under conditions other than dishonorable."[3] In other words, some veterans are denied the rights and benefits guaranteed by military service.

Hierarchy is a formal legal element of military service as well as an informal and social part of service (Soldiers and Marines are looked up to more than Airmen and Sailors, for example). Climbing the social ladder is not just about rank or time in service; it is about combat deployment and exposure to enemy fire. Tactical air control party (TAC-P) specialists, Airmen who deploy with frontline units to assist in arranging Air Force assets, socially outrank a Marine supply clerk. A cook with a Combat Action Badge is going to turn more heads than a field grade officer in Financial Affairs. The closer a soldier is to "the shit," the more credibility they possess. And nobody is closer to combat more regularly than grunts.

"GRUNT"

When I was in the Army, the definition of a grunt had a specific scope: any lower enlisted infantry soldier, military occupational specialty (MOS) 11B or 11C. It could not be used to describe every person with an eleven series MOS, because anyone with rank, like noncommissioned officers, lost the designation. Infantry commanders, MOS 11A, were similarly disqualified. As a forward observer for the artillery, MOS 13F, I was technically not a grunt even though I lived, ate, slept, shit, shaved, showered, and got shot at as part of my infantry platoon.

Forward observers, "FOs" for short, were the runts of infantry platoons, the tolerated nonmembers of an otherwise close-knit family. The main difference between an FO and a grunt was that the FOs carried more equipment and had higher test scores. Depending who you ask, I either *was* a grunt because I was a low-ranking infantry platoon member, or I was *not* a grunt because I was not an 11B or 11C.

A grunt is paradoxical, representing a mythological status that everyone wants to claim but nobody wants to inhabit. Although grunts are at the bottom of the *formal* hierarchy, they are at the top of the *social* hierarchy. Grunts are at the bottom of the heap, the lowest rung of the ladder. Grunts are also closest to the front lines in conventional warfare, and thus they are the ones who do most of the killing and the dying in battle. There's a perverted kind of social reward system for the guys catching all the shit as it rolls downhill: "You ain't shit unless you've taken shit." Grunts love to be at the bottom so they can look up their noses at POGs, any persons other than grunts.

Don't get me wrong, I'm flattered when civilians think I'm no different than an 11B. But most civilians don't know shit about soldiers. A couple of generations of cultural polarization have forced military personnel into an impossible choice: either love your armed service or hate it. The church exacerbates the military-civil divide by moralizing civilian bias, either villainizing or venerating soldiers en masse, assigning both guilt and glory by association.

The problem with this thinking is that it is not true. Few soldiers ever kill, and most military service is morally neutral. According to a 2010 study, the United States employed fewer combat specialties than the global average for developed nations.[4] Nonetheless, many Americans think the military is little more than a hammer looking for nails to pound. The image persists because soldiers have become instruments in the minds of most Americans.[5] Soldiers are humans, not hammers, and we should be treated that way. So long as soldiers are viewed in binary terms, as either heroes or monsters, we will never be seen as fully human. When people are deprived of their humanity, that's when things go bad and when bad becomes routine. Military suicide is no longer headline news because it has become so commonplace, a painfully poignant affirmation of Hannah Arendt's notion of the banality of evil.

A central feature of grunts is their quiet obedience; the very name evokes a guttural affirmation to barked orders. Grunting may as well be synonymous with silence, and therein lies the problem. Speaking up goes against everything enlisted soldiers are taught in basic training, which is all about conforming to survive. When grunts are expected to shut the fuck up and drive on, we will dutifully close our mouths and open our wrists. This is that time Martin Luther King Jr. spoke of in his controversial speech against the war in Vietnam: "when silence is betrayal."

Pastors and theologians treat soldiers and veterans as though the verdict is already in, as though their knowledge of military service is sufficient. The time has come to sound off, to grunt. It's good news that Jesus didn't come to give orders, but to empty himself, taking the form of a grunt, obedient to the point of death. If this is the model of Christian leadership, then it is especially good news for military families, which have been at the center of the Christian faith for thousands of years. If that's news to anyone, I hope this book helps set the record straight.

PART 1

SCRIPTURE

1.

WHAT HAVE WE DONE?
CAIN AND MORAL GUILT

I DID NOT REALIZE IT AT THE TIME, BUT WHEN I CAME HOME FROM
a yearlong combat deployment to Iraq in 2005, I needed to process what I had experienced. In the flurry of emotions that came in the wake of war, I opted instead to busy myself with my old habits and ignore the many feelings I had about my time on the battlefield. I needed to sort the good from the bad in what I had done, which, as a forward observer for the artillery, involved a lot of death and destruction. I had been trained on the *mechanics* of killing, how to do it, but nobody had ever prompted me to consider its morality and effects, why and when such violence might be justified. The Question of Killing should be about why and when, not only about how. Unfortunately, it was treated as one-dimensional, a simple formula for mission success: kill more of theirs than they kill of ours.

Reality is always much more complicated. Formulaic ways of thinking are pervasive, and soldiers and veterans have plenty of stories involving friends, family, and strangers so eager to hear whether they have killed anyone that it is the first question asked. Morbid curiosity has boiled down the Question of Killing to a "Have you done it?," placing the moral weight squarely upon the shoulders of soldiers. After civilians hear a yes or no answer, they move on, the "All Soldiers Kill" assumption confirmed. Besides making an ASS of U and ME (get it?), these assumptions rely on and perpetuate stereotypes and dehumanize our men and women in uniform.

TYPES AND TROPES

The word "stereotype" comes from the world of printing. It used to be that individual letters on small metal cubes had to be placed one by one in rows on a wooden shelflike contraption called a "chase," which would be slathered in ink and pressed to the paper to create one side of a page. Hundreds of chases were used to create copies of books, and then they were deconstructed when printing was done. If publishers underestimated a book's demand, then each chase would have to be typeset all over again.

Stereotyping allowed publishers to avoid the headache of reconstructing chases for popular books by making a more permanent way to ink pages in mass quantities. Instead of chases being made up of metal cubes representing individual letters, the whole page was cast as a single piece of metal. This convenience came at a cost, however, because no changes could be made after the stereotype was cast. For this reason, "stereotype" came to mean something that was repeated over and over again, from *stereos* (G4731), a Greek word meaning "fixed or unchanging."

A **stereotype** is cultural shorthand, a way of referring to something quickly without much detail. Stereotypes can be either good or bad, depending on how they're used, such as the stereotype that associates the ethnicity of a man with the size of his penis. If you're Black, this stereotype might benefit you; if you're Asian, maybe not so much. True or false, good or bad, stereotypes are a way to abbreviate our beliefs about ourselves and others in order to make sense of our lives. But they aren't the only way this happens.

Another Greek word, *typos* (G5179), means "example, impression, or mold." **Archetypes** are the originally intended version of a thing, what someone had in mind when the thing was first dreamed up. They outline our expectations; they rarely exist outside our own minds. In philosophy, they are not just how a thing was thought up, but also the perfect form to which a thing aspires to be. In this sense, Jesus is the archetype for humanity—a perfectly conceived human and the type of person Christians, at least, aspire to be. An archetype is about what a thing should be, based on its created purpose. Purpose and origin are important.

A **prototype**, on the other hand, is the first real-world attempt at a thing. Creation, to borrow a tech metaphor, is God's operating system, the underlying structure within which individual applications function. God spends six days creating at the beginning of Genesis, with each day concluding with the observation that what was made was *tov* (good, H2896): light (v. 4); earth and seas (v. 10); vegetation (v. 12); the sun, moon, and stars (v. 18); air and sea creatures (v. 21); and finally, creatures of the land (v. 25). Last but not least comes creation's flagship app, programmed with God's own *tselem* (H6754), or reflection. The Bible refers to God's prototype for humanity as *adam* (H120), a shortened version of *adamah* (H127), a feminine noun meaning "dirt or mud." We might call this person Clay, because that's what they are made of. Clay, *adam*, is Humanity 1.0 and the youngest of "the generations of the heavens and the earth" (Gen. 2:4). It is only after creating the first human that the whole ecosystem, operating system and apps alike, is called *me'od tov*, "very good" (Gen. 1:31).

If you remember one thing from this entire book, let it be this: You are good. You are good, full stop. Soldier or civilian, saint or sinner, grunt or POG, believer or atheist:

You

Are

Good

Let that sink in. Everything is created good. This is what is meant when theologians talk about human dignity, that God's likeness is fundamental to humanity, it cannot be degraded, only obscured. In the language of the Declaration of Independence, human dignity is "inalienable"; it is irrevocable and untouchable. If anyone tries to convince you that you are not good, tell them they're full of shit. If they are Christians, tell them to read their Bible.

The thing that violates creation's good design isn't *evil*, it's isolation. In Genesis 2:18, God says, "It is not *tov* that *adam* should be *bad* (H905)." The Hebrew word *bad* comes from *badad* (H909), which Isaiah 14:31 uses to evoke the imagery of a military deserter. It is not that evil is okay, but Genesis is careful to contrast goodness with alienation. Two things are written into the source code of creation: goodness and togetherness. According to Genesis, everyone needs a battle buddy, and that's where the second human comes in. Eve is Humanity 2.0, a little bit better but still not ideal. A prototype is always improving. Imperfect, but good.

Types of all kinds provide simplistic, two-dimensional ways of deriving meaning and sense from a sea of information and experiences. Would civilians spend money to watch the latest war films if Hollywood balanced out fight scenes by showing how much soldiers play video games and rub one out on deployment? Okay, maybe some would. But my point is that reality doesn't sell, it's too complicated. The value of types is in their brevity and lack of nuance; they rely on collective assumptions to move the story quickly and dramatically.

Stereotypes in media are called tropes, from the Greek *tropos*, meaning "a turn or pivot." Tropes shift our attention away from reality to embellishment, from complexity to simplicity. Storytellers use tropes as placeholders so the more important elements of a story can shine forth. Character tropes are figures in a story whose main purpose is to support the main character or message. The "redshirts" of *Star Trek* are a great example, whose narrative function is direct attention to Kirk and Spock. Like cannon fodder and bullet magnets, they act as little more than props; necessary, sure, but disposable. There is no dignity in being a prop. They usually don't even get a name; rather, they get monikers like grunts, GIs, or "the troops."

TROPES OR TROOPS

Stereotypes say more about the people who hold them than they do about the people they depict. When the Second World War came to an end, soldiers were welcomed home as the Victor. Never mind that the first war was supposedly the one "to end all wars"; who doesn't like a reason to celebrate? That changed a generation later when Vietnam veterans were attacked as the Villain. Never mind that the vast majority were drafted against their will, fuck those baby-killers! A little collective guilt over time, some overcorrection, and now we pity them as the Victim. Never mind that our wars never end. Cheap gas forever!

In reality, military service is always more complicated than we want to believe, no matter how many times we try to tell formulaic stories. Believe it or not, there are WWII veterans who hated *Saving Private Ryan* and there are Vietnam veterans who didn't kill a single baby. There are even Iraq and Afghanistan veterans who don't like being thanked for their service. I know; crazy, right? As a wise veteran once told me, "If you've met one vet, you've met one vet."[1]

Sometimes that doesn't matter, and shitty stories gain popularity because they make audiences feel better about themselves. Because soldiers and veterans are a demographic minority, the human dignity of military communities will never, on its own, outweigh civilian interests and desires. That is why the crisis of military suicide is framed through the lens of civilians coming to the rescue of soldiers and veterans.

Toward the end of my studies, I was contacted by *Christianity Today* asking for my permission to be photographed in connection with an article on an academic adviser of mine. The design director wrote, "One of the goals of photographing you is to show the toll of war and moral injury." She suggested I wear my old uniform and explained that editorial wanted my "face to speak to the pain of PTSD…to potentially allude to the darkness of the disorder." I had reservations about the preconceived notions she had but I supported the work my adviser was doing, especially because I'd had a hand in shaping it. An early draft of the article made clear that I and other veterans had shifted his thinking substantially, that it was *us* who had helped *him*.

After the photo shoot, I got radio silence. Then I saw the editorial director's Instagram feed featuring an image of a *Christianity Today* magazine with my face on it.[2] Scrawled across the cover in big, broken capital letters was the issue's title: "WAR TORN: How a Psychiatrist—and the Church—Are Deploying Hope to Soul Scarred Veterans." The feature article was not a carefully presented story about veterans helping other Christians; it was validation for civilians who patted themselves on the back for helping damaged-goods veterans.

A handful of other student veterans had been named and appeared in photographs as well. One said in an email, "I refuse to be categorized as the world wishes to see me (us)…I just want to walk away from all this." I couldn't walk away as easily; my face was on hundreds of thousands of print covers that went out to millions of Christians across the nation.

Another enlisted veteran from the story wrote a Letter to the Editor criticizing the editorial choices made by *Christianity Today*, but it couldn't be published in print until three months later.[3] In it, he described working as a combat journalist after being discharged from the Navy. Soldiers he was embedded with turned their backs on him because they didn't trust journalists, even those who had served. "They had made the mistake before," he wrote, "of trusting journalists to tell their story, only to be villainized." Recognizing war tropes, he went on to observe "CT's headline and cover treatment casts veterans as helpless victims."

Society rationalizes prejudice through totalizing stereotypes. We try to categorize things we do not understand, and our categories are not always accurate. There *are* things done in combat that are wrong, but that does not make anyone a Villain. Even those evils that we truly believe are necessary should not define us, as though we are only as good as our worst mistake. Likewise, there are things done in combat that are right and good, but to paint in such broad strokes that all soldiers become heroic Victors is equally misguided. As for being a Victim, I never saw myself as "war-torn" until a handful of civilian strangers told the Church that I was, and that psychiatry was there to save me. Who needs Jesus when you have a prescription pad?

We won't get rid of stereotypes, but we can reduce the harm they cause by challenging inaccuracies. One way to do that is through what philosopher Hilde Lindemann Nelson of Michigan State University calls counterstories, narratives *of* the military and *by* the military that normalize soldiers and veterans.[4] The church has plenty of these stories, and I continue to highlight as many as I can.[5] Another way is to expose the harmful stories for what they are, have a little laugh at their expense, and show them you are not going to take this shit lying down.

Things with *Christianity Today* got worked out in the short term; they gave me the remaining print copies with my face on them, and editors altered the online version based on our feedback. They even paid a few of us to edit and write an original web series called *Ponder Christian Soldiers*.[6] I was disappointed, but glad we got the opportunity to say our piece. That was until I found out that the original print cover was being used on a paywall to solicit subscriptions.

When I asked them to either remove or change the image, they resisted. They even got their lawyers involved. So, I decided to have a little fun with other tropes that Christians of the past have used to minimize and demean groups they sought to save. It was once common to applaud doctors for diagnosing tempestuous women with "Hysteria," missionaries for civilizing "Savage" Native Americans, and social workers for stopping "Profile Queens." I worked up three fictional covers and linked them together on Twitter with the hashtag #ChristianityYesterday, since the organization had forgotten the lessons learned about reducing human beings to caricatures.[7]

The All Soldiers Kill (ASK) stereotype deprives the Question of Killing of any meaningful depth. Until we can get away from the stereotype, the Question of Killing will never amount to much more than "Did you kill anyone?" Stereotypes persist because they *feel* true to enough people; ASK feels true, and killing is bad, so all soldiers must be (or feel) bad because they kill. But the reality is that *not* All Soldiers Kill, so civilians shouldn't.

(NOT) ALL SOLDIERS KILL...SO DON'T ASK

Imagine someone not drinking from the ASK tap, someone who knows there are a bunch of other things that soldiers do, things that modern war calls for, other than kill. What might be the first thing they say to a returning servicemember? Welcome home! How was your deployment? How much money did you put away? In a world where not all soldiers kill, why would a person ask a returning soldier if they did? Civilians can stop the ASK stereotype by not asking soldiers if they have killed, because the vast majority have not.

An army composed entirely of infantry would lose every war it entered; that's why militaries must balance something called the Tooth to Tail Ratio. The Tooth is combat arms specialties like infantry, artillery, cavalry/armor, attack aviation, combat engineers, and special forces. In between Tooth and Tail are combat support jobs like communication, intelligence, transport, and military police. The Tail comprises service and support occupations like ordnance, finance, legal, supply, and medical. According to a 2010 report that examined the militaries of thirty developed nations, the global average ratio was 63 percent Tail, or 3 support personnel to 1 combatant.[8] In other words, most armed forces are majority Tail rather than Tooth. The United States had the second-largest Tail at 77 percent, second only to Switzerland.

There are three times more fobbits[9] than there are grunts, but that didn't stop drill sergeants at Fort Sill, Oklahoma, from screaming that "everyone is an infantryman first" every chance they got. Their point was that every soldier, Tooth and Tail alike, had to be prepared without warning for frontline combat. But an emphasis on trigger pullers creates the impression that the essential quality of soldiers is the ability to kill. ASK creates a positive association with killing, inflating the egos of those who have and belittling those who have not.

A battle buddy of mine that I've known for over a decade reminds me whenever we talk about our service that my experiences are more important because I was an Army artilleryman, and he was an Air Force cadet. I always remind him that his experiences are just as valid as mine, that I don't outrank him at all. Unfortunately, his sentiment is the rule rather than the exception, and the military is filled with veterans who think they don't count. When these soldiers get ASKed, they feel inadequate because they haven't killed, were never deployed, chose the wrong branch…the list goes on. Those feelings multiply the many and varied circumstances that can lead to suicide because of the association of killing with credibility.

We have more to lose from the All Soldiers Kill stereotype than we stand to gain. But it's what we have, so let's return to Genesis and see what it has to say about the first person who killed.

KILLER AND CONFESSOR

Another way to translate *typos* is as a figure or mark formed by a blow or impression. Not just letters left by an inked chase on fresh paper, but also the impression left by God upon Cain. Some people see Cain as nothing more than his mark, just a typical killer. But this is not what Genesis 32 says.

The impulse to typecast Cain as an unrepentant killer, the embodiment of pure evil, has a long track record. First John 3:12 suggests that Cain was "from the evil one," and an early theologian referred to him as "the devil's seed."[10] The logic goes like this: if killing is bad, then Cain is bad because he killed.

This can hardly be further from the truth, and Genesis suggests that the mark is less for Cain than it is for everyone else. In Genesis 1:14, the lights in the sky are "signs" (*ot*, H122; and *semeion*, G4592), the same word later applied to Cain in Genesis 4:15. If the earlier use is any indication, whatever appears on or through Cain is for our collective benefit rather than for his own. Like the signs in the sky that mark seasons, days, and years, Cain's sign marks some kind of transition.

Genesis 4:1 contains zero evidence that the devil had anything to do with creating Cain. Remember, Genesis emphasizes that if you are human, then you are *tov*, good. As the first child, Cain inherited this goodness from his parents. The transition Cain "marks" for the watching world is from Humanity 2.0 to Humanity 2.1, a little bit better than his parents, but not a huge upgrade. To see what Cain's story is trying to tell us, we have to understand how he is an improvement over his parents rather than a setback.

In the Garden of Eden, there was only one rule: ignorance is bliss. If Adam and Eve wanted paradise, then they had to remain ignorant, without any help from the Tree of Knowledge of Good and Evil. When they eat the forbidden fruit—because *of course* they do—they act in typical fashion for anyone who has screwed up: they hide.

When we fuck up, we either hide *ourselves* by self-isolating or we try to hide *our sins* by justifying what we've done. In Genesis 3, they do something bad and then do something *bad* (H905), isolating first from God and then from each other. They isolate themselves from God by hiding "among the trees of the garden" (3:8), embarrassed at their nakedness. Then they isolate from each other and create a blaming crossfire: Adam blames Eve, and Eve blames the snake. Genesis 3:8–12 shows us how NOT to screw up. We make things worse by recoiling inward with our embarrassment and seeing everyone else as the problem.

Cain almost follows his folks' example but pivots and creates a new *tropos* for humanity. In each instance, God comes looking for humanity, asking Adam, "Where are you?" (Gen. 3:9); and asking Cain, "Where is your brother Abel?" (4:9), but there is no humanity to be found. Each of these early human prototypes reacts by withdrawing into themselves, making things worse by going against their nature. God made everything good, only isolation is *bad*. God seems unfamiliar with human embarrassment and shame, asking Eve, "What is this that you have done?" (3:13). People, symbolized by Adam and Eve, are distinct from "this" thing Christians call sin. There are no evil people, only evil deeds, and Genesis cautions against confusing what people *are* with what people have *done*. Nonetheless, we sometimes condemn ourselves by thinking we are either above guilt or beyond redemption. Whether by pride or by shame, Adam and Eve never object to being banished from Paradise. Cain will not make the same mistake, because he is Humanity 2.1.

When God asks Cain the closing question, it has changed slightly, as though God can now recognize sin, asking simply, "What have you done?" (Gen. 4:10). It is the Question of Killing, asking not just about mechanics, but about meaning and purpose. It might sound familiar to grunts, because it feels a lot like getting ASKed, "Did you kill anybody?" In Cain's case the answer is yes, but, unlike his parents, he confesses rather than be alone. Not a huge improvement, but definitely better than his predecessors. What follows is not

God punishing Cain, but rather explaining how his actions affect the togetherness in which creation thrives.

English translations have God telling Cain to expect to "be a fugitive and a wanderer" (Gen. 4:12), but those words lose meaning the more his story is told and retold. The Greek uses verbs, not nouns. Cain will *tremo kai stenon*; he will "tremble and shake." But they mean more than that; *tremo* (G5141) emphasizes dread and *stenon* (cf. G4728) means "narrow, tight, or enclosed." A derivative word, *steni*, means "prison." It would be a little more accurate to say that God says Cain will experience anxiety and avoidance. God is informing Cain that he will experience post-traumatic stress.

Cain's curse does not come from God, but "from the ground" (Gen. 4:10–11), humanity's older sibling in creation, which has been left to deal with cleaning up Cain's mess. The ground will do its job, Abel will be decomposed, but the earth can play games too: "Oh, you like your little garden? Good luck with that from now on, asshole." God is simply the messenger, letting Cain know that the earth didn't think using his brother as fertilizer was very funny.

Cain will feel alone, isolated from the presence of God and his family. Killing has that effect; friends and family don't know what to do with combat veterans, treating them as though they have changed. Douchebag theologians aren't shy about suggesting trigger pullers are the devil's seed. Worse, many grunts will believe the lie, either allowing it to destroy them or adopting it to survive. It shouldn't surprise anyone that Hells Angels was started by WWII veteran Otto Friedli. It feels like punishment to be looked at like there's something wrong with you, either because you are not allowed to feel guilt for the things you have done or because you are expected to feel shame for things you have not.

Cain is afraid of being alone, of being the embodiment of the thing God called *bad*. He is afraid that others will confuse *doing* bad with *being* bad. The mark God gives Cain is to protect him from shame, from what people might think of him and, by extension, do to him. For everyone else the mark is a sign. Just as the stars mark the seasons, Cain is a sign of transition we all must make from shame and embarrassment to guilt and confession.

GUILT OR SHAME

Guilt is about harmful actions, while shame is about harmful feelings. When we screw up, our guilty conscience reminds us until we fix it. We feel moral pain deep within ourselves. The Greek word used in the Bible for "soul" is *psyche* (G5590), like psychology. Our soul is a collection of our experiences, reflections, and dreams, both good and bad. It is not something detached or distinct from, but rather mysteriously bound up with, our physical bodies. Having a guilty conscience manifests both physical and moral pain.

Cain's uniqueness is found in his acknowledging his guilt and seeking reconciliation. Shame is about the feelings and beliefs we hold about ourselves or others, the degrading bullshit we inherit from our community. Shame exploits our sense of embarrassment; it occurs when a community assumes there is no separation between a person and their embarrassing acts. With shame, you *become* the embarrassment.

Unfortunately, God cannot force people to see Cain as he truly is: imperfect but good. Cain is still human; the only thing wrong is how people think and feel about him. Basil of Caesarea, a fourth-century bishop, stated, "By a conspicuous sign it was proclaimed to all that [Cain] was the contriver of unholy deeds."[11] However wrong an idea is, if it's repeated enough it becomes true. Tell soldiers that they're all killers over and over again, and they'll feel shame for things they may not have done.

Killing *is* bad, but it doesn't have the power to re-create us. All sin can do is obscure our humanity. It can hide a little of our created goodness. We can't hide from our own actions any more than we can hide from God. Grunts do some seriously fucked-up shit in war. They can try to ignore it, by burying it deep inside, or to justify it, as though one wrong makes it okay to do another one. But if all this hiding works, then why are so many soldiers and veterans killing themselves? The Defense Suicide Prevention Office (DSPO) reported 115 Total Force suicides in the first 90 days of 2021, for a rate of about 1.3 per day.[12] The most recent data from the Department of Veterans Affairs covers 2018, when there were 17.6 suicides per day.[13]

When we do things that are not good, that create isolation for ourselves or for others, we do not stop being human. Our humanity is obscured, but it does not go away. It is important to get the story of Cain right to understand what type of person he is and what the Bible wants us to take away from his story. Cain is not a killer; he is a human being who has killed. This is a critical distinction. What we do shapes us without defining us. If we believe we are created by God, then we can rest assured that God has determined that we are good. Cain is still human after he's killed his brother. The act only made it a little harder to recognize the goodness God put in him.

Make no mistake, Cain is not innocent. But guilt is not an invitation to shame. Cain is a prototype for repentance—an early, imperfect example of the sacrament of reconciliation. God's mark is reassurance to all those who seek God's face; it is the promise of protection from the self-righteousness of others. The mark is God's reminder to everyone, including Cain, that he was, is, and remains fully human. His story is about what he has done, not what he has become. This is good news for grunts, but it is a warning for anyone else who wants to lock soldiers in boxes to fit preconceived notions about armed service.

Soldiers are more than the stereotypes passed around about them. To be human is to have a soul, a mind capable of choosing either good or evil. It's terrifying, but true. It's normal to try to minimize the bad and overstate the good, but some people refuse to reckon with their own capacity for evil as though their shit don't stink. When I was living in a city I didn't particularly like (I won't say where), I kept a line of poetry near my front door to save myself from thinking myself better than those around me: "You shall love your [crooked] neighbor with your crooked heart."[14]

When confronted by God for killing his brother, Cain makes a halfhearted attempt at hiding, but it doesn't last. God leaves Cain a mark; not only is Cain left *with* a *typos*, a figure upon his brow, but he is also left *as* a *typos*, an example for others. He is not an example for murderers, but for those seeking reconciliation and community. This is what it means to do wrong; this is what sin and reconciliation look like. The tragedy is that he is still remembered only for his life's greatest mistake. But that's on us, not him.

2.

TYFYS:

MOSES AND LEVITICAL SACRIFICE

T HANK YOU FOR YOUR SERVICE" IS REPEATED SO OFTEN THAT post-9/11 veterans have begun giving it its own acronym on social media: TYFYS.[1] This stands in stark contrast with the open hostility experienced by soldiers returning from Vietnam. Some veterans appreciate the sentiment, but a growing number do not. According to a 2019 survey by Cohen Veterans Network, 90 percent of civilians polled reported saying TYFYS, despite nearly half of the military participants reporting discomfort at being thanked.[2] Words are supposed to convey meaning from speaker to hearer, but when TYFYS becomes little more than obligatory public ritual, veterans are forced to wonder whether it is "thank you" or "service" that has become meaningless.

I try to give civilians using TYFYS the benefit of the doubt by assuming their words mean something. When I am thanked for my service, I sometimes reply with "I was in for six years; which part?"

or "Oh, you've read about me! Do you want me to sign your copy of *Reborn on the Fourth of July?*" When I fail to perform the standard TYFYS rites, most people are confused but a surprising number are angered. "Hey, I was just trying to be nice!" is a typical response, which goes to show that *they* expect to be the ceremonial beneficiary, not me.[3] Sacrificial rituals are like that; they disclose more about the community that demands sacrifice than they do about those sacrificed.

If TYFYS were about service, then we would thank not only soldiers and veterans, but teachers, doctors, and more. At its best TYFYS affirms *and laments* that we live in a world where the few suffer so that the many can prosper. Diana Tsai, writing in *Forbes*, defends TYFYS because she sees the world as one in which "violence and destruction were things [she] saw on the news but never felt."[4] The dark truth is that TYFYS is for a community's sacrificial lambs, those thought to keep hardship at bay by taking unearned punishment upon themselves. Christian soldiers and veterans have frequently expressed to me how they feel like the sacrificial lambs of America. The good news for grunts is that it isn't all bad news, that there's something redeeming about the Levitical system of sacrifice. In fact, redemption is kind of the point.

PRINCE OR PAUPER

Sacrificial rituals might feel foreign to most modern readers, but they have been around for a while. Primitive societies sought to appease the gods to avoid natural disasters like famine, drought, and disease. Jan Bremmer, a historian of religion, describes ancient Greek scapegoat rituals "in which the elimination of one or two members saves the whole of the community."[5] That is sacrifice in a nutshell: a few suffer so that many may prosper. The mistreatment of a scapegoat, called *pharmakoi*, from *pharmakon*, meaning "drug or poison," provided a cathartic release for the community. These ceremonies were usually symbolic and involved temporary exile rather than execution. There are two sides of ritual, one stylized and the other pragmatic.

In the collective imagination, *pharmakoi* were expected to be the most valuable members of a society, esteemed royalty, wealthy merchants, hot pieces of ass. But no member with any influence was about to volunteer for abuse, so societies had to find a work-around. When it came time to select *pharmakoi*, it was "the poor, the ugly, and criminals" that were always left holding the short straw.[6] In order to fulfill mythical expectations, however, they put lipstick on a pig by dressing the *pharmakoi* up as "the attractive, aristocratic, and royal figures." Historically, the people made to suffer for the good of the many were always drawn from the lowest social classes. A token member of the bottom class would be treated like they were on the top of the world for the sake of ritual, before the climactic moment when they would be stripped, beaten, and run out of town.

Sacrificial rituals still exist today, only the reasons have changed. Maybe we aren't trying to appease the gods to avert disaster, but we all still need a little collective sigh of relief. In one unit, our company commander would relinquish control every so often and do morning physical training (PT) with a squad. The understanding was that the squad leader would get to order the captain around, do a little role-reversal. This usually resulted in an especially grueling morning for the squad, but everyone got their rocks off knowing their commander was occasionally at their disposal. The commander knew a squad would get good PT plus a boost in unit cohesion, a win-win. But this would be a historical exception rather than the rule; the ideal rather than reality.

Scapegoats, remember, were usually dragged involuntarily from the lowest classes to benefit the middle and upper classes. A modern (military) equivalent would be like taking a private and taping a few chevrons and rockers on his uniform and passing him off as a command sergeant major for a military review. Nobody likes drill and ceremony, so why should the CSM get a free pass? The scapegoat ritual is about sparing the many at the expense of the few. Like sending men and women off to unnecessary wars and calling it even by burying them in TYFYS greetings.

LEVITE OR LAITY

Ancient Israel was a radically equitable society, but it still had its social classes. At the top was the priestly caste, called Levites because they descended from Levi, Jacob's third-oldest son. Before the establishment of anything resembling an Israelite nation, the descendants of Jacob had no need of priests or sacrifice because they were essentially a clan rather than a sovereign nation. The turning point came as they were freed from bondage in Egypt under the leadership of Moses, a Levite.

Moses' name means "child of water," because he was spared the fate of other Hebrew children, which was drowning in the river Nile.

This reflects a pattern in the Bible of patriarchs avoiding death and rising to prominence. Joseph, the eleventh of Jacob's sons and the man who initially brought the clan to Egypt, was spared his own brothers' jealous wrath and sold into slavery instead. To cover their tracks, his half brothers smeared goat's blood on Joseph's coat to make it look like he'd been attacked by wild animals. Before Joseph, it was Isaac, whose father, Abraham, was instructed to slaughter him at Mount Moriah but Isaac was spared at the last moment by a ram.

The particular kind of killing in each instance foreshadows Israel's sacrificial system. The Hebrew word *mut* (H4191) can be used either passively, "to die"; or actively, "to make die." It is what God says will happen if Adam and Eve eat forbidden fruit (see Gen. 2:17), but it is also what Joseph's brothers plan to do to him (see Gen. 37:18) and what Pharaoh tells the Hebrew midwives to do to male children like Moses (see Exod. 1:16). Roughly equivalent to murder, *mut* is contrasted with *shachat* (H7819), carefully choreographed ritual slaughter. This is the method finally employed by Joseph's jealous brothers against a nearby goat (Gen. 37:31) and what God commands be done to Abraham's youngest son (Gen. 22:10).

The Bible does not adhere to the same social constructs as Greek and other Western cultures. It is the weakest and most despised to whom God repeatedly assigns the most responsibility and status, like Joseph or Moses. We might look up to pastors and priests, but when Israel was first made a people, every family was expected to perform the priestly rites that later became reserved for the Levites. The first collective sacrifice occurred when every house was told to slaughter, *shachat*, not a king or his pretender, but a lowly herd animal.[7] The tenth plague, when God killed the firstborn of Egypt in retribution for Pharaoh's murder of Hebrew children, became Passover, the first sacrificial festival.

The lead-up to the great escape from bondage emphasizes ritual sacrifice. We might have Charlton Heston in our head, bellowing out "Let my people go!" but that is only part of the story that Exodus tells. Moses is told to implore Pharaoh to let Israel go "so that we may sacrifice [*zabah*, H2076] to the LORD our God" (Exod. 3:18; 5:3). The Hebrew is slightly different here and coupled several times with *chagag* (H2287), meaning "feast or celebration." But the message is clear: "Party or plague; your choice."

Pharaoh's heart is too hard, so Moses tells the Israelites to prepare for the final plague, the first Passover. "The whole assembled congregation" (Exod. 12:6), presumably each family unit, served a priestly function in performing the sacrificial rites, a foretaste of God's hope that good people will be their own priests, not because God is obsolete, but because there is no separation between people and God.

When the time is right, they are to ritually slaughter a lamb or goat and spread its blood on their doorposts, like Joseph's brothers did to his coat. When the angel of death goes through the land, it won't have some psychic power to tell Egyptian from Israelite; if you don't have a horror show *on* the house, then you'll get a horror show *in* the house. When the dust settles, they are instructed to remind their children that God "passed over the houses of the Israelites in Egypt, when he struck down the Egyptians but spared our houses" (Exod. 12:27). The action God takes against the Egyptians is not bringing the hammer down on Israel's enemies like a badass. The word used, *pasach* (H6452), means "to limp along." Like Jacob walking away from his wrestling match with the angel, or soldiers dragging ass back home from battle.

A LAMB(?) FOR GOD

Substitutionary sacrifice is even more prominent in the Jewish High Holiday of Yom Kippur, which doubles as the new religious year. It's called the Day of Atonement, *kaphar* (H3722), which means "to pave over"; like paving a road makes a road even, so, too, does an annual shedding of blood even things out between God and Israel. Just like the Greek *pharmakoi* were ritually killed to smooth things over between gods and kings, every year Judaism repaves the way from God to humanity on Yom Kippur.

The main event is the sacrifice of two goats, one "for the LORD" and another one "for Azazel" (Lev. 16:8). There is debate as to what this Hebrew word *azazel* (H5799) means. One theory suggests it is a theonym, a name that describes God; combine *azaz* (H5810) with the divine suffix *-el* and you get "God strengthens." Another, more popular, theory combines *ez* (H5795), for "goat," with *azal* (H235), meaning "to deplete or run out." William Tyndale popularized this second theory, calling the second goat "the (e)scape goat" in his 1526 English translation of the Bible.

God's goat is slaughtered first and its blood is painted on the ark, like the Hebrew slaves did on their doorposts and Jacob's sons did on Joseph's coat. Then, before the carcass of God's goat is burned on the altar to complete the sacrificial ritual, the high priest returns for the scapegoat. Outside, where the people can see, he places his bloodied hands on the head of the scapegoat and "confess over it all the *iniquities* of the people" (Lev. 16:21, emphasis added). The Hebrew word used is *'aon* (H5771), the same term Cain used in his own confession in Genesis 4:13. When the priest places his hands, bloodied from the slaughter of God's goat, upon the scapegoat, the *'aon* is transferred from the people to the animal. The scapegoat is then set free, carrying away the people's guilt into the wilderness.

The word *azazel*, the "scapegoat," emphasizes this carrying away. "Escape" is one way to translate the Hebrew root *azal*, but it essentially means "gone, disappeared." *Azazel* is the *ez*, or "goat," who makes sin disappear by removing it entirely, *azaz*, as he wanders off into the wilderness. Only after the scapegoat has departed does the Levitical priest burn God's goat on the altar and wash himself off, completing the ritual.

Here's the thing. Sacrifice will later become a central theme of John's gospel and the letters attributed to him, including Revelation. Most Christians are probably familiar with the "Lamb of God who takes away the sin of the world" (John 1:29). At first glance, it is a callback to the Passover from Exodus 12. The crucifixion, after all, occurs over the Passover holiday, during which the innocence of Jesus is emphasized for dramatic effect. Lambs have a reputation for being docile and innocent; that's why early theologians picked up on imagery exclusive to John and blew it up. Augustine, for example, in his commentary on John 1:29, implies that lambs are synonymous with innocence.[8]

In Christianity, the dominant religion in America, sacrificial victims, "led like a lamb to the slaughter," are expected to be docile and

manageable, just "as a sheep before its shearers is silent" (Isa. 53:7
NIV). But this is a departure from the sacrificial imagery the church
inherited from Israel.

SPOILER: GOD IS THE GOAT

The Hebrew Bible never mentions a Passover "lamb" in Exodus.[9]
The essential qualities of the sacrificial animal are that it be young,
unblemished, and male. The type of animal named was any calf, *seh*
(H7716), a nonbovine herd animal. Which herd animal? God said
that families "may take it from the sheep [*kebes*, H3532] or from
the goats [*ez*, H5795]" (Exod. 12:5). The Passover sacrifice is not
necessarily a cute and cuddly little sheep; it might also be an ornery,
unpredictable goat. In fact, it would be more accurate to use the
image of a goat, because it is more in line with the Levitical sacrificial
system than a sheep.

Johannine imagery seems to confuse Passover and Yom Kippur.
Revelation uses *arnion* (G721), which is specifically a baby sheep.
John's gospel uses *amnos* (G286), which becomes the Latin word
agnus, also specifically a baby sheep. Taking away the sins of the
world, however, is done by the Yom Kippur scapegoat, not the Passover calf. John could have erred on the side of caution by using goats
more than sheep for salvation imagery, like other New Testament
writers, but he didn't. Paul, for example, does not share John's narrow focus on sheep over goats. When he mentions "our Passover
lamb" in 1 Corinthians 5:7 (NIV), he doesn't mention a calf of any
kind, only *pascha* (H3975), a transliteration of the Hebrew word
pesach (H6453). When the letter to the Hebrews addresses sacrifice,

it follows the language of Leviticus carefully by mentioning goats rather than sheep (see Heb. 9:12–13, 19; 10:4). John stands alone in the New Testament in insisting on using the symbol of a sheep rather than a goat. So what, though, right? Who cares; what's the difference?

Sheep and goats are *so* different that the gospel of Matthew uses them to illustrate the difference between good and evil. But the only purpose it serves is as a simile; it is *people* who are being sorted, not livestock. These people are so different that they must be sorted "as a shepherd separates the sheep from the goats" (Matt. 25:32). Sheep eat only grasses and weeds, limiting their range and making them more dependent on a shepherd and flock for safety. Their wool, which is valuable to people for clothes and blankets, must be sheared regularly, so they have a deeply symbiotic relationship with humanity. Goats' eclectic diet produces animals that are independent and physically agile, and their coats don't require as much maintenance. Frankly, they don't need people, and the feeling is more or less mutual. It doesn't help that, while sheep have secreting glands in their feet and face, goats smell awful because their glands are beside their butts. John, and most Christians, prefers the image of a sheep because it affirms a deep human desire for rainbows and sunshine. Sacrifice reveals much more about the *community* than the victims, and cultural associations about livestock teach us more about humans than animals.

The sweet and simple lamb, a symbol of prestige and fragility, always turned me off as a young soldier. The good news for grunts is that, if Jesus is the sacrifice of God who takes away the sins of the world, then God is the goat of Yom Kippur. That means the whole silent, stoic charade is unnecessary. Goats are ornery, disheveled, and downright dangerous, like a few soldiers and veterans I know.[10] The perceived low class of goats is not theologically disqualifying; the punchy, no-nonsense herd animals are just as sacred as the high-brow, cutesy sheep. God is the slaughtered calf whose blood stains the hands of the Levites as well as the scapegoat who carries our guilt away.

At the same time, God is the Passover calf (sheep or goat) whose blood spares us from the battle-hardened but war-weary angel of death who limps through the land. The gospel of John hints at this possibility. When Caiaphas "advised the Jews that it was better to have one person die for the people" (John 18:14), he was evoking the rites of Yom Kippur *on Passover*, combining two Jewish holidays to make Good Friday, where Jesus suffers so that we all might be saved. It's fair to evoke the meek and mild-mannered sheepish traits that Christians love so much. But we must not forget that Jesus can also be a hard-charging, head-butting cantankerous goat. And not just any goat, but the Greatest of All Time.

SCAPE OR SLAUGHT MATTERS NOT

Can you imagine being the scapegoat? Being paraded around for a day or two just so you can be banished to the wilderness? It's kind of how many veterans feel, and I'm one of them. Military families get paraded around their communities as American royalty for a handful of national holidays, but when the sun sets on Memorial, Independence, or Veterans Days, our carriages transform back into pumpkins, and it's back to the status quo. It should not surprise anyone that the military has a suicide problem; a lot of soldiers and veterans would rather be God's goat than the scapegoat.

Treating soldiers as sacrificial lambs says more about America's unresolved guilt than it does about military communities. Who really escapes in these rituals? Is it the goat left for dead in the middle of nowhere, or is it the rest of society, getting the benefits of citizenship without giving much up in exchange? The truth is that TYFYS is a canned remark that feels good to only those hoping talk isn't cheap. Nobody chooses to be the sacrificial lamb; they are recruited from communities with wealth gaps so big you could drive a tank between the rich and the poor.

Enlistment is driven more by economic considerations than by some patriotic calling. A 2018 RAND survey of lower enlisted personnel found that "the overwhelming majority of respondents had economic reasons for joining up."[11] This hasn't stopped civilians from viewing their service through the lens of some sacred vocation. According to more recent studies, civilians were most likely to think "that troops [serve] either out of patriotism or sense of duty."[12]

Jewish tradition held that the scapegoat would be pushed off a cliff. The metaphor may be apt: as a soldier you either die on the altar of war or live to fall off the proverbial cliff. For many enlisted grunts, military service can feel like a plateau, to go from a tight-knit community of deep meaning to literally being left at the side of the road with nothing but a DD214 in hand. The scapegrunt gets to live the high life only temporarily, for a few fleeting moments when all eyes are on you and no expense is spared. Then your service ends, your sacrifice complete. There's a saying disabled veterans use to describe their VA medical benefits: "You get what you pay for." Our "payment" was supposed to have been our service, the sacrifice of our bodies, but that still isn't enough to earn basic respect from the very agency responsible for us.

Diana Tsai, the civilian who penned the *Forbes* article cited at the beginning of this chapter, knows that veterans hear TYFYS a lot, but "it's important for [her] to try to express what" she means when she says it. As a rite within America's sacrificial system, TYFYS is about the person saying it, not the person it's being said to. It might be directed at veterans, but it is about civilians and their cathartic release. With nothing but good intentions, she goes on to say, "You never asked, and you never will ask, anything of me for these gifts you've given me." Civilians might hear her words as she intends them, but veterans of military culture familiar with the stigma associated with asking for help might hear them very differently. This is how expressions of gratitude from a place of privilege can strengthen social enforcement, transforming quaint sentimentality to code for "Shut the fuck up and drive on."

Tsai is listed as a cofounder of Veterati, "America's mentoring network for the military."[13] Although the idea came from Marine Corps veteran cofounder Daniel Rau, who had "become Diana's online confidant and kindred spirit," he was demoted to "Her Supporting Cast" in an online spread profiling Veterati for the *Atlantic*.[14] I might have dismissed that had I not experienced the same thing with *Christianity Today*. As a minority in America, veterans put up with being pushed out of the way so others can benefit. Once the sacrifice is complete, the community expects the *pharmakoi* to stay out of sight, out of mind. How can you live in peace if you're reminded of the suffering you pushed onto others?

Given the choice, would you rather go out in a blaze of glory as the sacrificial goat or get gussied up to take on the guilt of the community and pushed to the margins? Is it any wonder that some soldiers prefer serial deployments to discharge? Is there any real difference between sacrificial victim and scapegrunt? That's not a rhetorical question, at least not for military communities.

3.
TO PROTECT AND SERVE:
JOSHUA AND THE *MILITIA DEI*

BEFORE AMERICA HAD A UNIFIED MILITARY, IT HAD MANY STATE militias. These were groups of citizens willing to fight beside one another to oppose King George and other threats to our fledgling democracy. A few of today's fifty-four individual National Guard units trace their history to these militias. But as our nation grew up, it absorbed and organized them into a single modular force. The book of Joshua shows this process in reverse: Israel conquers the Promised Land as a cohesive unit under a strong leader before devolving into tribal forces competing for power and resources. Joshua also shows us God's plan for the military, which is inclusive of all public servants responsible for law and order in the human community.

JOSHUA THE MAN

Joshua is easily mistaken as little more than a military leader, the man in command of Israel's armies as they conquered Canaan in the book of the Bible that bears his name. But that is an oversimplification that obscures important details about who he was and what role he served in the history of the people of God.

According to the book of Numbers, Joshua was born a slave in Egypt named Hoshea (H1954, see Num. 13:8), meaning "salvation." The reason we don't see his birth name much is that, when he was recruited as a spy to recon the Promised Land, Moses "changed the name of Hoshea son of Nun to Joshua" (Num. 13:16) by adding the divine prefix *Jah-*. Biblical name-changing often adds something small for great effect. The Hebrew name *'Avram* (H87) belongs on a mug or a T-shirt; it basically means "world's best dad." But *'Avraham* (H85), or Abraham, means "father of many; father of all nations."

In Exodus 17, Moses puts Joshua in charge of repelling an enemy attack. But his military prowess is not the key to the Israelites' success. As if by magic, they hold the upper hand only so long as Moses holds his hands up, literally. "Whenever Moses held up his hand, Israel prevailed; and whenever he lowered his hand, Amalek prevailed" (Exod. 17:11). As a soldier, I couldn't help noticing that had Moses been better at cherry-pickers, an arm exercise used in physical training, he wouldn't have needed the help of Aaron and Hur. The point of the story is that human skill and dedication don't ultimately matter; we aren't in control, God is.

Joshua had plenty of experience playing second fiddle to Moses, something he seemed entirely content with. In the wilderness he served as little more than an "assistant" (Exod. 24:13; 33:11). This word, *sarat* (H8334), is also used to refer to what Aaron, the high priest and Moses' brother, did in the Holy Place. It is usually translated as "minister" (Exod. 28:35, 43; 29:30; 30:20), leaving the impression that Joshua serves a priestly role in the story as much as a military one. Joshua shows us how faith and service can, and should, coexist. He also foreshadows another, greater figure who will do the same by being both a military commander and a priestly servant.

Because there is no "J" sound in Hebrew, the divine prefix Moses adds is *Yah-* rather than *Jah-*. From the time Hoshea son of Nun serves as a spy, he is called *Yehoshua* (H3091), meaning "God is salvation." Upon the death of Moses, he is promoted to lead the ragtag militia of God in their first sustained military campaign as a nation. Throughout the harrowing battles that lay ahead for Israel, Yehoshua would serve as an ever-present, bodily reminder that God is and will be their Savior. They will need this reminder not just as a sign of hope but also as a word of warning; it is God who saves, not superior firepower or strategic advantage.

JOSHUA THE BOOK

The central promise God makes in the first five books of the Bible, of land and prosperity to Abraham's descendants, is fulfilled in Joshua, its sixth book. It follows Moses' assistant as he receives a battlefield commission in the militia of God to lead the people in becoming "a priestly kingdom and a holy nation" (Exod. 19:6). Unfortunately, to make an omelet, you have to break some eggs; the land given by God must be taken from its current inhabitants. There is no way around Old Testament violence, and nowhere is it as horrifying as it is in Joshua.

Before it comes to Israel's military campaign in Canaan, most biblical violence can be explained away as corrupt individuals pursuing their own self-interest. But in Joshua there is no mistaking God's frequent command to destroy every living thing that stands in the way of Israel possessing the land. The verb used is *herem* (H2763), "to reserve entirely to God by destruction"; while the thing devoted, a noun, is *haram* (H2764). If this feels familiar, it is because "Passover" (*pesach*, H6453) works the same way by naming the ritual as well as its victim; saying "Passover sacrifice" is like saying "basketball ball." Only the devoted things in Joshua are human beings, not calves.

The Ten Commandments of Exodus and Deuteronomy are Israel's constitution, but without land, people cannot be a nation. To get land, people have typically taken it by force, colonizing "new" worlds as if the land were empty when they got there. It's easier to live with ourselves when we tell our story in a way that preserves the facade that we are incapable of evil. To do that, we claim that our desires are the same as God's, that we are divinely ordained to do whatever the hell we want. What sets the book of Joshua apart is that not only does God *desire* Israel to possess the land, God also *commands* it. God has to, because the first time Israel was supposed to kick ass and take names, they got gun-shy (see Num. 13; 14).

When faced with what appeared to be an impossible task, the people lost faith that God would deliver on the promise of land. They were told by recon scouts that the land "devours its inhabitants; and all the people that we saw in it are of great size" (Num. 13:32). Most everyone cowered in fear and started talking about returning to slavery in Egypt. But not Joshua and Caleb. Their response to a superior force was classic grunt, gung ho rather than gun-shy, shrugging off grave danger with precisely zero fucks given: "The LORD is with us; do not fear them" (Num. 14:9).

"Gung ho" has gotten the same bad reputation as the overzealous soldiers who abuse it. A Mandarin word, *gonghe*, it was popularized by General Evans Carlson, one of the founding leaders of the Marine Raiders and twice a grunt.[1] He explained the inspiration behind the phrase, saying, "I was trying to build up the same sort of working spirit I had seen in China where all the soldiers dedicated themselves to one idea and worked together...Gung Ho. It means Work Together."[2] Used around the military today, however, gung ho implies that someone is dangerously overmotivated. Marines nowadays call people like that "motards."[3]

While the rest of Israel was gun-shy, Joshua and Caleb were gung ho; they had faith that, together and with God on their side, they could do anything. Unfortunately, fear won the day and Israel wandered another couple of decades. But let's fast-forward back to go-time.

The book of Joshua is short and sweet, and it shows in clear and concise detail what it means to serve in the military of God under Joshua's leadership. His battlefield commission occurs in chapter 1, but humans are not in command. Before fighting kicks off in chapter 6, Joshua encounters an imposing figure who identifies *himself* as the "commander of the army of the LORD" (Josh. 5:14).[4] Joshua knows he is outranked and is reminded that God doesn't follow people into their petty squabbles but leads them against impossible odds.

All of the fighting in the book occurs between chapters 6

and 11, and nowhere does Joshua make any command decisions. There are strict Rules of Engagement that change almost every time they enter battle. When people try to take things into their own hands, they lose. The first skirmish, against Jericho, is typical for those that follow, but by no means is it normal. What is described is unlike anything that can be called strategic. Israel conquers Jericho by performing something like a Mardi Gras parade led by a Chaplain Corps band with the Liberty Bell at the front. This ragtag formation of POGs must have been the laughingstock of Jericho, but they succeed because everyone does their own choreographed part.

There are more engagements that follow, but the emphasis of the book is not on battlefield prowess. Less than a quarter of the book describes expelling Canaanite inhabitants with violent force. A decent amount of material from chapters 6 to 12 details peaceful negotiations, and chapter 13 makes clear their victory was not total. Most scholars agree that the language of violent conquest is exaggerated and self-congratulatory, which is par for the course in the ancient Near East. Ten chapters, 13 through 22, outline in great detail how the Promised Land will be allocated to the tribes according to their size, a nod to the fairness and organization for which God's military serves.

TO SERVE AND PROTECT

The military is nothing more than an extension of human society so, to understand what militaries were intended to be, we have to understand what humanity was intended to be. When God created people, we were given "dominion" over the rest of creation

(Gen. 1:26, 28). The Greek word is *arche* (G757), meaning "first or original,"[5] which is odd because according to the story of Genesis, we were created last. As a family of creation, we are the babies, the youngest. Being given *arche* status means that, even though we are the youngest, human beings are expected to be the grown-ups in the room, the archetypes of how all creatures should be.

Some translations have God telling us "to rule" over creation, but that is not what dominion, *arche*, means. "Ruler" has a double meaning after all; rulers are not only inflated egos with a bejeweled crown perched on their heads, but they are also the things we count on for drawing straight lines and measuring out distances. By assigning us responsibility over all creation, God gave human beings custody of the whole world. What are we told to do with the earth? We are told "to till it and keep it" (Gen. 2:15). In Hebrew the words are *abad* (H5647) and *shamar* (H8104), literally "to serve and protect." This twofold imperative is the primary function of humanity, one Cain promptly undermines in asking whether he was "my brother's [*shamar*](Gen. 4:9)."

Serving and protecting is associated with law enforcement agencies around the nation. It began with the Los Angeles Police Department, which adopted "To Protect and to Serve" as the motto for their training academy in 1955. But a lot has happened since then to make average citizens question police officers' commitment to our fundamental human responsibility to serve and to protect. Although the LAPD credits the motto to Officer Joseph S. Dorobek, there is more to the motto, and police departments that adopt it, than meets the eye.

The Minneapolis Police Department's motto is "To Protect with Courage, to Serve with Compassion." An MPD officer was responsible for the death of George Floyd in May 2020 while he was in police custody, setting off nationwide protests and riots. A month after George's death, Joe Dorobek's granddaughter, Regina Varolli, revealed that it was his seventeen-year-old daughter, her mother, who actually coined the phrase for the LAPD that became synonymous with law enforcement.[6]

Varolli acknowledged, "It's not easy being a cop. You're underpaid. It's dangerous. It's thankless." Her family still lived in Los Angeles in 1992, when uniformed LAPD officers viciously beat Rodney King while he was in custody and managed to evade any real accountability. She called the riots that followed "selfish looting and senseless violence." But that did not excuse the officers sworn to serve and protect their community. "Those police officers who brutalized Rodney King betrayed their motto," she said.

When I was a cherry paratrooper, junior NCOs (noncommissioned officers) often warned us that "shit don't roll uphill." To grunts, it was a cynical reminder that officers' bad decisions would hurt us more than them, and that they could get away with "shit" by merit of their higher rank. Giving law enforcement officers a free pass is like letting shit roll downhill, from the servant-protectors to the people they are supposed to serve and protect. Shrugging off the great burden of responsibility by expecting shit to simply roll down the pecking order is just another way of saying we are not one another's *shamar*, of saying we cannot shoulder the full burden of our humanity; are we *really* our people's protectors, though?

Being the crown jewel of creation does not give us the right to "lord it over" (see Num. 16:13; Matt. 20:25; Mark 10:42; Luke 22:25) others by barking orders, but calls us to carefully tend creation as its custodians. If the earth is in our custody, it means we have a higher responsibility for protecting and maintaining the order God blessed it with. Not from the top down, but from the bottom up. If humans "rule" creation, it is not because we wield swords and shields, but because we are given gardening shears and a toilet plunger.

MILITIA DEI

One of the central lessons we are supposed to learn from Cain is that, yes, we *are* one another's protectors. In Greek, the word Cain uses for "keeper" is *phylax*, a root word of *phalanx*, meaning "a military unit."[7] Soldiers are a microcosm of humanity; militaries serve human communities the same way that all humanity serves creation. In other words, we cannot understand the function of militaries in the world apart from the function of humanity in creation. That function is to maintain the order God established over chaos in Genesis.

"Military" comes from *militia*: ad hoc local forces organic to a community rather than loyal to an absentee king. In Latin, *militia* comes from *miles*, meaning "soldier." The origin of *miles* is disputed, but many scholars insist that it comes from *mille*, one thousand, which survives in the metric system as the prefix *milli-*.[8] The intended purpose of militaries is to maintain the just ordering of communities, and that includes law enforcement as well as fire protection.

Any battles that might erupt are to serve that purpose; fighting was never supposed to be soldiers' primary function. The US Army still reflects this foundational truth, with its *lowest* organizational priority being "overcoming any nations responsible for aggressive acts."⁹

The same is true for the military of God. When you read about "armies" or "hosts" from Genesis to Joshua, the Hebrew word is *tsaba* (H6635). Its essential element is not to be heavily armed or highly trained, but to be carefully organized. The first *tsaba* is made up of the heavens and earth¹⁰; and Hebrew slaves are called a *tsaba* while they are still in bondage in Egypt.¹¹ The book with more "armies" than anywhere else is Numbers. Shortly after escaping Egypt, God tells Moses to take a census of all men "from twenty years old and upward, everyone in Israel able to [*tsaba*]. You and Aaron shall enroll them, [*tsaba*]" (Num. 1:3).

English translations usually word it something like "everyone in Israel able to go to *war*"; enroll them, *company by company*" (Num. 1:3, emphasis added). Americans really put their military on pedestals, which kind of skews the meaning here a little. It's truer to its original meaning to translate it as "Let those who are able to be assembled be assembled." One reason for assembly is defense against an enemy in war. But a much more pressing concern for Israel is to be assembled to get a piece of that sweet, sweet Promised Land. In fact, the majority of the book of Joshua is focused on the methodical distribution of land to all the different tribes according to their size. Battle is not the main story of Joshua; it is merely a prelude to fulfilling God's promise. When you read about armies and hosts in the Old Testament, you should not think first about weapons or strength. You should think of precision and order. This is what *tsaba* implies and it is what Israel under Joshua exemplified; not superior firepower, but discipline and accountability.

Just before the walls of Jericho came tumbling down, Joshua warned the people to "keep [*shamar*] yourselves from the things devoted [*herem*, v.] to destruction [*haram*, n.]," lest they "make the camp [*mahane*, H4264] of Israel a thing for destruction [*haram*]" (Josh. 6:18 ESV). There are two very important points to be made from this verse. The first is that Rules of Engagement (ROE) do not just protect noncombatants from injury, they also protect the protectors themselves from corruption and evil. Second, when soldiers and police play fast and loose with the moral structure of civilization, it is not just innocent civilians who suffer, it is society as a whole. The Hebrew word *mahane* does not distinguish between soldier and civilian. This word, like *tsaba*, can be translated as "camp," "host," "company," or "army." Here it refers to all of Israel, not just those assembling, because it is all of Israel that deserves to be *herem haram* if just one of them betrays their collective commitments.

After Jericho, Israel's forces suffer a debilitating loss in Ai because one soldier violated the ROE. The blue falcon is Achan, who had taken some silver and gold from the rubble of Jericho and hidden them in his tent.[12] When the people learn that their loss was caused by the betrayal of one of their own, Achan is stoned to death and his family burned alive to avert God's wrath. Rather than the whole *mahane* of Israel, Achan and his house are devoted to destruction. When one protector abuses their power, the whole community becomes morally polluted.

The *Militia Dei* in the book of Joshua is not defined by military prowess or advanced weaponry. Nor is it restricted to a select few who do the fighting when the need arises; all Israel is liable to serve in some capacity, from the priests to the musicians. If ancient Israel is our model, then the military includes all those whose service is marked particularly by the maintenance of justice and peace, from meter maids and traffic cops to the Joint Chiefs of Staff. It also means that our oaths and mottoes are not just empty words recited without meaning; they are profoundly significant. Not just to protect our people, but to preserve our moral integrity.

4.

IF JESUS IS GOD, THEN GOD IS A GRUNT:

JESUS AS DIVINE WARRIOR

B ESIDES FLOWING WITH MILK AND HONEY, THE LAND DISTRIB-
uted to the tribes of Israel held great value in its strategic location along both land and sea trade routes. Anyone who controlled it
could make easy money by taxing the goods moving through. That's
why Israel attracted the attention of great empires like Assyria and
Babylon who took the land and scattered the tribes of Israel. By Jesus'
time, it had come under de facto Roman control through treaties and
alliances with the Herodians, an unpopular dynasty that ruled by
force. Jews of the first century longed for a divine warrior who could
rally the faithful and lead them to independence. Hearing the news
that to them a Savior was born in King David's town and from his
family line, many Jews would have been justified in assuming that a

violent rebellion and spiritual renewal were imminent. Because they were, just not in the way that most expected.

SAY HIS NAME

According to Luke 1:31, Mary was the first to hear what name her first child would bear, *Iesous* (G2424). Regular folk in first-century Galilee spoke Aramaic on the streets and Hebrew in the synagogue. The name Iesous is a later invention of evangelists transliterating from Hebrew to Greek. Mary and Joseph were told to name the boy *Yehoshua*, meaning "God is salvation," "for he will save his people from their sins" (Matt. 1:21). Had they spoken modern English, they would have named him Joshua.

Jesus' birth name is a callback to the man who served as God's executive officer in the military campaign in Canaan. Devout Jews would hear his name and remember that God used one of the gung ho spies of Numbers 14 to redeem the people from the curse of exile in the wilderness. Another figure this name would have recalled in the minds of Bible-thumping Jews was the son of Jozadak, who served as the first high priest following their return from Babylonian captivity. After defeating the Babylonians, Cyrus II of Persia released Israel to return to their land and rebuild their temple. As high priest, Jozadak's son Joshua "set out to rebuild the house of God in Jerusalem" (Ezra 5:2), with the prophet Zechariah being told it is Joshua "that shall build the Temple of the LORD; he shall bear royal honor" (Zech. 6:13) alongside his battle buddy Zerubbabel.[1] The NRSV records the name as "Jeshua" because this section of Ezra was written in Aramaic, Joseph and Mary's native tongue. It was this "second temple," Joshua's temple, that stood in Jerusalem when Gabriel told Mary that her son's name would be...Joshua. It gives a little more meaning to John's phrase "the temple of his body" (John 2:21).

Jesus' namesakes were a soldier who led God's people in combat to take the Promised Land after the Exodus and a priest who led God's people in spiritual renewal after exile. Service and faith in one name, loaded with history and meaning for which "Jesus" would be its fulfillment. What gets lost in translation is the meaning of his given name. "Jesus" doesn't mean anything; it's linguistic filler. When you say his given name, Joshua, you are affirming that God is salvation.

The promise of God's salvation attracted a diverse crowd, from Zealots like Simon[2] to tax collectors like Matthew.[3] Four of the twelve, Peter, Andrew, James, and John, were common fishermen. So, what kind of man attracts the crowd Jesus attracted? Mark 6 suggests he was a carpenter, like his stepfather, a man of lowly status like the fishermen he hung out with. But that's kind of the problem: Jesus is both a man and also not a man. His name suggests he was destined to be a military and religious leader of unparalleled significance, soldier and saint in one, not an oxymoron but a paradox. This should not be an outlandish idea to people who believe in the incarnation, that God entered human flesh. In fact, Jesus' early years give us some interesting insight into his personal (military) history.

GOD'S HOME BASE

I spent my first two years on active duty stationed at Fort Bragg, North Carolina. Because young grunts must live in the barracks, their newfound wealth allows young soldiers to get into trouble and gives towns adjacent to military bases a bad reputation. As a young paratrooper, I was repeatedly warned against straying too far from base: "There ain't nothin' but trouble in Fayette'nam!" To the untrained eye, military towns are bad news. That's why Nathanael asks the apostle Philip, "Can anything good come out of Nazareth?" (John 1:46). Nazareth was Israel's Fayette'nam.

Palestine is and has been infamous for its shifting and contested borders. According to the Romans of the first century, it was a part of the province of Syria, which explains why it was patrolled by local *auxilia* rather than elite *legionarii*.[4] A brief but inspiring period of independence secured by the Maccabean rebellion would have rekindled devout Jews' biblical imagination. Mary and Joseph's generation may well have viewed the land through the tribal allotments of Joshua 19 rather than through the eyes of Roman boundaries. Those who did would have known Nazareth was dead center in the land of Zebulun, the commando clan of Israel, that Jesus was a military brat by birth as well as by residence.

Mary, as a blood relative (*syngenes*, G4773) of Elizabeth, belonged to the landless, priestly tribe of Levi (see Luke 1:5). Joseph, as a descendant of King David, would have a claim to live in the land of Judah. But it takes Quirinius's census to compel him to return to his ancestral homeland, and when he does, he takes his family only as far as the border town of Bethlehem. Surely there were carpenters in Judah, where he could have plied his trade. The holy family seems uninterested in living on the right side of the tracks, so to speak. When he comes of age, Jesus doesn't head to greener pastures in Judah either. He clings instead to the region belonging to Zebulun's battle buddy Naphtali, also known as Galilee. Not only does he grow up in a maligned military town, but operating in Galilee allows his healing to be received first by the disgraced military communities of Israel.

ZEBULUN AND NAPHTALI

Zebulun, whose name means "honor" (*zaval*, H2082), was the youngest of Leah's six boys by the patriarch Jacob. Naphtali (*naftul*, H5319), the youngest of Bilhah's two boys, foreshadows his father as a victorious "wrestler."[5] As the younger of the two half brothers, Zebulun gets primacy of place in the Bible, preceding Naphtali in nearly every mention.

In the desert, after their escape from Egypt, Zebulun's and Naphtali's descendants were relied upon for their military prowess. When the Israelites were on the march, Zebulun was in the front with the tribes of Judah and Isaachar, and Naphtali brought up the rear with the tribes of Dan and Asher.[6] Grunts will recognize this as standard operating procedure; the highest ranking leads the way and the second in command brings up the rear. When the people set up camp, Zebulun was part of Judah's regiment on the prestigious east side, closest to the rising sun and the entrance to the Tabernacle. Naphtali, part of Dan's regiment, was beside them on the north side.

After the successful campaign under Joshua to take the Promised Land, the two tribes become neighbors, with Naphtali as the northernmost tribe, above the Sea of Galilee, and Zebulun occupying land to the south and west. The book of Judges stands out as a dark time in Israel's history, with infighting and anarchy often prevailing over camaraderie and order. Zebulun and Naphtali rarely got into scuffles with one another, perhaps because of the bond they shared as Israel's troop-heavy tribes.

The oldest part of the Hebrew Bible, the Song of Deborah, describes how the two tribes "scorned death" (Judg. 5:18) at Mount Tabor against the forces of Sisera. Zebulun is singled out as the proud bearer of Israel's *shevet safar*, the marshal's staff or, more literally, "guidon of order"[7] (see Judg. 5:14). A chapter later, Gideon calls on the twin tribes (see 6:35) to fight near "the hill of Moreh" (7:1), where they defeat the Midianites despite being impossibly outnumbered.

Jesus seems to prefer the land of his people's most militant members not because Israel worshipped their soldiers but because they sympathized with the brokenhearted. In Isaiah 9, Zebulun and Naphtali, whose bloodstained boots once tramped all over Israel's enemies, have been consigned to live "in a land of deep darkness" (Isa. 9:2). Their mighty deeds "on the day of Midian" (Isa. 9:4) are recalled through the curse of hindsight, after the dust has settled and the stresses of combat have set in. How did the bearers of Israel's martial standard go from proud patriots to victimized veterans?

Israel's stature peaked under the unified kingdoms of Saul, David, and Solomon. Once the kingdom became divided, they fell back into chaos and infighting with leaders often competing for power. This left tribes on the margins of Israel particularly vulnerable to enemy attack, including Zebulun and Naphtali. They were the first to be carried off into exile in Assyria in the eighth century BCE, where Isaiah says they languished in a land of deep darkness. Perhaps the tragic irony that the first to be overcome were the most skilled soldiers is what drove Israel to regard them as such an embarrassment. Although the prophet watched as eight other tribes were scattered by Assyria, it was Zebulun and Naphtali in particular who were "brought into contempt" (Isa. 9:1). The good news for military communities like them was that the humiliation heaped upon defeated soldiers is precisely where Jesus chooses to begin his earthly ministry.

As soon as he learns of his cousin John's arrest, Jesus makes Capernaum in the land of Naphtali his new home "so that what had been spoken through the prophet Isaiah might be fulfilled" (Matt. 4:14). Isaiah's prophecy is militaristic, not in the narrow modern sense of war and violence, but in the ancient and true sense of structure and order. Soldiering is inseparable from this Jewish Messiah who identifies with Israel's disgraced commando clans.

The story of Zebulun and Naphtali is about a people, not just a place. Basing his ministry in their ancestral homelands meant Christ was redeeming those "who were in anguish…the people who walked in darkness" (Isa. 9:1–2). By privileging military communities, openly undoing their dishonor and rewinding their defeats, Jesus was pointing to God's reassurance in Isaiah's prophecy, "[Zebulun and Naphtali] have seen a great light…on them light has shined" (Isa. 9:2). Everyone looks to the light, like a shining city on a hill. God is reclaiming his military rank and redeeming the social stigma placed upon Israel's "war-torn" veterans.

Viewed in this light, Jesus' saving work takes the shape of a wildly successful military campaign, one that will mirror their great victory "as on the day of Midian" (Isa. 9:4) near the hill of Moreh. Not only was the historic battlefield in Nazareth's neighborhood, but the traditional site of Jesus' transfiguration also occurs at Mount Tabor, where Deborah and Ja'el claimed victory over Sisera. Jesus' ministry is distinctly militaristic. He is not an outsider to the military; he is its exemplar. He is, after all, the only Son of a Great Warrior.

DIVINE WARRIOR

Maybe you've noticed that I use the word "warrior" pretty sparingly. Besides being overused, it fails to describe what the military is meant to do. Most Christians since the third or fourth century have insisted that war should always be a last resort. Nothing exists solely for an activity it should rarely, if ever, engage in. The role of a military is order and justice, which may require violence. I refer to military personnel as soldiers because war is not supposed to be their main function and calling them warriors can imply that it is.

The popularity of a "warrior culture" in the United States Army can be traced to the March 2003 ambush of the 507th Maintenance Company in Iraq. The incident made clear that every soldier needed to be much more prepared for conventional combat, a real-world prooftext for the idea that every soldier "is a rifleman."[8] By the end of that year, the Army added a "Warrior Ethos" to the standard Soldier's Creed. Training and Doctrine Command head honcho General Kevin Byrnes told a *Washington Post* reporter that "[Soldiers will] tell you 'I'm a mechanic,' not 'I'm a soldier,' and we've got to change that."[9] When we think all our tools are hammers, all we see are nails. Field Manual 3-21.75 begins by contradicting federal law defining the Army's purpose, erroneously claiming, "Military service is…a profession with the enduring purpose to win wars and destroy our nation's enemies."[10]

Soldiers serve communities by protecting the fair and just ordering of creation established by God over chaos. If they fight, it is for that higher purpose; nobody fights for the sake of fighting. In Exodus 15, newly manumitted slaves have just witnessed an imperial force drowned at sea by God's miraculous work. In response, they sing out, "The LORD is a warrior; the LORD is his name" (v. 3). In Hebrew, God is literally "a man of *milhama* (H4421)," a term that derives from a verb that means "to eat or devour." God is a powerful figure who devours those who come against his battle buddies, just as the Egyptians were devoured by the sea. By calling God a warrior, the Israelites fundamentally challenge the ASK stereotype that assumes all soldiers kill (or should). On the one hand, this relieves us of having to fight our own battles, but it is also a warning against taking up the sword when it belongs to God.

In *God Is a Warrior*, scholars Tremper Longman III and Daniel G. Reid identify a five-stage development of the Divine Warrior motif that unfolds chronologically in the Bible.[11] In the first, God fights for Israel in Egypt, in the wilderness, and in the Canaan campaign. But almost immediately God shows that Israel is not immune to violent wrath, with God fighting *against* Israel at times in the wilderness and in Canaan, but particularly in the time of Judges. The third stage is reserved almost entirely to the time of the unified kingdom and exile, when the prophets speak of a coming deliverer who will be like David but even better. The fourth stage crosses the threshold into the New Testament, where God, in Christ, will directly engage the forces of evil and injustice. The fifth and final stage is only alluded to in apocalyptic literature of both the Old and the New Testaments, in which God's final victory is secured.

1. GOD FIGHTS FOR US

In Egypt, the Israelites would never have been allowed to produce or possess anything they might use to defend themselves. God is the only actor performing violence of any kind against Pharaoh and the Egyptians. The first nine plagues, Passover, and the final destruction of Israel's enemy by drowning is achieved entirely by God's power alone. As they fled, Israel was a ragtag cluster of political refugees who had just been freed from enslavement.

While they wandered in the desert, the people were workers and shepherds, not infantry and artillery. They were not an armed force moving about the land, they were nomads unlearning the ways of the so-called civilized world. Nothing could be taken for granted. If they took more *manna* (H4478) than they needed, the mysterious food would spoil overnight (see Ex. 16). If they planted a garden, the pillars of smoke and fire might appear, beckoning them to pick up and move. It was the same lesson I learned when I spent about nine months on a quick reaction force (QRF) in Iraq. We lived moment by moment because we never knew when we might have to pick up and leave, tasked with a new mission in a faraway area of operation. When you live out of your duffel bag, all you can count on is what you have. You *have* no control, so you stop trying to *be* in control. Before meditation and yoga became so popular, it was combat that taught me to be present in the moment.

Even when Joshua led the *Militia Dei* in taking the land promised to Israel, there was no consistent strategy employed, no standing orders, and no permanent rules of engagement. No two battles
in the book of Joshua are the same. This was not because Israel had
no moral code, but because their moral code had one simple rule—
obey God's commands. Deviate even slightly and there would be
painful consequences.

At first glance, it might appear that God is playing fuck-fuck
games with Israel in the desert. When a commander makes your life
more difficult than it needs to be, it may feel like they're just fucking
with you, making you want to fuck with them back. After the Iraqi
election in January 2005, we were supposed to return to Kuwait to
fly home, but it got pushed back. Talk about wanting to get back
at the brass for keeping us there…When we finally headed back,
rumors spread that a soldier died "playing Russian roulette," which
many of us took to mean that he took his own life. The delay was to
conduct an investigation and inform the soldier's next of kin. Had
we known at the time, it would have made sense and eased tensions
somewhat. Someone also could have prematurely blabbed about it,
so command rightly decided to keep it hush-hush.

Nobody likes fuck-fuck games but there is (sometimes) a method
to the madness, a reason for suffering. God wanted Israel on their
toes, to keep them from getting complacent and trusting in their
own abilities. When they thought they could stand on their own two
feet was when they started to have problems. When people think
they can fight, God is there to remind them they can't.

2. GOD FIGHTS AGAINST US

The scary truth is that the Divine Warrior fights *for* us as much as *against* us. God alone deserves the credit for freeing Israel from Egyptian slavery because God was both in command and in control. As the story unfolds, the people are given incrementally more agency; in the fight with the Amalekites where Joshua was introduced, God was with Israel only so long as Moses was able to keep his hands up. They continued to be given bit after bit of autonomy in the ensuing battles, but God was quick to recall control when they messed up.

As they were returning from Mount Sinai with the stone tablets, Joshua told Moses that he heard "a noise of war in the camp" (Exod. 32:17), but it was the people, acting like they just got their first pass during boot camp. In response, God had Moses call his Levitical tribesmen to his side and tell them, "Put your sword on your side, each of you! Go back and forth from gate to gate throughout the camp, and each of you kill your brother, your friend, and your neighbor" (Exod. 32:27).

The first thing Levites do as the ordained priestly caste for Israel is to kill three thousand of their own countrymen at the command of God. The Divine Warrior may fight for Israel, but that does not mean God always takes their side. When Joshua encountered the "commander of the army of the LORD" (Josh. 5:14), he asked "Are you one of us, or one of our adversaries?" (v. 13). The angel, his superior officer, had replied, "*Neither*" (5:14, emphasis added). God cannot be reduced to an either/or, a cheap talisman that simply reinforces our own preconceptions. Just because we have a covenantal partnership doesn't mean God runs to our side every time we call.

3. GOD (WILL FIGHT) WITH US

The prophets serve as the heralds of a coming day when God will step down from heaven and make war on evil in person. Some prophets are more worldly and realistic about this "day of the Lord," like Isaiah and Ezekiel, but others really go for a fantastical, hyperbolic approach, like Daniel and Zechariah. More on them later, but the basic message is the same: God's Anointed One, *mashiyach* (H4899), will come to earth to take matters into his own hands.

The day of the Lord will begin not with a bang (wink, wink), but with a birth: a young woman will bear this "God is with us" (see Isa. 7:14), who will be a suffering servant[12] and the "Prince of Peace" (Isa. 9:6) rather than a man of *milhama*. Since the Jewish day begins at sundown, many texts suggest his arrival will prompt evil to increase briefly as a messenger, thought to be the prophet Elijah, "prepare[s] the way" for a decisive battle (Mal. 3:1). The incarnate Divine Warrior will ultimately drive darkness away with force.

The Anointed One will be unique but not new, his "origin is from of old, from ancient days" (Mic. 5:2). Whatever this Divine Warrior is or does, his identity and mission are thoroughly determined by God's covenant with the descendants of Abraham and the line of David. Israel will have their Savior and be exalted before the nations.

4. GOD IS A GRUNT

The fourth phase of the Divine Warrior motif is the promise realized, when God comes to earth to fight alongside us, to show us what to fight for and how to fight. The appeal of a Divine Warrior coming to liberate the Jews was widespread by the time the Romans oversaw Palestine. Many Jews led uprisings with promises of independence, using more of the hyperbolic violent imagery than that of the suffering peaceful servant. The Maccabees did not make messianic claims, but many rebels did, including Simon of Perea, Athronges, Judas of Galilee, Theudas, and Simon Bar Kokhba.

As God, Christ is the Divine Warrior. Humans are not called to be warriors, for we cannot fulfill Jesus' role as God. But as a human, Jesus chose to be little more than a lowly grunt. As he was arrested, Jesus made clear that, as Commander in Chief, thousands of angels were at his disposal. His choice at that critical moment was to remain an earthly soldier. He would serve by *giving* his life rather than lead others in *taking* life.

Paul, the only apostle with theological training, told the Christians in Philippi that Jesus, "though he was in the form of God, did not regard equality with God as something to be exploited, but emptied himself, taking the form of a slave, being born in human likeness. And being found in human form, he humbled himself and became obedient to the point of death—even death on a cross" (Phil. 2:6–8).

His description has overt military connotations. In 42 BCE, Philippi was the site of a battle between legions loyal to the new emperors, Mark Antony and Octavian, and legions loyal to the old republic. The imperial forces prevailed, and the republic was effectively over. Octavian's Twenty-Eighth Legion was near the end of their twenty-five years of service, and it was customary for legionaries to be discharged with land and money, the equivalent of modern veterans' benefits. In honor of their service, the city was called a "Victory Colony." Twelve years later, in 30 BCE, Octavian retired more veterans, this time from his secret service unit, the Praetorian Guard. Philippi is a military community, and we cannot fully appreciate what Saul wrote without reading it through their eyes.[13] What he says here about Jesus is so important he states it twice for emphasis: he emptied himself; he humbled himself. If Jesus is God, then God is a grunt.

Most soldiers of modest means would not have owned slaves. They would not have understood Saul to be saying Jesus is below them. Rather, they may have felt like slaves themselves insofar as their primary task was to obey orders, to serve the interests of others rather than their own. Jesus meets us where we are at. In Philippi, as in most military families today, Jesus meets us as a grunt, at the bottom of the heap. The good news for grunts is that Jesus does not grasp at high rank but demotes himself to a lowly grunt. Though he might look and act like an E-1, as our Commander in Chief, he is ready and willing to die for his subordinates, whom he calls his battle buddies.

To be a part of Jesus' movement we are invited back to earth, to the bottom rung of the ladder. Whether you call it "emptied," as Paul did (Phil. 2:7), or "lowliness" (*tapeinosis*, G5014), which Mary preferred (Luke 1:48), there are plenty of appropriate metaphors to describe Jesus' chosen social status. Military communities have another term for making the best of a bad hand: "embracing the suck." The beauty of this maxim is unveiled as Paul continued, "Therefore God also highly exalted him and gave him the name that is above every name" (Phil. 2:9). The humility Yehoshua embraces is the direct cause for his exaltation. That name is important, it is not some transliterated nonsensical sound; when we say his name and accept his low status, we are affirming God's promise of our salvation.

When we are at our lowest, our Commander in Chief is there with us. There is nowhere, in heaven or on earth, that God cannot accompany us. And if he is there with us, he can lead us from suffering to glory. And if anyone knows what suffering is like, it is the men and women who spend every waking hour taking orders, serving their community, and bearing the weight of glory.

5. GOD PREVAILS

The fifth stage of the Divine Warrior in the Bible is the conquering of chaos and injustice in a final showdown. Apocalyptic prophets provide the foundation for the New Testament to bring the motif full circle. Nowhere is there more metaphor and hyperbole than in John's Revelation. It is in this final book of the canon that the Divine Warrior is imagined in all its glory, bringing Exodus's Warrior God full circle to apocalyptic war-maker.

Exodus's Warrior God emerged in response to a crisis of his covenant partners, and the story is not that different in Revelation. Written toward the end of the first century, it was composed from exile after Roman forces had destroyed the Second (Yehoshua's) Temple. The final showdown with evil happens in Revelation 19, when we get a glimpse of the long-awaited victory over sin. It is important to notice that the "multitude" (vv. 1, 6) does not engage in battle, God alone is the Warrior. Humans and angels alike, regardless of rank or status, are mere "comrades" (Rev. 19:10) whose primary task is to collectively bear witness to our Commander in Chief.

What we are shown when God rides in on a white warhorse is another key to understanding him as a Divine Warrior. His garments are stained in blood (see Rev. 19:13), not because he has a high kill count but because he threw himself on a grenade. As the atoning scapegoat, he rides a horse to avoid limping from the many injuries we, as enemies of God, inflicted upon him. The so-called "armies [*strateuma*, G4753] of heaven" (v. 14) that follow him have no bloodstains on their uniforms and are completely unarmed. The Divine Warrior wields the only weapon on the battlefield, but a sword "from his mouth" (v. 21) is not a sword in his hand.

There is no mistaking that the Divine Warrior is Jesus Christ. But the crucial distinction cannot be overstated; we are not God, he is. Premeditated violence is God's alone to undertake. The good fight of the faith is to remain humble and to persevere hardships as godly grunts. Although we may aspire to be stealthy operators or become ordained, that is not our primary calling. Rather, we are to be a people who live by example rather than by force. That's why God's battle dress uniform is made up mostly of defensive instruments rather than offensive weapons.

GOD'S ARMOR

We get a detailed accounting of God's armor in Ephesians 6:11–17, where, according to someone claiming to be Paul, we learn what items believers are issued from heaven's central issuing facility (CIF):[14]

Put on the whole armor of God, so that you may be able to stand against the wiles of the devil. For our struggle is not against enemies of blood and flesh, but against the rulers, against the authorities, against the cosmic powers of this present darkness, against the spiritual forces of evil in the heavenly places. Therefore take up the whole armor of God, so that you may be able to withstand on that evil day, and having done everything, to stand firm. Stand therefore, and fasten the belt of truth around your waist, and put on the breastplate of righteousness. As shoes for your feet put on whatever will make you ready to proclaim the gospel of peace. With all of these, take the shield of faith, with which you will be able to quench all the flaming arrows of the evil one. Take the helmet of salvation, and the sword of the Spirit, which is the word of God.

Paul's authorship of this letter is suspect because it stands out like a sore thumb from other letters, and one of the ways it does so concerns this passage about God's armor. Compare it to an undisputed letter like 1 Thessalonians, which is considered the earliest text composed to make it into the New Testament. In the fifth chapter we get a slightly different version of God's armor. Paul instructs believers to "put on the breastplate of faith and love, and for a helmet the hope of salvation" (1 Thess. 5:8). This earlier text soft-pedals the metaphor in a noticeable way by omitting the belt, shield, shoes, and sword.

The book of Revelation seems familiar with these two accounts, but its author prefers an even older tradition found in the books of Isaiah and the Wisdom of Solomon. The oldest is Isaiah, where God has "put on righteousness like a breastplate, and a helmet of salvation on his head; he put on garments of vengeance for clothing, and wrapped himself in fury as in a mantle" (59:17). The Wisdom of Solomon passage is longer, likely inspiring the passage from Ephesians: "The Lord will take his zeal as his whole armor, and will arm all creation to repel his enemies; he will put on righteousness as a breastplate, and wear impartial justice as a helmet; he will take holiness as an invincible shield, and sharpen stern wrath for a sword, and creation will join with him to fight against his frenzied foes" (Wis. 5:17–20).

To make the final showdown flashy and dramatic, John leans heavily on the prophetic imagery of vengeance and fury. Where Paul tones down the violent imagery, John ratchets it up, giving the Divine Warrior a far sharper edge. The wrathful sword from Wisdom and furious mantle from Isaiah are combined in a way that comes off as a rebuttal to Paul's peacenik sandals. Rather than proclaiming peace, Jesus' feet "will tread the winepress of the fury of the wrath of God the Almighty" (Rev. 19:15).

Paul wants to paint a detailed picture of the Divine Warrior not just so we know what God does as a soldier, but so we know how God operates. Paul's interactions with soldiers give us a detailed and consistent picture of Roman service, which we will get to in the next chapter. Between his many arrests and time spent serving pretrial detention, Paul becomes intimately familiar with the soldiers guarding him. For his letters he borrows what he sees and combines it with the traditions he is familiar with to flesh out the metaphor a bit more.

God's standard issue, according to Isaiah, includes righteousness, salvation, vengeance, and fury. It's a bit more tooth than tail when compared to Paul's, even if it lacks a sword. The Thessalonians version has the same vestments, a breastplate and a helmet, but is considerably...softer. Paul sees a more conciliatory God than the prophets of old, just as he sees the main military force with less animosity than other authors like Mark and John, who really have a chip on their shoulders for their oppressors. Even the Wisdom version is couched in zeal and ends with wrath, evoking more of Isaiah's fiery vision, but Paul strikes a necessary balance.

The first century was filled with messianic pretenders leading the charge against injustice and evil only to be struck down by the powers of the world. God the Son no longer fights against enemies of flesh and blood, as when God the Father fought for (and against) us before we were given the prophets. This is why Paul emphasizes that the real battle is "against the spiritual forces of evil" (Eph. 6:12).

Romans are not the problem so much as our animosity toward them. We confuse evil with evildoers, as though by getting rid of the latter we rid the world of the former. That's not how it works. Jesus is here to remind us that the fight against evildoers belongs to God, not to us. We are called to battle our *own* sense of self-righteousness and entitlement by humbly emptying ourselves, as our Commander has shown us.

5.
EARLY ATTITUDES, OR *THE EARLIEST* ATTITUDES?
GIs IN THE NEW TESTAMENT

ALL CHRISTIANS DESCEND, SPIRITUALLY, FROM THE EARLY church. The differences between traditions and denominations all grew out of disagreements that came well after the first few centuries. So, the earlier we can trace our beliefs, the less we should disagree, right? If one person can prove that the earliest Christians believed that military service was wrong, then it's on the other person to prove that the early Christians were mistaken. This was a popular tack taken at academic conferences and journals I followed as a student veteran in seminary.

Every weekday in my first graduate theology program at Duke Divinity School, I would watch the *Colbert Report* on my lunch break. There was a running bit that I got a kick out of in which the faux-conservative satirical host would fluster progressive interviewees by asking "George W. Bush: a great president or *the greatest* president?"[1] Professors at my school talked about soldiers in Scripture as though Jesus and his disciples could barely contain their disdain. Dean Richard Hays, a New Testament scholar, had argued in an influential book that the narrative function of grunts in the Gospels was to represent "the most unsavory characters."[2] That wasn't my impression when I read the Bible, and I imagined myself asking New Testament scholars about Christian soldiers: Are these early attitudes, or *the earliest* attitudes?

As it turns out, Christian soldiers have been right in front of us the whole time. Either soldiers in Scripture are historical figures and members of the earliest church, or they are inventions that disclose an ambiguous (Mark) to positive (Luke–Acts) attitude toward soldiers held by the earliest Christians. Any academic who makes broad claims about the early church being pacifist is not doing scholarship; they're doing punditry. It was only later, when I began to push back against blatant intellectual laziness, that I realized a lot of pacifists mirrored Colbert's satirical anchorman: "well-intentioned, poorly informed, high-status idiot[s]."[3]

CHRISTIANS WITH ATTITUDES

Across the ideological spectrum, Christian scholars I encountered in my studies took it as a given that there was little evidence that Christians served in the military until the second century. Arguments focused on older arguments, as theologians debated one another across time about which talking head had the best theory about the idea of military service. A few references to the *earliest* Christian soldiers, as in the followers of Jesus right there in the Bible, served as little else but prooftexts. In one book published in the middle of my studies, Christian anarchist Andy Alexis-Baker somehow read Matthew 8 and Luke 7 to suggest a soldier in the New Testament possessed a "faulty view of Jesus" that put Jesus within "the demonic imperial chain of command."[4]

Alexis-Baker may be on the left edge of scholarship, and the essay was not peer-reviewed (the gold standard for academic publishing), but his argument would have been laughed out of the room had it been argued in a space that was ideologically diverse. After about a decade in the fields myself, I've found that Christian theology and ethics is not all that diverse. Twentieth-century Christian scholarship has skewed hard toward the left because studies of the early church are dominated by pacifists claiming to know early Christian attitudes. For example:

C. John Cadoux, *The Early Christian Attitude to War: A Contribution to the History of Christian Ethics* (London: Headley Bros., 1919)

Roland Bainton, *Christian Attitudes toward War and Peace: A Historical Survey and Critical Reevaluation* (Nashville: Abingdon, 1960)

Jean-Michel Hornus, *It Is Not Lawful for Me to Fight: Early Christian Attitudes toward War, Violence, and the State,* trans. Alan Kreider and Oliver Coburn (Harrisonburg, VA: Herald, 1980)

John Howard Yoder, *Christian Attitudes to War, Peace, and*

Revolution: A Companion to Bainton, (Harrisonburg, VA: Herald, 1983)

George Kalantzis, *Caesar and the Lamb: Early Christian Attitudes on War and Military Service* (Eugene, OR: Wipf and Stock, 2012)

Of these authors, only Cadoux and Bainton served in war, in British WWI ambulance units run by Quakers, a pacifist denomination. Kreider, who translated Hornus's work, and Yoder were Mennonites, another pacifist denomination. Yoder was too young for WWII and too old for Vietnam, and Kreider spent the 1960s at Princeton and Harvard. But that doesn't necessarily matter, because college students and clergy have historically been exempt from conscription. Anybody who enters college young and becomes a minister can avoid military service indefinitely, and their understanding of (and commentary about) war will always be through degrees of separation. The end of the draft in the midst of a war in Vietnam just made it easier by forcing the burden of service onto the shoulders of those for whom it represented the best of only a very few options. The result is that over the last century, the lived experience of soldiering has become increasingly alien to "educated" faith communities.

By the time I entered formal theological training, what I didn't know was that I was also entering an intellectually incestuous echo chamber without a mechanism or incentive to self-correct when so-called scholars veer off into crazy town. Richard Hays, for example, published his belief that "the place of the soldier within the church can *only* be seen as anomalous."[5] In a 2010 exchange with pro-war ethicist Nigel Biggar in the *Journal of the Society of Christian Ethics*, he insisted "the three or four texts that mention soldiers…[were] the oddities," that stood "in tension with the great weight of the [New Testament] witness."[6] At a 2012 conference of the Society of Christian Ethics (SCE) focused on war, only professors or PhD students could submit papers and participate in panels; I had to listen and comment from the audience. When I did happen upon a veteran SCE member, we commiserated over dinner about the pressures to conform to antimilitary sentiments prevalent in the society and Christian academia more broadly. He wasn't going to endanger his career though; challenging bias would have to wait until he reached tenure.

If you accept that the military is primarily about organization and structure, you will notice that the New Testament overwhelmingly shows soldiers doing what they are supposed to do: keeping order, protecting the innocent, and governing in partnership with the local populace. The soldiers, centurions, and tribunes of the New Testament are first and foremost human beings; good but imperfect. But to hear it from prominent theologians, Christian soldiers are little more than anomalous oddities, "the unlikeliest people" to be sought out by Jesus, "complete outsider[s]" to the story being told in the New Testament.[7]

This might explain how George Kalantzis, cited above, saw no issue with publishing his belief, transposed onto second-century Christians, that "what is asked of soldiers is to kill."[8] The only place I was told my primary responsibility was to kill was in boot camp. Believing all soldiers kill is like the *Left Behind* series taking John's

Revelation literally; it mistakes hyperbole for reality. It's pretty crazy when academics do it. But that's what happens when ideology drives theology. So let's rewind all the partisan rhetoric and look at what the New Testament and the context within which it was composed actually have to say about *the earliest* attitudes toward soldiers.

MILITARY SERVICE IN THE NEW TESTAMENT

A lot is actually known about the soldiers in the Gospels and Acts, some of whom can be called Christian. To get a sense of the diverse military representation within the New Testament, however, it will be necessary to understand militaries and their organization in first-century Palestine.[9]

First there were militaries formed and maintained by client states like the Herodian kingdom in the Roman province of Judea. The imperial name for these local forces was *numeri*, and they were little more than expendable barbarian hordes the emperor could lean on against external threats. They served under the authority of their own king and had little to no investment in imperial culture or customs. They might have been conscripted against their will and served with no pay, or they may have been incentivized by monetary or other rewards.

Then there were *auxilia*, armed forces made up of locals recruited into lengthy terms of service through the promise of basic pay, good food, and Roman citizenship at discharge. As locals, they spoke whatever language was common to their area of operation. They also typically spoke Greek to interact between and across client state boundaries and had to understand some Latin in order to take orders from their Roman superiors. They often had dual loyalties to their regional political apparatus as well as to imperial interests. For this same reason, they might have been treated with some suspicion by both.

These two types of forces, *numeri* and *auxilia*, were the overwhelming majority in Palestine during Jesus' lifetime. Christopher Zeichmann, a scholar bridging Roman military history and the New Testament, has shown convincingly that the soldiers Jesus and his followers encountered would have been ethnically similar to them, and some would have been Jews themselves. Whereas it is common knowledge in academia that Jews were not drafted into Roman military service, "there is no indication that this prevented them from serving of their own accord."[10] In 6 CE, the region was annexed after disputes between Herod's heirs forced Rome to intervene. Herod Antipas secured the emperor's blessing, but the trade-off was much closer Roman supervision. Before the kerfuffle, military forces active in Judaea were mostly Herodian *numeri*, but the effect of Roman intervention was an influx of *auxilia* from their new parent province of Roman Syria. These Syrian forces aspired to be Roman but were rooted in their own indigenous culture, which would not have been all that different from their Judean neighbors' to the south.

The common misconception that soldiers in the New Testament were fair-skinned, Italian foreigners comes from gospel authors, whose political situation differed significantly from Jesus' own context. No gospel was composed until after the Jewish War of 66–70 CE, the result of which was the destruction of the temple that the high priest Joshua established. Without a sacrificial system, not only did Jesus' movement attract mourning Jews, but it also became more palatable to Gentiles, like the *legionarii* assigned to Judaea after the war. The uprising suggested that the *numeri* and *auxilia* had failed by being either too friendly to Judaeans or simply incapable of containing threats. From about 70 CE onward, the situation went from regional policing to outright occupation.

Legionarii were citizens from birth, directly employed by Rome, whose service and loyalty differed from that of the *auxilia*. Because Rome couldn't use citizenship to get them to enlist, their standard pay was higher, they were offered frequent bonuses, and they were all but encouraged to extort the locals. These soldiers were usually native Latin speakers who spoke Greek only as necessary. Although they found ways around it, legionaries were prohibited from marrying while on active duty. Where they went, sex workers followed. Debauchery and extortion were two of the biggest objections Jews made about *legionarii* in and around the Holy Land.

The Gospels and Acts were written in the wake of the Jewish War by communities under foreign occupation, but the events they describe were not so polarized. Soldiers that Jesus and his followers encountered were Middle Eastern by modern standards, not European. What you read in the New Testament is about a community reacting to a more oppressive governance than the settings they describe. And because none of the writers were soldiers themselves, their descriptions are approximations at best and caricatures at worst.

Whereas soldiers are attentive to the importance of rank and grade (do I salute? go to parade rest?) and the power systems inherent

therein, the words used by New Testament authors are not historically reliable. At the bottom of the heap are *stratiotes* (G4757), from
the root word *stratia* (G4756), an assembly. They were the rank-
and-file cannon fodder grunts. Hard to fuck them up, literally and
figuratively. "Centurion" (*hekatontarches*, G1543), however, was
used to indicate anyone the evangelists assumed was in charge of one
hundred soldiers, with no consideration for military rank or social
status. This lack of familiarity with the military marred the telling
of the story before it became canon, and the same problem skews its
interpretation by biblical scholars today.

Romans used *hekatontarches* the way today's Army uses "sergeant"; it both *is* and *is not* a formal title. There are many different
modern ranks that use the word, prompting questions from military
insiders: staff, platoon, first, or master? Likewise in Latin, there are
titles for varying centurions in charge of the basic Roman military
unit known as a *centuria* (from *centum*, meaning "one hundred").
Just like the Army has companies within battalions within brigades,
Rome had *centuriae* within *cohortes* within *legiones*. And just like
there are noncommissioned officers at every level of Army leadership, there were centurions nested like Russian matryoshka dolls in
units of varying size and status.

The only true *hekatontarches* was the *primi ordines*, equivalent to
a first sergeant (1SG), whose only responsibility was the one hundred soldiers of a century. Six centuries made up a Roman cohort,
with the highest ranking of six centurions serving as *piles prior*, the
equivalent of a master sergeant (MSG). His century was filled with
only the best one hundred soldiers but he held sway over all six

hundred, technically a *sescentarches*. Ten cohorts made up a legion of about six thousand soldiers and their sixty centurions, the highest ranking serving as *primus pilus*, the equivalent of a command sergeant major (CSM). This was the lifer of the legion who ascended the ranks from the bottom and who was the brawn to the officers' brain. Because Latin titles do not lend themselves to Greek, and because civilians wrote (and interpret) the New Testament, these distinctions disappear.

Commissioned officers in the Roman military were tribunes, men in their twenties who came from the senatorial class of Rome. In the New Testament they all are *chiliarchos* (G5506), "head of one thousand," but there were no Roman units of that size. Concentrated in a legion's headquarters were five junior "narrow stripe" and a senior "broad stripe" tribune. Technically these officers commanded one cohort each, with the oldest serving as a kind of "first among equals" like the centurions, but they rarely left the headquarters element of a legion. The junior officers, roughly approximate to captains in the Army, were of the upper equestrian class preparing for a political career that served a mostly administrative role. The senior tribune, something like a colonel in the Army, served as the executive officer, or second in command to the politically appointed commander, the *legatus*.

With this brief overview of military service during the first century, the particularities of soldiers in the New Testament become clearer. As we will see from the following examples, the first evidence of Christians serving in the military occurred well before the second century. In fact, our earliest examples, from Luke's gospel, can be doubted as Christian only because they preceded Christ's active ministry. Let's go from military service during the New Testament to military service within it.

JOHN BAPTIZES SOLDIERS

The baptizer named John comes "proclaiming a baptism of repentance for the forgiveness of sins" (Luke 3:3). Religiosity ran thick in his family, and not just your garden-variety religion either. His mother, Elizabeth, descended from the tribe of Levi through Moses' brother Aaron, and his father, Zechariah, "belonged to the priestly order of Abijah" (Luke 1:5). Abijah was one of twenty-two "priests and Levites who came up with Zerubbabel son of Sheatiel, and Jeshua" (Neh. 12:1) from captivity in Assyria to rebuild the temple.[11] The reference to Abijah's "order" is about Zechariah's place in the rotation of sacrificial responsibilities in the temple. Luke's language will be familiar to grunts because it is essentially a work detail; Zechariah's "section was on duty" (Luke 1:8).

Out of twenty-four priestly lots cast, Abijah and his descendants were made eighth in rotation and Jeshua (aka Joshua) was ninth (see 1 Chron. 24:11). Jeshua, or Yeshua, is a shortened version of Yehoshua, the son of Jozadak, whom we like to call Joshua. Attentive readers will notice that Zechariah's duty fell immediately prior to the lot once reserved for Zerubbabel's high priest, who was responsible for building the second temple. That means that, like his ancestor Abijah, John precedes and prepares the way for Yehoshua, whom we like to call Jesus.

Anyway, back to Luke 3. John's initial followers are fellow Jews, whom he reminds not to feel too high and mighty simply because they are descendants of Abraham. His "baptism of repentance" is no easy pill to swallow, and he chastises the very people who come to him, calling them "a brood of vipers" (Luke 3:7). The crowd responds by asking what they should do, a question repeated by a tax collector and soldiers.

The text suggests the first cluster of onlookers are Jews, descendants of Abraham, implying that the tax collectors and soldiers are not. There were Jewish tax collectors, like the apostle Matthew, called Levi, and there were Jewish soldiers in both the Herodian *numeri* and the Roman *auxilia*. Although we do not know if the tax man or his bodyguards are Jewish, it's a distinct possibility. There is no evidence in Luke that the soldiers are just wandering around and happen upon this disheveled shaman shouting down passersby. While it *is* possible they are simply accompanying the tax collector, who "came to be baptized" (Luke 3:12), that doesn't explain why they speak up. Their interaction with John signals that they are intrigued by his particular mission, his "baptism of repentance," and want to know more.

If it is their identity *as soldiers* that is driving their moral curiosity, violence would not be top of mind. For ancient and modern soldiers alike, the amount of actual combat they perform represents a negligible proportion of their time. Most of their days are spent policing, supporting governmental administration, and providing humanitarian aid. When the soldiers ask John what to do, he responds by addressing their most egregious abuse, which is extortion.[12] He doesn't tell them to leave the military because the military did as much, if not more, good than evil. Nobody present at the baptism saw soldiering itself as a sin.

Although Luke 3 is ambiguous, there is good reason to believe they were baptized. First, John tells "*all* of them...'I baptize you with water'" (Luke 3:16, emphasis added). Seems pretty clear. As if that's not enough, Luke refers back to this episode four chapters later in the midst of another encounter with a Roman soldier. Jesus is reminding another crowd of what his cousin John had done, and Luke tells his audience in a parenthetical remark, "*All* the people who heard this, including the tax collectors...had been baptized" (Luke 7:29, emphasis added).[13] The soldiers weren't seen as the worst of the lot; the tax collectors were! The only question is whether those John baptized were properly "Christian," a term that didn't exist yet, as John and Jesus thought of themselves as Jews. Insofar as the soldiers believed in their twin ministries, it's perfectly reasonable to think of them as Christian.

CAPTAIN MARVEL

The soldier at the center of Luke 7 (and Matthew 8) is usually remembered as the centurion of great faith, but that's kind of a mouthful and it tells us little about him or his service. That's too bad, because there is plenty to know about the soldier who makes Jesus *thaumazo* (G2296), which the English Standard Version translates as "marvel" (Luke 7:9; Matt. 8:10).

The encounter occurs in Capernaum of Galilee (see Luke 7:1; Matt. 8:5), a region governed by Antipas since 4 BC after the death of his father, Herod the Great. A decade later, in 6 CE, Antipas became the last Herodian in power after the emperor Augustus removed his brother Archelaus from power in Judea, to the south.[14] Judea was annexed by Rome, and Syrian *auxilia* were sent to supplement Antipas's Galilean *numeri*. It is unlikely that Rome would install their own forces in Galilee, an area already maintained by a trusted ally like Antipas, so the centurion is probably part of the Herodian *numeri* rather than the Roman *auxilia* transferred from the province of Syria.

By pointing out that Jesus marveled at this Galilean soldier, Luke is setting up a contrast with Nazareth, Galilee's Fayette'nam. The last time the word *thaumazo* appears is in Jesus' hometown, where the locals marveled "at the gracious words that came from his mouth" (Luke 4:22). But they turned on him, becoming "filled with rage" and trying to "hurl him off [a] cliff" (Luke 4:28–29). As Jesus' ministry expands to the Gentiles, his own people reject him, first in Nazareth but eventually in all of Israel. Walking to Capernaum from Nazareth would take less than a day and wouldn't require leaving Galilee. Where once he was the one making people marvel, now it is this outsider who is, ironically, also a local.

What is more, the centurion is wealthy and well regarded, another contrast with Nazareth. Not only does he own a slave (see Luke 7:2), but he has also built a local synagogue (see Luke 7:5). Not only does he have military power, but he also has money and influence. Royal forces of client states were generally smaller; if he truly commanded one hundred *numerii*, they would have constituted a larger portion of Antipas's total force than would be the case for the same number of Roman *auxilia*. His proportionate rank, and therefore his social status, is understated by an author unfamiliar with the local nuances of social and martial hierarchies. Although in Roman forces the leader of one hundred soldiers is an enlisted man, as a member of the *numeri* it is safe to suggest he is a Judaean noble. Considering the posh assignment, it is likely he was an aristocrat and/or had close ties with Antipas or his inner circle. Nobles are not enlisted, and he commands approximately a company of soldiers so he is the equivalent of a captain.

Then there is the matter of what this centurion does. A beloved servant has fallen ill and he asks Jesus to heal him. Not only does he not seek personal gain, he violates the status quo by saying a noble is "not worthy" (Luke 7:6; Matt. 8:8) to have a rejected preacher under his roof, which presumably is also in Galilee. According to the NRSV, Jesus is "amazed" (Luke 7:9; Matt. 8:10) at this remark, but about half of all English translations render *thaumazo* as "marvel" instead. Captain Marvel may be an asset of a big, rodent-centric corporation, but he is also a wealthy Gentile officer in Antipas's Galilean army. When he saw one of the kids from back on the block performing miracles, CPT Marvel threw his trust behind him to heal a battle buddy.

As for whether he was truly a Christian soldier, the usual entrance requirement is either confession or baptism. While he is not baptized, he does confess Jesus as Lord (see Luke 7:6; Matt. 8:6, 8), who in turn affirms the soldier's great faith (see Luke 7:9; Matt. 8:10, 13). Who are we to argue with God?

CORNELIUS'S *FAMILIA*

Next up is Cornelius, probably the most well-known Christian soldier, in Acts 10 and 11. The good news for grunts is also good news for military families. That is because Cornelius is not the only Gentile baptized when Peter comes through town. Acts is the sequel to Luke's gospel, and Captain Marvel's faith is mirrored in Cornelius. Unlike the unnamed indigenous *numeri*, Cornelius is given plenty of identifying details. As "a centurion of the Italian Cohort" (Acts 10:1), he would have been a birthright Roman citizen. What we do not know is if he is still serving when he has his vision or if he has been discharged and is a veteran.

If Cornelius is a soldier in Acts 10, then scholars can pinpoint the most likely unit in which he served, *cohors II Italica*.[15] Cohorts like these were led by low-status Roman citizens (criminals, former slaves, etc.) and made up of *auxilia* from the local province. The Cornelii name saw a flourishing after 82 BCE when Lucius Cornelius Sulla freed thousands of slaves who then adopted his name,[16] one of whom may have been our Cornelius's father or grandfather. As the Italian descendant of slaves, Cornelius would have been shipped off to Syria to serve as one of five 1SGs in charge of one hundred local grunts or the MSG in charge of all six hundred in the cohort.

Alternatively, Cornelius may be a veteran by the time he has his dream and encounters Peter.[17] The vague phrase used in the text may just be a reference to the last unit Cornelius served in before his discharge. If that's the case, then he may have found himself in Caesarea because, as the Roman capital of Judea, it was one of many colonies where veterans were resettled after service. If so, he would represent the embodiment of Roman culture as an ethnic Italian and former noncommissioned officer.

Whether he was a salty, low-status soldier or a prestigious Roman veteran, what stands out is his piety. *Pietas* was a central feature of Roman domestic culture, where the *paterfamilias* was lord of his house. Oddly for Roman eyes, however, his piety was distinctly Jewish. Cornelius's vision occurs at 1500, the same time of day that Jews observed "the hour of prayer, at three o'clock."[18] The implication is that he is praying when the angel appears, the same thing that happens to the priest Zechariah while the people are outside praying (see Luke 1:10). Just as Zechariah leads his people in prayer, Luke's description of Cornelius suggests he, too, piously leads his extended Gentile family.

Although Cornelius is the central character, his *familia* plays a crucial role. The pious devotion described does not just apply to him, but "all his household" (Acts 10:2). He does not reflect the role of *dominus*, lording over his household by centralizing power in himself. A Roman *domus* referred to the nuclear domestic family; it was a unit of legal power and social status in the ancient world. The Greek work used throughout Acts 10 is *oikos* (G3624), which was used to refer to *all* the people living under one roof, sometimes even pets and livestock.[19] This inclusive term is evidenced by (1) the participation of servants and a fellow soldier in finding Peter; (2) Cornelius's invitation of "relatives and close friends" (Acts 10:24) to Peter's arrival; and (3) his family's enthusiasm for baptism (evidenced by their request that Peter remain a few days). His family's piety does not seem forced; rather, they are following the humble example of their loving father.

As New Testament scholar Laurie Brink puts it, "Cornelius stands as the antithesis of the braggart warrior."[20]

From a Roman military perspective, the most glaring detail is a noncommissioned officer's deference to a lowly Jew. The text builds up the Romanness of the setting to heighten this effect; Caesarea was the provincial capital of Judea and mention of "the Italian Cohort" acts as a caution against trusting imperial loyalists. If Cornelius is a veteran, he may simply have abandoned Roman pantheism for what would be seen as "monolatrous" Judaism. But if he is still a soldier, his calling a low-status member of a client state "lord," in the only Roman city in Judaea, is tantamount to treason.

And yet, Cornelius and his family are the example for all Gentiles who follow them into Jesus' movement. He is the first undisputed Christian soldier because he confesses *and* is baptized; he does not run *from* or cling *to* his military service. He does not allow his patriotism to outrank his piety. What I love about Cornelius is that he doesn't stand alone in his faith, even if ancient biases did put him at the center of his family's story. Acts 10 and 11 is a reminder that we have our family to help us honor our commitments, to keep us walking the right path. Always, fam. Semper, familia!

PAUL(US) AND THE JAILER

Finally, there are two minor characters who merit consideration as Christian soldiers. The first, Sergius Paulus, is the only Roman governor to become a Christian; and the second is the unnamed prison warden of a military town who Paul and Silas save from an all-too-common fate for soldiers.

Sergius Paulus (Acts 13:4–12)

Despite the friendly military encounters they had with Cornelius, Jesus' disciples were being killed with the tacit approval of the state throughout Acts. Stephen, a Hellenistic Jew and member of the church in Jerusalem, is stoned after preaching the good news to "the synagogue of the Freedmen" (Acts 6:9). Similarly, James, son of Zebedee, was "killed with the sword" by Agrippa I (Acts 12:2).

It is with these unfortunate events fresh in the minds of believers that Saul and Barnabas are called to preach in Cyprus, a Roman island province with a large Jewish population. To be assigned proconsul there meant that other aristocrats didn't trust you. As a quiet province, the military presence was negligible and there were few things to screw up. Sergius Paulus was the lucky loser; he had class without friends, power without might. But word of Stephen's and James's deaths would have spread quickly, and Saul and Barnabas likely expected that any time with state officials was time on the chopping block.

When the missionary preachers first meet Paulus, he has been familiarized with Judaism by a magician and false prophet named Elymas (see Acts 13:7–8). A fiery proclamation from Saul leaves Elymas blind and Paulus convinced: "When the proconsul saw what had happened, he believed, for he was astonished at the teaching about the Lord" (Acts 13:12).

Insofar as Sergius Paulus commanded what little armed forces Cyprus possessed, he was a part of the military apparatus. Technically not a grunt, but still a soldier in the most inclusive sense. As the governor of an entire Roman province, he is the single most powerful person in the New Testament to be converted to the faith. Why his conversion has been largely overlooked is beyond me.

The Jailer of Philippi (Acts 16:23–36)

The final Christian soldier who appears in the New Testament is an unnamed prison guard in Acts 16. The setting is Philippi, a veteran colony established by Octavian after a nearby battle in 42 BCE. Saul and Silas encounter a demon-possessed girl enslaved by local Roman businessmen to tell fortunes for a profit. Apparently she was good at what she did; of Saul and Silas, she foretold that "these men are slaves of the Most High God, who proclaim to you a way of salvation" (Acts 16:17). When they expel the demon her abilities cease, and with her abilities goes the businessmen's profit. So they drag Saul and Silas to court.

Although located in the province of Macedonia, Philippi was called a "little Rome." It probably had this special relationship with the imperial city because it was the site of the "Liberators' Civil War," where the first official emperors defeated the republic's forces and unified the empire. The "magistrates" in charge of Philippi were *duoviri*, two men appointed by, and who answered directly to, Rome. To appease the businessmen's accusation that they are offending Roman customs, the *duoviri* have Saul and Silas beaten before telling the jailer to lock them up.

Although a civilian or slave might serve as a municipal jailer, that seems highly unlikely in the case of Philippi. The jailer answers to the city's military leadership, its *strategoi* (G4755, a compound word used exclusively in Luke–Acts that combines *strateuo* (soldiers,

G4754) with *agos* (leader, G71), and its *rhabdouchos* (G4465, the Roman "police" responsible for capital punishment).[21] Furthermore, as a city independent of the surrounding province and with a close connection to Rome, the jailer probably dealt frequently with political prisoners. A job like that is unlikely to be trusted to lower classes with doubtful loyalty.

Chaos ensues when an earthquake frees the prisoners in the middle of the night. The perceived consequence (dishonor? imperial retribution?) is so high that the jailer prepares to commit suicide. Saul intervenes, reassuring him that none of the prisoners have fled. Recognizing a miracle when he sees it, the jailer asks, "[Lords], what must I do to be saved?" (see Acts 16:30).[22] He is the only person in Acts to call a man *kyrios* (G2962) besides Cornelius, suggesting the jailer does not think the emperor has a monopoly on lordship. Saul corrects him: there is one Lord and it's neither Saul nor the emperor. "Believe on the Lord *Jesus*, and you will be saved, you and your household" (Acts 16:31, emphasis added).

The jailer takes Saul and Silas to his home and washes their wounds. It may be that the same bloodied water was used to baptize him and his family, who "rejoiced that [the jailer] had become a believer in God" (Acts 16:34). It may also be that the jailer's house was the first church in Philippi, the same to which Saul would write many years later on his way to Rome, following his appeal to Caesar after a similar arrest and beating.[23]

6.

FREEDOM ISN'T FREE:

P(S)AUL AND CITIZENSHIP

BIASES ARE LIKE PRIVILEGE BECAUSE WE ARE BORN WITH THEM. We don't see them until we get out of ourselves a little bit. That is what education is about; the word comes from the Latin *educare*, from *ex-* (out of) *-duco* (lead). The nature of bias is that it becomes harder to see the more we surround ourselves with like-minded people. If everyone thinks the same, we'll mistake bias for scholarship. This is what happened with theology and pacifism.

I've spoken to several Christians tired of American exceptionalism and manifest destiny who would change their nationality if they could. But the desire to forfeit your passport and move to a tropical island to live out your days is a privilege of the few. The earliest Christians were of low status, marginalized by the same systems of power they relied upon to get by. For most people in need, the promise of full citizenship and the freedoms it affords are too valuable a prize to forfeit. Military service was and remains one way of achieving that goal. Grunts who hope for a better tomorrow know that "freedom isn't free" because they must earn it. Whereas some privileged Americans may see the phrase as manipulative, others see it as a fact of life. Sometimes privilege shifts, as we see in Acts, where it is Saul whose untainted birthright means he effectively outranks the most powerful Roman official in Jerusalem.

NATIONALITY AT BIRTH, RIGHT?

Modern birthright citizenship is unique to North and South America; the rest of the world grants citizenship based not on where one is born, but to whom one is born. Most nations still practice *jus sanguinus*, Latin for "rights from the blood," meaning nationality and citizenship are inherited genealogically. The United States adopted the notion of *jus soli*, or "rights from the soil," from old English common law. We didn't adopt this system from birth, however; it took us until we were fourteen amendments old to guarantee due process and equal protection to all citizens.

The promise of birthright citizenship can appear dangerous to some; one person's inheritance is another's anchor baby. Israel was no different. During its infancy as a nation, there were warnings against becoming impure by introducing foreign ideas and people through marriage or immigration. In Exodus the people are warned against taking a foreign spouse because they and the children they produce will "prostitute themselves to their gods" (34:16). In a parallel account in Deuteronomy, the reason is toned down, but it remains essentially the same. If Israelites were to marry the inhabitants of the Promised Land, that "would turn away your children…to serve other gods" (Deut. 7:3–4). This is *jus sanguinis*, the restriction of national privileges to only those who can trace their lineage by blood.

Judaism is matrilineal, passed from mother to child, rather than patrilineal, from father to child. Wealth, however, was treated no differently than other ancient cultures; it was a gift only Dad possessed and only Dad could pass down. Hebrew birthright(s), *bekowrah* (H1062), followed the pattern in ancient cultures of awarding the largest inheritance to the *bekowr* (H1060), or firstborn son. Also known as primogeniture, it is a custom still followed in many cultures even though it is consistently subverted in the Bible.

Some of the biggest protagonists of the Old Testament were the youngest of their families but exalted above their siblings: Isaac over his older half brother Ishmael; Jacob over his older twin brother, Esau; Joseph over his half brothers[1]; Moses over his older brother, Aaron (and older sister, Miriam); and David over his seven older brothers. Notable exceptions to these Cinderella stories include Abraham, whose birth order is unknown[2]; and Joshua, who was an only child (of Nun). God apparently doesn't have much regard for the oldest child or the human tendency to elevate age over character.

The problem with "birthright" is that it can create a sense of entitlement; it can make people expect unearned privilege. Cain, for example, assumed that Abel and his sacrifice were inferior because he had come to expect special treatment. His mother rejoiced at his birth (see Gen. 4:1); he inherited the family business of tilling the earth (see Gen. 2:15; 4:2); and even God seemed to prefer chatting with *him* over his little brother.[3] Cain could be forgiven for thinking that the world revolved around him, because it sure *seemed* to.

Maybe the Bible upends the birthright script because people born into privilege so often turn out to be arrogant and selfish.

America is a great place to live, and people born here are lucky to have a free life full of liberty and justice for all. We are seen by the world as a shining light on the hill, a land of the free *because of* the brave. Or so we are told.

After WWII, the United States increasingly engaged in unnecessary and costly conflicts around the world, losing much of its global social capital along the way. This had a profound effect on soldiers who fought in forgotten, failed, and forever wars in Korea, Vietnam, and Iraq, respectively. Disillusioned with themselves and their nation, countless veterans either left the land of their birth, becoming expatriates, or wished they could, becoming "ex-patriots."[4]

The phrase "Freedom Is Not Free" on the Korean War Veterans Memorial in Washington, DC, can feel manipulative, like civilians owe something to veterans. By making service the stick that dangles the carrot of freedom, it's the evil twin of TYFYS. The sacrificial lamb equation is reversed, in which a debt is *created* rather than paid. Veteran entitlement is a thing, but it exists in direct proportion to civilian privilege and guilt.[5] It also is a direct result of the ever-increasing benefits and "entitlements" recruiters dangle in front of prospects to get the few to serve so that the many can live free (of responsibility, sacrifice, and other inconvenient shit democracy demands).

LYSIAS THE TRIBUNE

Roman citizenship was the primary recruitment tool for the *auxilia*, which gives us quite a bit of information about the tribune of

Acts 21–23. As "the tribune [*chiliarchos*] of the cohort" stationed at Fort Antonia (Acts 21:31), adjacent to the holy temple, he was the highest-ranking Roman official in Jerusalem. The governor resided in Caesarea and made trips to the city only for special occasions like Jewish holidays or urgent crises.

Officers were young Romans either appointed by governors or promoted from within a legion after acquiring some experience. Lysias was different; his freedom was not freely inherited from his parents but rather came at the cost of "a large sum of money" (Acts 22:28). This put Lysias below Saul in the social pecking order, outranked by a local agitator. Although he commanded a cohort of six hundred *auxilia* under Rome's control, it was he who must follow Saul's orders as a birthright citizen.

There is only rare evidence of selling and buying citizenship,[6] and Lysias's name provides clues as to how he managed to skip ahead and get his citizenship before his discharge. In a letter to the governor preserved in Acts 23:26–30, he gives his name as Claudius Lysias. We do not have his birth name, but Lysias, his family name, is Eastern, probably Greek or Syrian. Clan names like Claudius, when possessed by a non-Italian, suggest an ancestor freed by a member of that clan, the same way Cornelius of Acts 10 probably inherited his name. But Lysias wasn't a birthright citizen; he was a bought-and-paid-for citizen.

Emperor Claudias's third wife, Messalina, was accused of selling citizenship sometime during his reign, from 41 to 54 CE.[7] As a grown-ass man by the 60s, when some scholars believe Acts to have been written, Lysias's "large sum of money" probably stuffed the empress's coffers. Being a newly minted citizen might explain why this butter bar is so deferential to both his enlisted leadership and birthright citizens like Saul. In two episodes that would have offended a "real Italian," Lysias allows others to question his judgment and determine his actions. First, the cohort's MSG questions his order to flog Saul in Acts 22:26; then Paul's nephew orders him around in Acts 23:21. Whereas some may see this as a leadership flaw, it may not be the case.

As a grunt, I had more respect for the lieutenants who invited feedback and welcomed healthy criticism; that contributed to the cohesiveness of the unit. Officers who hold tightly to their status, who insist on strict adherence to decorum like saluting, are ridiculed the moment they are out of earshot. Lysias does not grasp at the power given to him because he knows what's it's like to be at the bottom of the barrel. He's something like a "prior," not the Latin title for noncommissioned leaders, but military slang for a commissioned officer who has prior enlisted experience. We have no evidence that Lysias was ever a regular *auxilia*, but if he had to buy his citizenship, then he knew what it was like to live on the margins of Roman society.

Lysias states explicitly that his freedom was not free, but he does not hoard what he has acquired. It is the mark of an honest person, not someone racing to the top for the sake of being there. He is prodigious in giving away the freedom he has over others. Although he is not called devout or "God-fearing" like Cornelius, he clearly knows something about being a good person and protecting the good he sees in others.

God's grace is so amazing because it *is* free. God doesn't give grace to us based on what we've done, and there's nothing we can do to earn more of it than we need. God doesn't owe it to us; grace is a gift rather than a debt. Birthright citizenship, whether we like it or not, isn't much different. So long as a person is born here, they aren't supposed to have to earn the rights and protections afforded to American citizens. Freedom, for those born in America, is *supposed* to be free—even if it isn't.

The truth is that some Americans are born especially free. Some of us never experience racism, sexism, ableism, or other prejudices. Those who have know what it is like to fight for rights that are supposed to be bestowed upon them at birth according to the Fourteenth Amendment to our Constitution. Inequality is un-American, and patriotism can make progressive activists feel like they are the problem unless they fight with the disadvantaged. And if you fight long enough without real progress, you can become disillusioned with yourself and your nation. There are plenty of patriotic Americans who have lost faith in America, who feel like their only option is to walk away, to wash their hands of the privilege they never asked for and disassociate from a nation they are no longer sure loved them in the first place.

Getting something at someone else's expense can feel like thirty pieces of silver burning through our souls. But just because something is wrong doesn't mean you are to blame. I cut my theological teeth around Christian anarchists like Andy Alexis-Baker from the last chapter, a lot of whom expressed disgust at their own national identity. It might feel like a solution to try to give our privilege back, but what does that accomplish? Rather than trying to pretend we're something we're not by trying to wash the America off ourselves, we could make citizenship mean what we all think it should. As a noncommissioned officer told me when I was feeling hopeless, "Play the game before it plays you." The problem (and solution) is that you can't change how you were born; you might as well accept it and make the best of it. Saul of Tarsus certainly did.

SNIPPED OR DIPPED?
P(S)AUL'S HARD-TO-FOLLOW FAITH

The man from Tarsus is complicated. Both he and his namesake, King Sha'ul (H7586), were from the tribe of Benjamin.[8] Contrary to what many Christians might believe, he never changed his name. As the Jewish movement that followed Yehoshua began to grow among Roman Gentiles, the Latinized versions of names became dominant; Yehoshua became Iesous the same way Sha'ul became P(S)aul.

Tarsus, a one-week journey by foot from Jerusalem, was a major urban center when Saul was growing up. His parents, who were devout Jews, possibly Pharisees, had him sent to the Holy City to study under Gamaliel, the most famous rabbi at the time. While the Bible depicts Gamaliel as a moderating voice on the Jerusalem Sanhedrin, who encourages the council to stop persecuting the apostles in Acts 5:33–39, the same cannot be said of young Saul, who was present for the stoning of Stephen. The student clearly did not take after his teacher, so what does it mean to be a Jew? Was Saul a better example of their faith, or was Gamaliel?

Saul the Jew

To Greek-speaking Romans, the term *Ioudaios* (G2453) was a reference to a place, not a religion. The province of Judea was a diverse region that included groups with very different and even conflicting religious beliefs. For example, Samaritans were always at odds with Jews, but both would have been clumped together in Roman eyes. There were also urban centers within the province that were decidedly non-Jewish, like its capital, Caesarea Maritima. There were Gentile Judaeans of little or no faith, and there were also devout pantheistic Judaeans. Jews of middle or low social status might make a big deal out of their religious identity, as Saul often did, or they might downplay it if they wanted to fit in with other Romans. After all, the Jewish standard for membership wasn't exactly publicly disclosed.

At first glance, the oath God made with Abraham *was* circumcision: "This is my covenant...Every male among you shall be circumcised" (Gen. 17:10).[9] But what if nondescendants wanted to enter the community of God? The earliest instructions for converts to Judaism came after the firstborn of Egypt had been slain by the final plague. According to Exodus 12:48–49, aliens who wanted to partake in the first Passover had to be circumcised. In other words: no snip; no salvation. For men like Saul, Jewishness was not something you wore on your sleeve; it was something you wore in your pants.

Circumcision was expected of all *males*, newborns and converts alike, but that was not the only requirement. For all prospective Jews, including people ineligible for circumcision (like women or eunuchs), the requirement of full immersion in a ritual bath, called a *mikveh*, was just as strict. These expectations persisted until about the first century, which led the Jesus movement to convene the Council of Jerusalem in Acts 15. Relaxing the requirement of circumcision, whatever else it may have represented, was, in effect, a leveling of the gender dynamics that elevated circumcision over *mikveh*, which Christians call baptism. One faith; one entrance requirement (penis optional). The fact was that nobody was technically born a Jew, you *became* a Jew by snipping and/or dipping.

We don't have to see the evidence to believe Saul when he makes a big deal about his Jewishness. But what about his claims about being the thirteenth apostle? What made him, or anyone else at the time, a "Christian"?

Saul the Christian

According to Acts 11:26, the first time Jesus' followers were called "Christian" was in the city of Antioch.[10] The Antiochenes spoke Greek, so the word was originally *christianos* (G5546), and they had a strong reputation for giving nicknames. Apparently this reputation was so widespread that the nickname reached Herod Agrippa more than four hundred miles away in Judea, who mocks Saul in Acts 26:28 for trying to make the king a *christianos*.

The word combines Greek with Latin, a language used mostly in and around the Roman capital by high-status types. The Greek part, *christos* (G5547), means "anointed one," and it is the word used in Greek versions of Daniel 9:26 to describe the Jewish *mashiyach* (H4899), or Messiah. The Latin part is the suffix *-ianus*, which was used to express ownership over something, as in slavery. "Christian"

66666666666666

was an insult hurled at the slaves of a Jewish Messiah who had been executed by Rome. A more respectful name for Jesus' followers, given by other Jews, was *nazōraios* (G3480), or Nazarenes, after the town in which Jesus grew up (or perhaps a reference to "consecrated ones" called Nazirites, which we'll explore in a later chapter). The Hebrew equivalent of "Nazarenes," *Notzrim*, occurs in the Babylonian Talmud, and is still the modern Israeli term for "Christian."

Ultimately, the new faith community undermined the pejorative by adopting the term as its own. Believers are told that anyone who "suffers as a [*christianos*]" should not consider it a disgrace, but should "glorify God because you bear this name" (1 Pet. 4:16). This ringing endorsement of the former insult led to its being preferred over the less disparaging "Nazarenes," and later writers like Ignatius, Polycarp, and Justin Martyr cemented its status as a title of honor.

In the decades after Jesus' crucifixion, non-Jews flocked to his faith, which was Judaism. The Council of Jerusalem had to address circumcision because it was the highest hurdle for most Gentiles. To accommodate the influx of aspiring believers, the council adopted James's proposal that restrictions be eased significantly. Converts could be circumcised or baptized if they really wanted to be, but it was no longer obligatory. To become a member of the newly emerging subset of Judaism that eventually became Christianity, all they had do was refrain from eating unclean food and sleeping around (see Acts 15:28–29).

Although Saul's zeal motivated him initially to persecute what appeared to be rogue Jews, his experience on the road to Damascus would flip that on its head. Assuming Saul was circumcised, he went the extra mile and also indicated his membership in the Jewish sub-sect that followed Jesus. As soon as the scales fell from his eyes, "he got up and was baptized" (Acts 9:18). While this did not disqualify him from being a card-carrying Jew, it definitely complicated things.

SAUL'S DUAL(ING) CITIZENSHIP

Some early Christian writers suggested Saul's parents were enslaved, then released and granted citizenship.[11] If this is true, then Saul would have inherited his citizenship from them. Saul is a great example of how Christians can and should wrestle with their birthrights, in his case not as a Jew, but as a Roman.

Saul never claims, or even acknowledges, his citizenship in his own letters. It may have been a sore issue for him, as many of his peers may have found Saul's enthusiasm as a Roman citizen a little distasteful. Many, if not most, Jews would have had a low opinion of Rome. The transition from republic to empire was not kind to independence-minded regions like Judaea. Their temple was repeatedly desecrated and the people had been slaughtered and oppressed. If Saul wanted Jewish friends, he needed to be discreet about the fact that he was "one of them."

Luke seems to be unaware of or unsympathetic to Saul's discretion. The sequel to his gospel, Acts of the Apostles, does not depict Saul as being in any way shy about his citizenship. The first instance is in Acts 16, after the jailer of Philippi, a newly baptized Christian soldier, tells Saul and Silas they have been released. Saul refuses to leave, insisting that, since they were beaten in public, the authorities should free them publicly. It serves them right to be exposed like that, he suggests, for treating Roman citizens without regard to the law.

Tarsus was a major city that enjoyed imperial favor, so it is not impossible that being born there brought great privilege. Those privileges would have traveled with Saul to Jerusalem when he left to study under Gamaliel and may have created social tension between the highly regarded Jewish teacher and the young buck with Roman privilege. There is some academic debate as to whether Saul possessed citizenship, but it apparently did not matter since even to claim it was enough to influence the behavior of several Roman administrators and commanders. Nowhere is this made clearer than in Saul's interaction with Lysias the tribune.

P(S)aul the Roman

In Acts 22, Saul has narrowly escaped death at the hands of Jewish purists who accused him of defiling the temple of Jerusalem by allowing a Gentile to enter. The mob became so violent that soldiers had to carry Saul inside Antonia Fortress, where Lysias could question him in relative peace. Safely within the barracks' confines, they tie him up and prepare to perform an "enhanced interrogation" but suddenly stop after learning P(S)aul is one of them, that he is a Roman.

Most English translations of the passage use the words "Roman citizen" or "Roman citizenship," suggesting that Saul somehow *became* a citizen (What kind of citizen? A Roman citizen). If Saul can attain it, then anyone can. It's like the fabled American Dream; we want to believe that it is within everyone's reach. But in the era of #MeToo and #BlackLivesMatter, we know that "reach" is relative. "Freedom is not free" because it is kept out of the reach of some people, either by chance or design.

In the original Greek, no word appears for "citizen" in Acts 22: 25–28. In verse 25, P(S)aul asks if it is legal to flog *anthropos rhomaios*, "a Roman [person]." The centurion, either a 1SG or the MSG of the cohort, hears this and tells the butter bar, who asks P(S)aul in verse 27 if he is *rhomaios* (G4514), which P(S)aul confirms. This seems to irk the officer, and his remark in verse 28 is one of only two places where *politeia* (G4174) appears in the Bible. Some translations render *politeia* "citizenship," but others use "freedom." How did P(S)aul acquire his freedom? The detainee replies, *egō kai gennaō*: "I was born."

Saul did nothing to acquire citizenship; it wasn't the result of his strong work ethic or positive attitude. He was born into privilege. There's nothing wrong with birthright citizenship, is there? The Fourteenth Amendment promises American citizenship to anyone born here. Freedom is free, right?

Not exactly. There are plenty of ways to live by the letter of the law while shitting all over the spirit (of the law): voter suppression, racial profiling, gaslighting, redlining—the list can go on. Some of us are born with "invisible knapsacks," while others are issued rucksacks and expected to carry everyone else's baggage. Peggy McIntosh began exploring sex-based bias in the 1980s but quickly discovered bias also acted in ways based on race. She writes, "Privilege is like an invisible weightless knapsack of special provisions, maps, passports, codebooks, visas, clothes, tools and blank checks."[12] It may also be at work in relationships between soldiers and civilians if civilians can hide behind stereotypes that make military personnel out to be "war torn" and "unsavory."

Why should some Americans bear the weight of other people's bias? God-fearing Americans may also ask why it has been so difficult to repair the damage done by racism, sexism, and other forms of oppression. Where does that leave people who want to do justice, love kindness, and walk humbly with God?

Notice how "Paul" uses his privilege strategically; he does not run from the fact that he is a fellow member, by birth, of the Romans right in front of him. He was born into an ambitious republic-turned-empire with which conscientious individuals had a litany of moral qualms. Many, if not most, Jews of his generation had very good reason to be suspicious of anything Roman. So what are we to do if our birthright, our privilege, is unwanted?

US, TOO, BRUT(AL)?

Too often, we rush to wash our hands of our forebears' sins or our nation's evils, as though Meyer's soap and a juice cleanse are next to godliness. Privilege has become a guilty pleasure—we love our gentrified neighborhood, but we hate gentrification. There's a better way, a way to own our privilege by using it responsibly. But that requires coming to terms with our love-hate relationship with justice, as well as our love-hate relationship with the privilege of citizenship.

Combat experience makes the value of our freedoms painfully and inescapably clear. Even a decade and a half after my discharge, my heart is still warmed by the mere idea that I might suffer or give my life so that others can enjoy the liberties and justice our

Constitution promises for all. There is another way that my military service changed the way I thought about citizenship and privilege, and it brings us back to Saul in Acts 22.

Notice how it is *the soldier* who is underprivileged in this situation. He had to pay a boatload of money for this thing, *politeia*, that Paul has done nothing to earn and can take totally for granted. I don't care what time or country we're talking about, it's fucked up that a soldier must purchase their own freedom from the same empire they might die protecting. In America, "purchase" and "freedom" go together like "states' rights" and "heritage."

As a student veteran in seminary, I learned to decenter myself and use my voice to amplify others'. But seeing myself *only* as a cisgendered white evangelical male masked the fact that privilege is like a chain—only as strong as its weakest link. When I found myself in Christian academia, disproportionately influenced by pacifist theologians, I noticed that I started to identify more centrally as a veteran. It was a part of my identity that my peers expected me to hate, like Saul's birthright. Many of those same book-smart pacifists privately turned to me for advice on military congregants or estranged family members. Professors turned to me so often for advice on the influx of student veterans after the 2011 drawdown in Iraq that I finally just wrote it out.[13] But if I veered too far from the established party line, if I rocked the boat, I learned that I could be deprived of any privilege I thought I had.

When push came to shove, institutions and influencers repeatedly leaned on socially acceptable stereotypes to link my veteran status with mental illness, emotional instability, even intellectual impairment. I had to put being an ally on hold because I started *needing* one so desperately. When I cried out for allies, most Christians turned me down, either refusing to risk their privilege or accusing me of ignoring mine. Acts 22 is a reminder that the benefits of citizenship, like privilege, cannot be assumed. To shut down contrasting voices, all the majority has to do is suggest you need psychiatric care.

I once tallied up the number of soldiers and veterans who turned to me in private about civilian bias and mistreatment; it averaged out to more than one person a month for fifteen years. I've always protected their identity, but backchannel communication creates more problems than it solves. The problem is not that grunts don't feel guilty enough for what they may have done; the suicide rate makes that crystal clear. The problem is that civilian bias goes unquestioned by the communities it hurts most. As long as soldiers and veterans only complain in private, military communities will continue to be seen as the problem, the broken thing in need of fixing.

It is not up to soldiers and veterans to change a culture that has alienated them. I've heard and seen enough to know that martial complaints about civilians are legitimate. Instead, I have found myself inviting civilians into a church they never realized was already there, a body that has always included soldiers and their gifts, led by a nonviolent military commander proclaimed by a self-styled general with dual citizenship and a proclivity for martial metaphor. If you don't believe me, then keep reading. If Christian faith and military service are incompatible, the church must forfeit some central traditions and practices because many of them grew out of or arose within soldiers' experiences.

PART 2

TRADITION

7.

DEATH BEFORE IDOLATRY:

GEORGE AND MARTYRDOM

URING THE SECOND WORLD WAR, JAPANESE FORCES DID NOT
consider using suicide dive-bombers until June 1944, when it
was becoming clear that Germany and Italy would fall to the Allies
in the wake of D-Day. It was common for combat pilots to try to
crash into an enemy craft as a last resort, but a looming defeat made
military brass put every option on the table. Japanese culture had
already been influenced by Bushido, the "way of the warrior," which
codified loyalty over survival for ancient samurai. Children had
pledged to offer themselves sacrificially to the state since 1890, making for starry-eyed aviators easily recruited to "divine wind special
attack units."[1]

Samurai and chivalric knights both held honor in the highest
esteem, such that they would rather take their own lives than bring

humiliation on themselves or their families. That's probably why "Death before Dishonor" is a popular refrain in the Marine Corps in particular. If there is honor in war, then death pales in comparison to the dishonor of defeat; I'd rather die than watch the higher good I fought for be destroyed. The early church may have been okay with the routine, largely administrative duties of soldiers, but they saw little honor in war. Their rallying cry was not to sacrifice their lives in the face of humiliation, but to give up their lives rather than dishonor Christ.

SURVIVAL IS NOT A VIRTUE

As it turns out, you *can* die in combat. Between two "forever" wars in the last twenty years, you'd be hard-pressed to find a soldier who didn't realize their service put them at high risk of death. Grunts nowadays know that their mortality is on the table as soon as they don the uniform. Put another way, survival is far from guaranteed when you're a soldier. The thing that makes that gamble worth it is usually a higher good that one's death may point toward—something worth dying for.

In the philosophy of ancient Greece, the highest good was happiness. But this was not the plastered-smile positivity of Joel Osteen or Dave Ramsey. The thing that virtuous people lived and died for was *eudaemonia*, well-being. You became virtuous by practice, by making virtue habitual. Well-being came from, well, *doing*. Happy people were those who were good, and people *became* good by making it a habit of *doing* good. Make no mistake, this is not the biblical worldview, which insists everything is good from the get-go. But ancient virtues are the lifeblood of the military profession, and survival is not a martial virtue.[2]

Nancy Sherman, a virtue ethicist with prior appointments at the Naval and Air Force Academies, has made the case that it was stoic virtues that most influenced the profession of arms. The first line of her book *Stoic Warriors* says it all: "This book is about 'sucking it up.'"[3] Her claims, however, are descriptive rather than prescriptive; it's not that soldiers should be stoic, it's that they act stoic. Martial stoicism is an offshoot of its Greek predecessor, one that appeals to grunts as a kind of rugged isolationism, one that promises "one's happiness could depend solely on one's own virtue."[4] Even before the high rate of military suicides was well known, Sherman acknowledged that the stoic impulse to shut the fuck up and drive on, variations of which appear every day throughout the military, takes a psychological toll. If we didn't know then, we certainly do now that stoic virtue causes more problems for soldiers than it solves.

Servicemembers know that the good guy doesn't always win, that survival is not necessarily a mark of honor. Survival might even work against a soldier's character. Lieutenant Dan, as much of a caricature as he may be, spoke the mind of many a soldier when he told Forrest Gump, "I was supposed to die, in the field, with honor!"[5] The purpose of life, in Greek-inspired Western civilization, is to be honorable. The surest way to do that is to die an honorable death, and where better to die than in battle, for your country? The Roman poet Horace captured this sentiment in one of his odes, writing,

Dulce et decorum est, pro patria mori ("It is sweet and right to die for one's country").[6]

Horace served in the Battle of Philippi as a tribune, but for the losing side. He remembers it without affection, as he learned the hard way that survival is not a virtue. The Romans inherited Greek culture from the Athenians as well as the Spartans. The Spartan version of "Death before Dishonor" was a warning to young men rather than a rallying cry: "Come back with your shield, or on it."[7] Victorious forces would confiscate equipment from survivors, and if you made it home without your shield, it meant you were a deserter. To the hyper-militarized Spartans, the only options were victory or death, in which case your shield served as a stretcher.[8]

In our own world, patriotism gets a lot of playtime from both sides of the aisle. But is it truly the highest good? Horace's idiom got another treatment in WWI at the hands of British lieutenant Wilfred Owen. While recuperating from combat stress at the Craiglockhart War Hospital, Wilfred called Horace's dictum "the old Lie."[9] He objected to the war and leveled sharp criticism at elites who needlessly sent "half the seed of Europe, one by one" to die.[10] What good does dying for your country serve if you've lost faith in it? As if by design, the same year Wilfred publicly called bullshit on Horace's line, it was inscribed above the west entrance to Arlington's Memorial Amphitheater near our nation's capital.[11]

...IT IS A FORM OF RESISTANCE

Just because death isn't the worst thing that can happen to us doesn't mean dying is a good thing. Soldiers know, and their lives make clear, that surviving is not always the best thing we can do with our lives. Some things are so important that they are worth dying for. One of those things might be our country, if we believe that our country is worthy of our lives. But the danger there is self-interest: Is my country good by its own merits, or is it good only because it is my country? Our lives are good, but not because they belong to us. Our country, on the other hand, is only as good as the ideals it continues to embody and promote.

The Japanese Bushido code, which emphasized honor and loyalty above all else, was exploited by modern imperialists to recruit young men to become suicide bombers in the waning years of World War II. If Spartan mothers held out the hope of victory with "Come back with your shield or on it," Japanese society effectively told its young men simply, "Don't come back." Kamikaze pilots were compared to ancient samurai, who would commit ritual suicide to avoid the shame of failure or capture. Dive-bombers sometimes recited death poems on their way to their final mission, much the same as samurai who would address spectators present at the suicidal *seppuku* ceremony.

There is something of the ancient honor system still operative today in our nation's veterans. Too many stories exist of soldiers or veterans convinced that their family is better off without them, making suicide some kind of inverted virtuous act. Somewhere underneath the heartache and pain is a faint ember of goodness, an enduring desire to serve others. We were made to be and do good, to go with the grain of a universe God made good just like us.

As for Horace, he returned from the Battle of Philippi as a

deserter.[12] Despite all his patriotic bluster, Horace had fled in the heat of battle, leaving his shield there on the same field in which the Roman Republic breathed its last. When he got home, he found that his family's wealth had been confiscated and given away to veterans loyal to the empire in the same process that made Philippi a military colony. Although he had failed to "suck it up" sufficiently in battle, something inspired him to endure. Rather than take his own life as a failed soldier, as his stoic commander, Brutus, had, Horace took up the pen as an aspiring poet.

Sometimes, as we will see with the Christian tradition of martyrdom, the good is served by laying down our lives. But virtue is situational rather than universal; what may be good in one instance may not be in another. Even though the military (and the church, as we will see) teaches us that survival is not a virtue, sometimes it is a form of resistance. In battles both physical and spiritual, we may be called upon to lay down our lives. The tides of war shift, however, and we must remain vigilant against unseen scars or demonic forces that fuck with our heads. The lesson we should take from military experiences is "Don't be afraid of death." But that is not an invitation to run toward it and embrace it either.

MARTYRDOM

Laying down our lives can serve a good and noble cause, but it is not the ultimate sacrifice. That honor belongs to Jesus, who alone could redeem people, families, nations, even the world, through his death on the cross. As much as Christians might be called to imitate his life, we cannot imitate his death; Christ's cross does not belong to us.

By inviting his disciples to "take up their cross and follow me" (Matt. 16:24), Jesus is the ultimate example, his cross the only universally redemptive act. The life of discipleship brings salvation to others when we serve as an example of him, when our lives bear witness (*martyreo*, G3140) to his.

A martyr (*martys*, G3144) is someone who testifies in a court of law. Under Jewish law, "a single [*martys*] shall not suffice to convict a person of any crime" (Deut. 19:15).[13] When Jesus is tried before the Sanhedrin, the high priest Caiaphas gets flustered when he fails to find matching *katamartureo* (testimony against, G2649) from two witnesses (see Matt. 26:62; Mark 14:60). When Jesus finally speaks up for himself, Caiaphas rips off his clothes and shouts, "Why do we still need [*martys*]?" (Matt. 26:65; Mark 14:63).[14]

Before any Christian was killed for preaching the good news, the apostles and believers were *all* martyrs in the proper sense; they were testifying to the world that Jesus was Lord and God in their words and their deeds. In the years that followed, as his movement gained popularity, some were a bit overzealous to partake in Jesus' suffering, seeking out hostility to the faith, *odium fidei*. In later centuries anti-imperialist theologians leveraged the history of state persecution to great effect, just as some believers today seem to have a martyrdom complex, in which they are perpetual victims. While martyrdom is real, even in affluent countries like ours, the threat is too often over-stated to advance a political agenda rather than spiritual maturity.

Before Rome ever cared about Jews or Gentiles proclaiming Jesus as the Messiah, the earliest persecution was something more like intramural Jewish hostility that got the earliest Christians killed.

John the Baptist died at the hands of Herod Antipas (see Matt. 14; Mark 6; Luke 9); Stephen's stoning by members of the Sanhedrin (see Acts 7:54) was instigated by mostly Greek Jews in Asia Minor (see Acts 6:9); and James, son of Zebedee, was killed by Herod Agrippa (see Acts 12:2).

It wasn't just establishment figures who wanted Jesus' followers out of the way. Zealots and anti-imperialists did as well. Although sentiment cannot be truly known, the Christians' disinterest in joining Jewish efforts to expel Rome seemed to be at least one animating feature. According to the Jewish historian Josephus, Jesus' brother James was killed in 66 CE by the high priest Ananus, who became a leader in the Jewish Revolt later that same year.[15]

There is no evidence of a general state-sponsored persecution for almost a century after Jesus' death. In 64, the emperor Nero blamed the Great Fire of Rome on Christians of the city, whom he "punished with the utmost refinements of cruelty," but this was the exception to the rule, inspiring "a sentiment of pity" among residents, rather than imitation.[16] Despite all the talk of martyrs in John's Revelation, it might be more bluster than substance. "Antipas my witness" in Revelation 2:13, for example, might refer to an Antipas of Pergamum killed under Nero's reign, or it could refer to (Herod) Antipas, who killed (rather than represented) "the *martys*, my faithful one" (i.e., John the Baptizer; see Matt. 14:10; Mark 6:27; Luke 9:9). Only a small handful of scholars believe that Domitian, a later emperor who exiled John the Apostle to Patmos, ever directed any official policy of suppression toward the messianic Jewish sect.

Any martyrs made prior to the third century would have been

few and far between. Emperor Trajan, for example, counseled a provincial governor on sentencing Christians on trial, but he could barely conceal his lack of interest.[17] There was an uptick in persecution under Marcus Aurelius, but most incidents described by early church historians appear exaggerated. For example, Eusebius made a big deal about a persecution at Lyons in 177 CE,[18] but its bishop at the time, Irenaeus, made no mention of it in his many writings. That is not to say that martyrs were not made, but that persecution was not widespread or organized, even if imperial figures were aware of and allowed it to happen.

If there ever was an "Age of the Martyrs," it was as much about sporadic mistreatment as about increasing popularity of the faith. At the same time persecutions increased under Marcus Aurelius, we have evidence of Christians serving in the Roman military from a non-Christian source. Eusebius's account of the "Thundering Legion"[19] also appears in Cassius Dio's history of Rome.[20] In 173, the *Legio XII Fulminata*, as it was known, was surrounded by enemies only to be saved by the prayers of its Christian members. Persecutions must not have been formally sanctioned from the top, since Christians were appearing openly in increasingly high-status positions.

The earliest official persecution that scholars can reliably confirm came from Emperor Decius in 249 CE. Concerned that a cultural decline was the result of divine displeasure, he demanded that everyone verify their loyalty to the gods by performing a sacrifice before a local magistrate. Jews were exempted because the Romans admired the great age of their traditions, but Christians were seen as lapsed Jews who actively sought to recruit others to monolatry. The

Galilean religion was not exempt since it was seen as a "pernicious superstition" and a "disease" threatening the empire because of its followers' impiety.[21]

Many Christians refused to honor false gods and were killed or otherwise punished, but nearly as many buckled under pressure. When Roman authorities went church to church demanding that copies of Scripture be surrendered for destruction, Christians who complied were condemned as *traditores*, the "ones who handed over," and stripped of authority. The Decian persecution was not *directed* at Christians, but it became a precedent that later emperors imitated in their anxiety over the looming collapse of the Roman world.

GEORGE (AND) THE GREAT (PERSECUTION)

This anxiety only grew following Decius's attempt to restore conventional Roman *pietas* by force. However seriously the Christian community took his edict, on the whole it was minimally enforced and probably would have been forgotten at his death just a year later had it not been for an even more zealous successor. In the late 250s Valerian ordered all Christians, including senators and members of his own staff, to be stripped of their property unless they recanted their faith.

The "Age of the Martyrs" is far from a simple story about oppression and violence, because Christians were being promoted to the highest positions of power. The Decian persecution may have been a setback for the faith, but it did not succeed as a deterrent. Valerian wanted to change that by directly targeting Christians, whose numbers and practices he saw as an affront to the Roman gods.

Unfortunately for him, Valerian spent most of his time away on military campaigns unable to ensure strict enforcement. His death in 260 left his son in charge, who repealed the law and restored (a temporary) peace to the church.

When Diocletian rose to power in 285, he was willing to let bygones be bygones and made no effort to revive Decius's edict or issue his own. That changed when Christian members of his own staff interfered with pagan fortune-telling rituals. According to the historian Lactantius, when they made the sign of the cross on their foreheads "the demons were chased away, and the holy rites interrupted."[22] This was the final straw, and the Christians finally became the target of formal imperial ire. The first focused and systematic persecution to create martyrs of the faith was initiated by Diocletian on February 24, 303, and "began with the brethren in the army."[23]

Diocletian's persecution is known as the "Great Persecution" for the same reason Jesus' execution is called "Good Friday." Neither was *morally* good, but good in that they overcame evil *with* good. Under an earlier persecution, a theologian had insisted that "the blood of Christians is seed" for the church.[24] There was no better way, in other words, to show the world you believed in Christ than to suffer his same fate. Soldiers led the way because they were most proximate to the jilted emperor. Once called on to die for their country, soldiers were now made to die for their faith. The Great Persecution lasted ten years, from 303 to 313, when Constantine I legalized Christianity.

Although there were many military martyrs before him, none

have had as devoted a following as Saint George. So little is known for certain that he is like Christianity's "unknown soldier," historically traceable but culturally malleable. So long as we ignore, or fail to unearth, his real identity, he can be anything to everyone. As little more than another golden calf, George has been abused to justify any "Old Lie," from the Crusades to colonialism. The good news is that we know enough about this soldier-saint to undermine those impulses.

What we do know about the *megalos martyras* (Great Witness) is that his name, Georgios, is Greek and most of his biographies (the earliest dating to the fourth century) agree that he was from nearby Cappadocia in Asia Minor. That he was an officer in the army, perhaps even the Praetorian Guard, is also probably true given the military's proximity to the emperors. Archaeologists have found ancient churches dedicated to George that can be dated to the various persecutions, but they allow us to narrow the timeframe only so much. We know George was a historical figure, but what made him a martyr is a murkier matter.

The first reference to George is by the aforementioned Lactantius, an intellectual connected to Diocletian, who converted to Christianity and resigned his posts prior to the emperor's edict targeting the church. Writing just a few years after Constantine I ended the persecutions, Lactantius remembers how "a certain person tore down [Diocletian's] edict, and cut it in pieces."[25] He does not approve of the act, calling it "improperly" conceived, but he admires the man's "high spirit" and "admirable patience under sufferings," which included torture and being burned alive.

Ten years later, Eusebius recalls a similar event but from further remove. Whereas Lactantius probably could retell the event from more direct sources, Eusebius has little more than rumor colored by the zeal of George's swift popularity. His *Ecclesiastical History* draws from Lactantius's account and adds some embellishment: "A certain man, not obscure but very highly honored with distinguished temporal dignities, moved with zeal toward God, and incited with ardent faith, seized the edict as it was posted openly and publicly, and tore it to pieces as a profane and impious thing."[26] Eusebius records the location as Nicomedia, Diocletian's imperial capital and the city in which he assigned Lactantius to teach rhetoric before becoming a Christian.

Lactantius and Eusebius come from very different theological perspectives, but they both keep silent on the name of the person in question. It is reasonable to assume the story was unlikely to spread without the reference point a name provides, so why the silence of two prominent commentators? It could be that the brash provocation by one of the emperor's own soldiers was hard to justify. George could not have been ignorant of the consequences of his actions; was his death really martyrdom, or something more like suicide?

For as long as there have been martyrs, there has been a debate in the church about this very problem. Christian purists might insist that believers who seek after their own death are dishonoring the great value of their own lives or causing their executioners to be guilty of murder. The command to nonviolence, they may say, is as binding upon our own bodies as it is upon those of our enemies. Knowingly bringing about your own death is not martyrdom, but suicide. Lactantius acknowledges the great popularity this "certain man" has already accumulated, such that it must be mentioned, but he will not contribute to venerating someone he sees as having brought discredit to the faith.

MARTYRDOM: COMPLEX OR COMPLICATED?

After *Reborn on the Fourth of July* came out, describing my conviction to lay down my weapon but remain in the military, Joe Carter, a former Marine Corps gunnery sergeant, accused me of having a "lack of interest in life." Ignoring the conjecture (we've never met and he never reached out), the sentiment is not a far cry from Lactantius's highbrow distaste for George's apparent enthusiasm for death. But his distrust of martyrdom was the minority view in the early church, most often held by Christians with comparably high status and great wealth who had more to lose. The more widely held view was that of Eusebius, who helped popularize martyrdom by praising George for his "zeal" and "ardent faith."

Eusebius's position was so popular that many early believers felt martyrdom was the surest way to heaven. The problem this created was to confuse celebrity with conviction; some were more interested in the *idea* of martyrdom than actually enduring it. The earliest account of Christian martyrdom makes a point to describe one such believer, Quintus, "who forced himself and some others to come forward voluntarily."[27] He is condemned as an apostate not because he gave himself up, but because when the time came to witness, to follow through with the suffering he sought, he shrank from the burden.

Likewise, today, many Christians act like victims to gain political points; our own suffering is leveraged to great effect while we ignore the suffering of others. Journalist Jonathan Merritt called it a "persecution complex" and pointed out the disproportionate outrage a vocal minority of American Christians expressed at JCPenney hiring Ellen DeGeneres as spokesperson while remaining silent about the exodus of Christians from Iraq in the wake of the withdrawal of American forces.[28] This impulse relies upon the idea that the early church suffered a lot more than history suggests it did. The irony is that an overemphasis on martyrdom, in the absence of any suffering, is precisely what the early church was unified against. A fascination with our earthly lives, over and above the possibility that we might suffer for our beliefs, is consistently condemned by the historic church. For early Christians, suffering was a privilege, not a talking point.

What sets Saint George apart from other martyrs is the great number and diversity of his sufferings. He knew survival was not a virtue, but he never abandoned what he believed to save his own tail. The historical accounts confirm that "he was not only tortured, but burnt alive," and the legendary accounts of the later medieval world are comical in their embellishment upon this theme.[29] One modern scholar lists no less than twelve tortures contained in various accounts from the eleventh to fifteenth centuries.[30] Even the earliest accounts emphasize how many times George suffers death, then is resurrected and encouraged by Christ, only to be killed again. If this serves to say anything of any substance, it is that George resists, that he does not give in, even to death. Survival isn't a virtue; it's a form of resistance.

His testimony stands to remind soldier-saints of today that death may not be the worst thing to happen to us, but it also should not be the answer to problems we face. We should not avoid the dark truth that, occasionally, our "desire is to depart and be with Christ, for that is far better" than to suffer endlessly (Phil. 1:23). Rather, like George, the soldiers of Christ do not give in to the promise of peace and rest by abandoning our lives. The enemy may take our lives, but not without a knock-down drag-out (spiritual) fight.

8.

LIFE, LITURGY, AND THE PURSUIT OF HOLINESS:

PACHOMIUS AND MONASTICISM

T O BE HOLY IS TO BE SET APART; THE WORD IS USED TO TRANS-
late the Hebrew verb *qadas* (H6942). In the very beginning,
"God blessed the seventh day and hallowed it [*qadas*]" (Gen. 2:3).
The King James Bible swaps "hallowed" with "sanctified," a word
closely related to "saint" and "saintliness." Whereas the Sabbath is like
a "selectee," drafted involuntarily into holiness, the saints are people
who enlist voluntarily for holiness. The martyrs were the first believers held up as the highest expressions of faith, but as the faith grew
martyrdom became exceedingly rare. Attention turned to monks and
nuns who gave up the basic comforts of life as a commitment to
God. Grunts love the self-denial, of doing without life's luxuries, and
often boast at how much shit they can take. Veterans can seem like

latter-day monastics, with their penchant for rural solitude and distrust of so-called authority emanating from urban centers.

The Greek word *monos* (G3441) means "alone or solitary," but it can also be used to imply "forsaken" or "cast off." In his first letter to the Thessalonians, Paul says he and his companions felt orphaned, "when we could bear it no longer, we decided to be [*monos*]" (1 Thess. 3:1). The phenomenon of early Christians fleeing the corruption and superficiality of the urban centers reflects similar sentiments of American veterans migrating from the cities. According to the Council on Foreign Relations, four of the five states with the highest proportion of 2020 enlistees were in the South, including South Carolina, Florida, Georgia, and Alabama.[1] These states are also alike in being relatively dense, or at least above the national average of 88.4 people per square mile.[2] Data from the National Center for Veterans Analysis and Statistics shows that the veteran population is concentrated primarily in rural states of very low density, including Alaska, Montana, Maine, and Wyoming.[3] Across the nation, veterans make up about 6.2 percent of the population, but these northern states all fall above 8 percent. With the exception of Virginia, this depicts the average military trajectory as going from the moderately dense Southeast to the least populated rural states of the North.[4]

The data suggest that veterans as a population prefer rural rather than urban locales, even if the reasons are hard to pin down with certainty. A majority of living veterans served in or during the unpopular war in Vietnam, meaning retirement could help explain the migration (whether or not feelings of civilian resentment added fuel to the fire). Despite the hostile homecoming, at least soldiers and activists felt the same way about that war; a veteran and a civilian could find common ground in condemning the war in Vietnam.

The military-civilian divide has only grown in the decades since, and Iraq and Afghanistan veterans have cause to feel even more alienated from regular Americans than prior generations. According to the Pew Research Center, Iraq and Afghanistan veterans were almost twice as likely as civilians to feel the "forever wars" were not worth fighting.[5] The military-civilian divide is one not just of service, but of experience; veterans cannot escape the reality of military service, and civilians seem unable or unwilling to understand it.

ASK(ESIS), AND YOU SHALL (NOT) RECEIVE

As long as there have been cities, there have been reasons to hate them. As economic centers, they supply not only life's necessities, but also personal indulgences. Unlike modern housing associations or gated communities, military towns preserve the primitive function of ancient outposts; every grunt knows where to go off base to press their uniform, pawn their shit, and pay for sex. Under the various persecutions, the density of cities could provide cover for Christians, allowing them to escape into the crowd. Where people congregate, however, power follows.

About a decade after Diocletian's anti-Christian edict began the Great Persecution, the emperor Constantine ended it once and for all. At the Battle of Milvian Bridge in 312, Constantine appealed to the Christian God by adorning his soldiers' shields with a Christian symbol. The letters *chi* and *rho*, which look like an *X* and a *P* respectively, are the first two letters of the Greek word *christos*. Constantine legalized Christianity when he prevailed, signaling imperial patronage of the Christian God.

Christianity became popular and officials throughout the empire started jumping on the bandwagon to show their alignment with the emperor's favored religion. Not surprisingly, the slaves, women, and other outcasts who had carried the faith that far would return to their marginalized state as churches began to look and act a lot like the cities in which they were found. Rather than stay in the still-just-as-corrupt urban centers with all the so-called "Christians," many of the most devout left cities for the surrounding deserts where they could live out their faith with less distractions and corruption. Leaving the high-density city life for the rural wilderness was what inspired many early ascetics, and we see it in the civilian to soldier to veteran pipeline as well.

John the Baptizer was a prophet and proto-ascetic who wore camel skin and lived in the wilderness eating bugs and wild honey. His lifestyle was not unfamiliar to his audience, however, nor was it politically neutral. The hair shirt was a direct criticism of the luxury of power, for "those who wear soft robes are in royal palaces" (Matt. 11:8). Unlike Jesus, John fasted often and called his followers to similar patterns of penance. As the forerunner of Christ, John couldn't model himself off his cousin. He had to look deeper into the Hebrew Scriptures for ascetic inspiration.

There was another, long ago, "a hairy man, with a leather belt around his waist...Elijah the Tishbite" (2 Kings 1:8). During the reign of the corrupt King Ahab, Elijah challenged rampant corruption and impiety in Israelite society. Although he gained little sympathy at the time, Elijah became a prominent figure in the Bible, second only to Moses. Elijah was so pious that he never suffered death. When his time came, there appeared "a chariot of fire and horses of fire… and Elijah ascended in a whirlwind into heaven" (2 Kings 2:11). It is this amortality, of Elijah being neither mortal nor immortal, that has people in Jesus' time asking whether the great prophet of old has returned (see Matt. 16:14; Mark 8:28). Jesus makes it clear that he is not Elijah but points to John as "the Elijah who is to come" (Matt. 11:14; 17:11–13). This was foreshadowed early in Luke's gospel when Zechariah is told by an angel that his son John will possess "the spirit and power of Elijah" (1:17).

Elijah and John both preferred to wander the wilderness, denying themselves creature comforts as a not-so-subtle critique of urban elites. Another proto-ascetic movement active during Jesus' time was the Essenes, a Jewish doomsday sect that lived away from the cities in anticipation of the end of time. They referred to themselves as "*osey haTorah*, 'doers' or 'makers' of Torah."[6] As in, everyone else fails to do Torah, but not us. It's like saying "the real America," as though the coasts don't count.

Asceticism goes hand in hand with social critique, dancing on the thin line between self-righteousness and self-denial. It's no coincidence that John's ministry was a call to repentance and the Essenes looked down on the rest of decadent society as doomed. But biblical asceticism has not always been so holier-than-thou. *Askesis* appears only once in the entire Bible. In Acts 24, Paul argues that self-righteousness doesn't earn anybody any brownie points, that there is no justification for looking down on people we think are unrighteous. He uses *askesis* in its historically grounded sense, not as self-denial for self-righteousness' sake, but as practice or training: "Therefore I do my best [*askeo*, G778] always to have a clear conscience toward God and all people" (Acts 24:16).

The earliest Christian ascetics were Syrian Christians who practiced self-denial without self-isolation. For Syriac *askesis*, "contact with the outside world seems to have been *cultivated* rather than shunned."[7] They lived among the people, living lives of pious hospitality, not self-righteous elevation. They never felt the need to run from the corruption of urban elites, but chose to live their lives in public contrast to affluence and indulgence. They built shanties attached to city walls, like Rahab, or lived itinerantly within city limits as wandering vagrants, doers and makers of good news. Distinct from the Christians in densely populated areas of Rome and Egypt, Jesus' adherents in Syria inhabited a middle ground between the imperial imagination of the Roman west and the anti-imperialist resistance of the Egyptian south. To Christians of Syria and Palestine, "following Christ meant active engagement, as Christ's representatives, with the 'world' they had renounced, rather than permanent social withdrawal."[8] They knew that when piety is inspired by frustration at the world the object of attention is not God, and the exercise of separation is self-righteousness rather than self-devotion. By standing out rather than standing apart, the lifestyle of Syrian ascetics bore a closer resemblance to biblical practices than later Egyptian anchorites who left everything to live alone in the desert.

HERMITS—RUGGED ISOLATIONISTS

Both combat and Christianity taught me that I am never as great a person as I tell myself I am. I think that is why the eremitic impulse strikes me as self-indulgent; the idea of living off the land apart from society is an introvert's dream, one within reach for many military veterans. But if rugged individualism is spiritually healthy, then why is there still this issue of veteran suicide? I think the answer has something to do with the fact that getting away isn't always the solution; sometimes it's just avoidance. Sure, Jesus went away from the crowds for a time, but God had said of isolation, "It is not good that the man should be alone [*bad*, H905]" (Gen. 2:18). Christians who make heroes of hermits have wandered from the biblical story, and it started in 360 with Athanasius's *Life of Antony*.[9]

According to Athanasius, who wrote his biography of Antony around 360 CE, Antony came from a wealthy Egyptian family of Christians. He was homeschooled as a child, "not caring to associate with other boys."[10] His parents died unexpectedly when he was about nineteen years old, so their estate passed to him, including the care of his younger sister. Shortly thereafter he was inspired by a sermon on Christ's words to believers to "sell your possessions, and give the money to the poor...then come, follow me" (Matt. 19:21). Antony liquidated the estate, gave the bulk of the profits to his neighbors, and had his sister "committed...to known and faithful virgins."[11] Having freed himself of worldly responsibilities, he began the ascetic life. Far from a heroic leap of faith, Antony seemed to be indulging his own introverted desires, in morally dubious fashion. That's how I read it through the lens of a community predisposed to self-isolation. But I'm not most people, nor are soldiers and veterans. Even if you're not an introvert like me, to see Antony's heroism reflected in his eremeticism distracted from the whole story. He wasn't even the first to do it.

That distinction falls to Paul of Thebes, whose story was recorded in Jerome's *Life of Paul the First Hermit* around 375 CE.[12] According to Jerome, Paul was born in a time when "Christians would often pray that they might be smitten with the sword."[13] His parents died when he was sixteen and left him an enviable inheritance, which his sister's husband tried to acquire by turning Paul over to the persecutors. Despite the popularity of martyrdom in Paul's early life, he decided to flee "to the mountain wilds" instead. There he found a cave with "a large hall, open to the sky, but shaded by…an ancient palm." Nearby "was a secret mint [from] the time of Anthony's union with Cleopatra."[14] Jerome describes Antony meeting with Paul in his desert enclave and telling his followers, "I have really seen Paul in Paradise!"[15] Although it may come across as referring to heavenly residence, Paul is still very much alive. An admittedly cynical reading of Jerome could be taken to depict Paul as having traded one rich inheritance for another. Who wouldn't spend the rest of their days "in prayer and solitude" (wink, wink) in a cash-strewn desert oasis?

The timing of Jerome's *Vita Pauli* is important, as it was the same year Athanasius's Greek biography of Antony was translated into the same "vulgar tongue" (i.e., Latin). With the expectation of martyrdom all but dead, Christians were looking for another way to signal their virtue to God and their neighbors. Athanasius sees a viable alternative in Antony's rugged isolationism, but Jerome wants to pump the brakes, depicting eremitic monasticism as having less than austere origins. Not to pooh-pooh monasticism, but to dissuade people from putting Antony on a pedestal, or Paul for that matter. The "first hermit" did not pursue piety; he fled from persecution. Don't get me wrong, nobody can blame Paul for being afraid of martyrdom; at least he didn't try to steal the valor of the martyrs by pretending he was up for the task like Quintus. There is an important distinction between running *to* faith and running *from* death.

Jerome saw the time of Paul and Antony as a shift in spiritual strategy by the Enemy. Slow but deadly tortures, like those inflicted upon George, were supposed to break the spirit before finally destroying the body. Martyrdom, however, deprived death of its sting as flocks of Christians actively sought out the very tortures intended to break them. The late third century was a time of massive social change for the church from Diocletianic persecution to Constantinian endorsement. Some scholars see this shift toward imperial assimilation as corruption, a sentiment shared by at least some of the Christians at the time. But it can also be interpreted cosmically as a time when "the spiritual forces of evil" were forced into a tactical pause against the army of God. By taking the fight to the spiritual plane, ascetics were the new and improved *Militia Dei*. Just as the adversary had, the earliest monks were forced to experiment with trial and error, and proto-monastics Paul and Antony got some things right and other things wrong.

Rugged isolationism is appealing to veterans sick and tired of superficial civilian bullshit. But people were not made to be alone, and our desire to get away can be as self-indulgent as it is self-destructive. Athanasius makes the case for rugged isolationism by making Antony a model for the most devoted faithful, while Jerome seems to urge caution. The soldiers of Christ were once led by the martyrs, who knew that survival is not a Christian virtue. But as power shifted and the church became a dominant institution, ascetics were the next generation of godly grunts learning that sometimes survival is a form of resistance.

NAZIR-ISH: PIETY, PLACE, AND PEOPLE

The clearest form of self-dedication in the Bible is the Nazirite vow described throughout Numbers 6. People who wanted to live particularly devout lives were not to separate themselves from the world but "to separate themselves *to* the LORD" (Num. 6:2, emphasis added). Nazirite vows were open to men and women alike and were usually time-limited rather than lifelong. For the duration of their vows, Nazirites were forbidden to consume alcohol, cut their hair, or make contact with a human corpse. The prohibition on alcohol was so severe that it extended to grapes and grapevines.

In many prominent cases, like with Samson and Samuel, a vow could be undertaken by the Nazirite's parent. In most cases, however, becoming a Nazirite required only a public statement followed by adherence to the three prohibitions. Compared to abstinence from alcohol and contact with corpses, the shaving prohibition was visible. Nazirites' long, flowing hair was a public sign of a *r'os nezer*, or "consecrated head" (see Num. 6:9, 12, 18, 19). To bring the ascetic period to an end, a Nazirite would be expected to go to the temple to be baptized and make three offerings with the assistance of the priest on duty: a burnt offering with a young male sheep, a sin offering with a young female sheep, and a peace offering with a mature ram. Because "their consecration to God is upon the head" (Num. 6:7), Nazirite vows formally cease when they shave their luscious locks and add their hair to the fire below the peace offering, which they then eat with the priest. After all that, they could go back to drinking wine. Because who wouldn't need a chaser after eating hair-smoked ram chop?

Outside the Book of Numbers, there are scattered references to Nazirites in the Bible. Zechariah is told in a dream that his son John "must never drink wine or strong drink" (Luke 1:15), reminiscent of a lifelong Nazirite vow. In the book of Acts, after a run-in with an angry Jewish mob in Corinth, Paul "had his hair cut, for he was under a vow" (Acts 18:18). Later in Jerusalem, James, bishop of Jerusalem and Jesus' brother, tells Paul, "We have four men who are under a vow. Join these men, go through the rite of purification with them, and pay for the shaving of their heads" (Acts 21:23–24). Just like in Corinth, Paul has been accused of encouraging Jews to not observe the ancient customs, so James tells him to take, and quickly conclude, Nazirite vows to ease tensions. The vows he has taken, and will take again with the four believers, are used as evidence that the Jesus movement is in fact Jewish. Not only are Nazirite vows distinctly Jewish, there is reason to think they are a family tradition for Jesus.

The New Testament consistently refers to Jesus' hometown as Nazareth (*nazara*, G3478), a cognate of "Nazirite." Before the Gospels, however, there was no record of a town by this name. The earliest references to Nazareth outside the Bible don't appear until the third century, when Eusebius mentions *Desposyni*, residents of Nazara who claimed relation to Jesus through his siblings.[16] Matthew's gospel is alone in claiming Jesus settled in that specific location "so that what had been spoken through the prophets might be fulfilled, 'He will be called a Nazorean [G3480]'" (Matt. 2:23). There is no prophecy in the Old Testament to this effect, but Matthew uses the Greek Septuagint, in which "the angel of the LORD appeared" to Samson's mother in Judges 13:3, telling her, "You shall conceive and bear a son…The boy shall be a [*nazireon*]" (v. 5).[17] As a judge, Samson will "deliver Israel from the hand of the Philistines" (v. 5), much the same way Jesus will "save his people from their sins" (Matt. 1:21).

Was Jesus a Nazirite? No. He drank plenty of wine and touched the dead body of Jairus's daughter (see Matt. 9:18–26; Mark 5:21–43; Luke 8:40–56). Besides, Jesus taking an ascetic vow is something the evangelists wouldn't miss and certainly wouldn't purposefully omit. But his cousin John the Baptizer sure seemed like one; the angel Gabriel implemented a prenatal prohibition on "wine or strong drink" (Luke 1:15), and he paraded around Galilee wearing "clothing of camel's hair with a leather belt around his waist" (Matt. 3:4). His appearance would not only evoke Elijah, "a hairy man, with a leather belt around his waist" (2 Kings 1:8), but also the unshaven aesthetic of Nazirites.

As if to emphasize the family's proclivity to holiness, Jesus' brother James was "holy from his mother's womb. He drank no wine or other intoxicating liquor, nor did he eat flesh; no razor came upon his head."[18] This is the same James who encouraged Paul to take vows with other believers to show Jews how Jewish Jesus' movement was.

Like the problems with "warrior," calling ascetics "monks" can be misleading because it misplaces the linguistic emphasis. One way to read monasticism is as coming from *monos*, "single or alone," which names the cell or room an individual ascetic occupied. But the Greeks called them *monachos*, "single," as in celibate, as in only one monk per bed. The earliest title reserved for particularly pious Christians was *Ihidaya*, a Syriac equivalent of *monogenes* (G3439), "only begotten one" (see John 1:18). In other words, the non-needing, non-procreating ones.

Biblical piety is about standing *out* from the crowd rather than standing *apart*. Naziritic vows, Nazi-rites if you will, gave regular people a means to take up holiness by giving up personal indulgences. Before the evangelists named the city Nazara, the word brought up imagery of harried and haggard holy folk on a race to the bottom of the social pecking order. To be Nazir-ish, *nazarenos* (G3479) is to be associated with the person, place, and piety of Jesus, his brother, cousins, and the whole *familia* of faith.

PACHOMIUS—FAITH WITH FRIENDS

Pachomius was born just before the fourth century near the Nile River in southern Egypt amid the Great Persecution of Diocletian. Around 313 CE, at age twenty-one, he was conscripted into the Roman *auxilia*. As in our own day, new soldiers were processed in central hubs near their homes before being shipped off to training. For Pachomius, his first stop was not MEPS, but a recruit depot in nearby Thebes (now called Luxor). After processing, he was shipped four hundred klicks north to a now-destroyed city of Antinopolis where he was to conduct his one year of basic training.[19]

The only intact Roman military training manual was written by a Christian civilian named Vegetius a generation after Pachomius's brief time in service.[20] With a title translated roughly as "Concerning Military Matters," it described the initial training of recruits with some detail, including the twice-daily requirement of exercise with mock weapons. Roman recruits would use wooden swords, but grunts are more familiar with "rubber duckies."[21] Vegetius calls this training *exerceo*, and its Greek equivalent would have been *askesis*. Without knowing it, Pachomius was paralleling the monastic novitiate, the rigorous process of becoming Nazir-ish. That's because even the hermits modeled their lifestyle on Roman military.

As a conscript rather than a volunteer, Pachomius was under close watch that included lock and key. When he arrived for his basic *askesis*, he was imprisoned with other draftees whenever they were not training. Although all soldiers were well fed, it was common for the lowest echelons to get shorted. It was behind bars that Pachomius first encountered Christians bringing food to prisoners as a corporeal work of mercy, and their witness inspired him to imitate their example.

Pachomius was released from his military service obligation before his one-year training was complete, what we might call an entry-level separation, and immediately set out to imitate the heroes of Christianity. One thing he learned from the military was to build and restore fortifications, from hasty fighting positions to long-term occupations. When he eventually pursued the Nazir-ish life, he put his military training to spiritual use by restoring abandoned forts rather than simply inhabiting them. Antony was an inspiration, but even our heroes aren't perfect. Pachomius improved upon Antonian monasticism by making it a community affair, by encouraging faith with friends rather than being a lone wolf.

Historian Christian Barthel suggests military culture continued to find a home in the emerging cenobitic, or communal, monastic movement under Pachomius's leadership. Entry into the community was marked by "Trials of Commitment," and it wouldn't be a stretch to call what some monastic novices endured a kind of hazing.[22] If successful, they would take vows, like the military oath Pachomius didn't last long enough to profess. Vows were to be made publicly, just as the Nazirites had to make a verbal commitment before witnesses. Monastic rank was based not on age or social status, but on the date of profession. An elderly novice was expected to defer to a younger, more established ascetic.

Pachomius was the first to establish rules, *regulae*, that, like the voluminous military regulations, ordered the lives of his recruits. Monks who violated the *regulae* were "out of regs" and could lose rank and find themselves back at the bottom of the pecking order the same way Nazirites who became defiled had to start their period of consecration over again. Monastic correction was made a public affair to promote mutual accountability and, like Roman military punishment, involved the symbolic loss of their belt or girdle, called a *cingulum*. A dishonorable discharge, which meant a loss of all privileges of citizenship and veterans' benefits, was symbolized by stripping a soldier of his *cingulum*. When a Pachomian monk faced correction, they could signal penitence by loosening their *cingulum* before the whole assembly and thereby avoid full expulsion.[23]

Borrowing these symbols and rituals from the military was not Pachomius's contribution to monasticism. Antony and other ascetics before him had already laid the groundwork for reinventing or subverting martial imagery. Antony struck out on his own in 285, right as Diocletian assumed power. The site Antony chose was an abandoned military fort at the base of a mountain about fifty klicks from what is now known as the Suez Gulf.[24] There, in the emptied husk of Roman military might, Antony fought the forces of evil with the armor of God, "like a good soldier, seizing the shield of faith and the helmet of hope" to protect him from the dangers he faced.[25] After twenty years of sustained spiritual combat, Antony would have emerged a "veteran" with his citizenship (in heaven), at which point he would have been expected to help train (catechize) incoming recruits (catechumen).

Why the emphasis on military training? According to recent scholarship, "The level of endurance and conviction he displayed to withstand this onslaught put him in direct succession of the true confessors—the martyrs."[26] Christians looked to the martyrs as the most reliable representations of Christ's mission on earth, many of which were thought of in military terms. The *militia Christi* was led by those who most adhered to the example that Jesus set, but the end of the persecutions made martyrdom almost impossible to come by. Antony and the other eremitic ascetics are to be commended, but they fall short of the glory of God in so far as they sought isolation rather than communion. Pachomius improved upon their witness and offered the church a way to testify to the holiness of God by calling communities rather than individuals. By the time Pachomius died, he oversaw thousands of monks, both men and women, who showed us what it might mean to be called *into* a broken world as a broken people.

9.

"I AM A SOLDIER OF CHRIST":

MARTIN AND HAGIOGRAPHY

WITHOUT THE GOSPELS, THERE IS NO TELLING HOW RADICALLY
different Christianity, and by extension global religion,
might be. Jesus did not keep a record of his life, so the only information about his life we have is through his friends and followers.
People who wrote about themselves could be seen as prideful, and
the earliest autobiographies focused on self-deprecatory themes, as
with Ovid's *Tristia* (Sorrows) and Augustine's *Confessions*. To be great
was to have your actions do the talking and someone else do the writing. There's a saying with veterans and combat: "Those who talk don't
know and those who know don't talk." If you need people to know
who you are and what you've done, then chances are you ain't shit
and you haven't done shit.

Martin of Tours was one such great man, a quiet professional
of the faith who got shit done and didn't spend much time talking

about himself. He wrote nothing, but left his mark on history in more ways than one. As a soldier-saint, he inherited a story that destined him to martyrdom, but it turns out he was in the right place but the wrong time. Instead of entering the great cloud of witnesses, he would shape the cult of the saints by being the kind of person others wanted to write about. After a dishonorable discharge, Deacon Martin made his life amid rural communities while urban Christians fawned over biographies of desert hermits like Athanasius's *Life of Saint Antony*. Before he could depart this life in peace, he would acquire his own cultlike following thanks to a stan named Sulpicius Severus, whose *Life of Saint Martin* would become a hallmark of the burgeoning tradition of hagiography.

SOLDIER OR CIVILIAN, CHRISTIAN OR PAGAN?

Humanity has this horrible tendency to form cliques, to create groups of insiders and outsiders. Romans during the republic called these outsiders *pagani*, literally "of the countryside." Calling someone a pagan was the ancient equivalent of calling someone a redneck or a hillbilly; it was synonymous with being uncivilized. Pagans could hold citizenship and even Latinize their names, as Saul did, but they would never escape the prejudice of being *idiotae*—dumb, indigenous country bumpkins who couldn't be trusted.

As Rome aged and fell into imperialism, the meaning of *pagani* changed with the surrounding culture. When the ruling class no longer wanted to defend the country they controlled, they "professionalized" the military by making it economically attractive to the

---

poor. Incentives included such luxuries as food, clothing, shelter, and veterans' benefits. There was an unintended consequence, however: to be a fully realized citizen was still thought to include military service. Romans who never served in the military were eventually lumped together with the *pagani*; by the first century it came to refer to civilians.

This was the state of things when Christianity emerged from an odd coupling of Roman society and Jewish faith. Gentile followers had no problem being soldiers. But the church's Jewish heritage opposed all that reeked of imperialism and idolatry. Christian soldiers like Captain Marvel and Cornelius were treated as exemplary by Gentile believers but with caution by Jewish believers. When the dust settled, toward the second century, a compromise was struck in which the martial element of belief, soldiers, was dependent upon the divine object of service, God or Christ.

Although it does not appear in the New Testament, Christians began referring to themselves very early as *milites Christi*, or "soldiers of Christ." Even outspoken pacifists like Tertullian relied on this military nomenclature. Writing *Against the Military Crown* in the early third century, he contrasts the *paganus* (civilian/citizen) with the *miles* (soldier).[1] The *pagani* were those who did not serve God, or who served false gods. In using this language, the church reflected the Roman normalization of military service as well as the irreligious "pagan" connotations of yore. Distrust of pagans under the republic was because they either failed to observe cultic traditions at all or they sucked at them when "civilized" Romans came to town. Pagans were both nonsoldiers (of God) as well as nonbelievers (in Christ).

Plenty of modern Christians turn to Tertullian's text to bolster weak claims that early Christians were pacifist, but it's not that simple. The church was mostly decentralized until 325, before which little consensus on extrabiblical subjects formed, like predestination or the perpetual virginity of Mary. After all, Tertullian promoted a then-unpopular belief that God was three persons in one, now known as the doctrine of the Trinity.[2] A martial hermeneutic is no less credible than the Trinity; in fact, it may be more credible. At least grunts can claim it started with Saul.

Saul would have been a pagan to Romans in both the religious and the civic senses, but that didn't stop him from identifying with soldiering. In what may have been Saul's final epistle before his death, he encourages Timothy to "share in suffering like a good soldier [*stratiotes*, G4757] of Christ Jesus" (2 Tim. 2:3). Timothy was not serving in the military; he was serving God in his missionary work alongside Saul. Educated Romans hearing these words would pick up on the contrast with *paganus*, its Latin equivalent; "don't be a pagan outsider; be an insider, a soldier." Saul's words are not just a reminder that suffering is a cardinal virtue of godly grunts but an early endorsement of a martial hermeneutic.

CHRISTIAN OR COMBATANT,
TO SERVE OR TO FIGHT?

The earliest Christians insisted that they served God just as soldiers served the empire, so there's no reason anyone in the church cannot identify as a soldier (of Christ). The question is not *whether* Christians can be soldiers, but what *kind* of soldiers Christians are called to be. Saul makes it clear in his second letter to the soldiers of Christ in Corinth that "we do not wage war according to human standards" (2 Cor. 10:3). The weapons we wield, he continues, "have divine power" (v. 4) rather than regular worldly power over flesh and bone.

It is unclear whether Saul thinks worldly service is incompatible with divine service. In the New Testament, Jesus never condemned military service and no converts went AWOL so Saul's ambiguity was standard for centuries. Despite a vocal minority, Christians continued to serve in the Roman military without cause for concern (likely because most soldiers served in the equivalent of municipal administrative roles). The subject of Tertullian's antimilitary treatise is a Roman "soldier of God" who refuses to wear part of his uniform in faithful defiance. If this Christian felt empowered to object openly to ceremonial saber rattling, then he probably had seen or heard of others who did so before him. Christians in the military would have stood out, been seen as set apart and, dare I say "holy," for their conscientiousness, for refusing to do things other Romans were fine with. And therein lies the problem.

The age of martyrs did not really *start* in the military, but that was where it got kicked into high gear. As we have seen, if an emperor wanted to enforce anything, it was easiest to start where he exercised the most control, and that was in his armed forces. Closest to him was his own Praetorian Guard, next would be the commanders of legions and their tribunes. This is why most of the military martyrs were officers; nobody cared enough about the enlisted grunts or the auxiliary corps, or if they did, it was not feasible to enforce an unpopular edict the further you went from the emperor's central court. When shit started hitting the fan, Christian soldiers stuck out like sore thumbs because they would refuse to do things that violated their conscience, like saying powerful people were inherently godly. As more faithful soldiers spoke up, the more the Church had to face the dilemma of Christian service. Like the person he wrote about, Tertullian likely followed the trend rather than started it.

Martin was born a military brat straddling the line between God and country; his father was an army officer and his mother was a Christian. The year was 316 and Diocletian's "great" persecution was over.[3] Although Constantine the Great had begun the long process of Christianizing the empire, feelings were still mixed about the question of Christian soldiers. Traditionalists, like Lactantius, insisted Rome was a wolf in sheep's clothing and saw military service as immoral. Sympathizers, like Eusebius, saw divine intervention in the ascendency of the faith and saw no problem serving in Rome's army. Martin's home was split; his father named him after Mars, the god of war, and pressed him to serve, but his mother encouraged his keen interest in religion.

Perhaps fortunately for him, Martin would not have to choose sides; a law at the time made military service mandatory for all able-bodied male children of veterans. He was inducted at age fifteen into a heavy cavalry unit guarding the emperor. Even before being baptized, he gained a reputation as a devout Christian by washing his servant's feet and preparing his meals. To incoming members of his unit, "he was regarded not so much as being a soldier as a monk."[4]

He served entirely without incident, following the emperor around Europe as a member of his personal security detachment. Perhaps the nature of his service, protecting someone from harm, never conflicted with his strong religious convictions.

One winter campaign proved to be particularly brutal, fatal for unsheltered people. In what is now Amiens, France, an unclothed beggar was asking members of his unit for help in the bitter cold. Nobody had obliged the doomed man until Martin reached him, so he cut his luxurious Praetorian cape in half to share, thus saving the beggar's life. That night Martin dreamed that his charitable act had clothed Christ himself, so the next day he was determined to be baptized.

Despite being baptized the following day, Martin made no effort to leave military service. Perhaps he was serving under Constantine, the same emperor who had legalized Christianity.[5] If so, his experience as a soldier would have been very different from his later service under Julian the Apostate, who famously tried to roll back Constantine's religious toleration. The incident in Amiens sealed his devotion to Christ, but it did not inspire him to leave the military. That would come almost twenty years later.

For the vast majority of his service, Martin was a baptized Christian soldier. If he had misgivings, they were not strong enough to compel him to seek discharge. In 356, Julian was preparing his imperial guard for battle against enemy forces at Worms, in Germany. It was Martin's first recorded encounter with combat, but it also would have been the last year of his required term of service.[6] Whatever his reason, he took it as the final straw and made his stand. Julian was reviewing his troops on the eve of battle when Martin proclaimed loudly, *Christi ego miles sum, pugnare mihi non licet* ("I am a soldier of Christ, it is not lawful foir me to fight").[7]

Martin distinguished between one who serves (*miles*), which he was; and one who fights (*pugnare*), which he was not. This is not some foreign concept, then or now. Most Roman soldiers served long, boring careers and saw little, if any, combat, which could also be said of America's military before 9/11. But more important than the amount of actual combat soldiers perform is the important distinction *within* militaries between trigger pullers and pencil pushers, the "Tooth to Tail" ratio I described in the introduction.[8] As a member of the Praetorian Guard, Martin would have fallen between combat and support, just like the Secret Service. Warfighting is far from their primary responsibility, and the violence they might expect to commit would be in direct defense of another human being. After all, emperors are regular old human beings whether or not they force their people to say otherwise.

A BITTER PARADOX

Up until this moment, Martin's story was in no way unique. Many other Christians had served in the Roman army, and he would have heard of many godly grunts like George who were put to death when their faith was discovered. Sometimes they were outed by jealous battle buddies, as in the cases of Callistratus of Carthage and Victor of Milan. These stories were cautiously passed around by word of mouth during the persecutions before being committed to writing after Constantine popularized Christianity. We know this because in the recorded stories, called hagiographies, it is the non-Christian soldiers who are called pagans and outsiders.

By the time Martin entered the military in 331, Christianity was firmly established as the norm, even if under Julian there was a brief attempt at restoring the pantheon and its cults. The vast majority of these hagiographies depict certain death upon disclosing one's service to Christ above Caesar. There had been peace for Christian soldiers when Constantine issued his Edict of Milan in 312, but Julian represented a dangerous return to the old ways. At the Battle of Worms in 356, Julian was the junior of two Caesars, the lowest ranking of the imperial tetrarchy. As soon as he was made a full Augustus in 360, he made every effort to roll Constantine's religious reforms back.

When Martin proclaimed himself a *miles Christi*, he was fully prepared to suffer the fate of countless military martyrs before him. Julian was an asshole of the first degree, which Martin would have known from personal experience. Martin would have heard whispered stories, proto-hagiographies, describing soldiers being martyred for declaring Christian soldiers were called to die rather than to kill. In 388, the Christian influencer John Chrysostom eulogized two praetors, Juventinus and Maximinus, who had been beheaded by Julian for speaking ill of his religious policies.[9] Martin served in the same capacity under the same emperor, but had escaped their fate. The soldier of Christ had stumbled upon what Dag Hammarskjöld called "the bitter paradox: the meaningfulness of death and the meaninglessness of killing."[10]

In response to Martin's bold declaration, Julian got his undies in a tangle and accused him of being a malingerer, to which the saint replied, "If this conduct of mine is ascribed to cowardice, and not to faith, I will take my stand unarmed before the line of battle tomorrow, and in the name of the Lord Jesus, protected by the sign of the cross, and not by shield or helmet, I will safely penetrate the ranks of the enemy."[11]

Not knowing what to do, the emperor threw him in prison overnight, during which time the enemy forces surrendered. Martin was dishonorably discharged and suddenly found himself in a very awkward position of possessing "no story because the design was already complete."[12] Everyone else he modeled his life upon had been martyred, but the life of Saint Martin had not ended in martyrdom. Hell, it hadn't even been written yet.

When the saints' stories were finally recorded in writing, tales of martyrs' torture and deaths were called "passions," *passiones* in Latin, after Christ's own suffering. They were not immediately recorded since Christians remained suppressed and the *passiones* were restricted to local oral tradition. Each region had its own venerated saints who were loose composites of several figures whose real stories were lost. As persecutions slowed to a halt, saints who escaped death were called "confessors," and their lives, or *vitae*, were propagated more quickly and accurately. The first was Athanasius's *Vita Antonii*, which many scholars date to 356, the same year as Martin's dishonorable discharge under Julian.

Recently allowed out from under the rock they had to live under, Christians went cuckoo for Cocoa Puffs over the *Vita Antonii*. When Jerome wrote his corrective in *Vita Pauli*, he may have smelled blood in the water, because he went on to write three more hagiographies in 373, as well as a collection he titled *De viris illustribus*, "Of Illustrious Men." The popularity of Antony's *vita* would not be surpassed until after Jerome turned from hagiography to focus on his translation of the Bible for the *vulgus*, or "unrefined people." The life of Saint Martin would finally be written in the 390s, hot off the press before his body was in the cold hard ground.

HIGH CHURCH LOWLIFES

Between the publication of Athanasius's *Vita Antonii* and Jerome's *Vita Pauli*, Martin had been living an obscure life as an itinerant deacon. His mentor, the anti-imperialist theologian Hilary of Poitiers, had pleaded unsuccessfully with him to be ordained a priest. As a praetor, Martin had rubbed elbows with plenty of the top Roman brass during his twenty-five years of service and apparently had little patience for dog and pony shows. Instead, he built monasteries, planted churches, and made his life among rural pagans that the elites loved to hate.

At a time when desert hermits were all the rage, Martin attracted a devoted and diverse following. Without ever writing a single *vita*, theological treatise, or open letter, Martin converted both country bumpkins and imperial households.[13] His reputation was so great that he was made bishop against his own will. In 371 the residents of Tours lured him into town with a ruse about healing a sick woman and even had to plant guards along the road to prevent him from turning around. At his reluctant elevation to lead the Christians in the large urban center, other bishops remarked that "he was unworthy of the episcopate, that he was a man despicable in countenance, that his clothing was mean, and his hair disgusting."[14]

As a bishop Martin was the first to maintain monastic habits, living in a cave across the Loire River from Tours rather than in the bespoke residence attached to the cathedral. It may have been his service at such a large city that increased his reputation exponentially, with some eighty disciples attracted to his way of life, including several who had left affluent lifestyles to follow the disgraced veteran turned brutish bishop. Deacon Martin had been content within the Loire River valley, but Tours was an influential bishopric and he found himself caught up in churchwide disputes that only increased admiration of him across Christendom.

Martin wielded his newfound influence to condemn the use of capital punishment to enforce orthodoxy, an affirmation that his conscientiousness toward violence was lifelong. When members of the clerical class tried to have Priscillian of Avila executed for heresy, Martin inspired Ambrose of Milan to excommunicate the parties responsible in dramatic fashion. In a letter to Valentinian, Ambrose turned away the two bishops leading the persecution of a fellow Christian.[15] This put the emperor and many prominent clergy in a difficult place politically, but it endeared him to the vast majority of Christians at the time. In 385 Priscillian was executed over Martin's objections, leading him to recede from public advocacy in disappointment, which served as a rebuke of the marriage of clerical and imperial power.

His spiritual maturity and political engagement appealed to people from all walks of life. He was a champion of the poor but a friend to the rich and powerful who reminded rank-and-file Christians that the faith was not just ritualistic smells and bells. Although he preferred the rugged lifestyle typical of a lowly grunt, he wasn't off-putting to the high and mighty in either the church or the state. Earlier monastic movements mostly attracted the faithful poor, but Martin was distinct for his popularity among both the poor and the rich. Unlike most Christian leaders, Martin happily practiced the austerity he preached and provided an example for others to follow. His was a movement of Christians giving up the Low Church high life to become High Church lowlifes.

One of Martin's devotees, a well-connected lawyer named Sulpicius Severus, took it upon himself to record the details of Martin's life. What set his *vita* apart from those of Athanasius and Jerome was that his subject was not yet in the ground. Sulpicius would be the first to write a hagiography accountable not only to history but to its subject as well. This fact may have propelled the *Vita Sancti Martini* and the cult of the saints from backwater hobby to popular pastime.

CAPE AND BONES TO CROSS AND SPEAR

Severus's *Vita Martini* was unique in that he expanded the cultlike following of a saint, in this case Martin, before he had a chance to become one. Since Athanasius did not begin his *Vita Antonii* until after the famous recluse was dead and buried, the saint would not be bothered by the flood of starry-eyed believers seeking their own Christian celebrity sighting. The cult of the saints exploded after the persecutions ended, but the intense devotion to *vitae* and *passiones* began long before the fourth century. Hagiography is not just about the texts that survive to remind us of great lives, but also about relics.

Christians believe that death is little more than a necessary threshold we must cross from this life we know to the hereafter we have yet to experience. When ancient Christians died, they were thought to be "asleep in the Lord," waiting for that moment when the dead would be raised just as Christ had been. Particularly exemplary believers were celebrated every year on the anniversaries of their deaths, the days their bodies were deposited into the earth to await resurrection. The Christian community would visit their graves for a feast that included partaking in the bread and wine of Communion. Some of the wine would be poured out for the saint and people would tell stories about the life he or she lived, not just to remember them by, but to model their own lives after.

Imagine a group of battle buddies huddled around the grave of a dead friend, pouring one out for their homie. Except rather than a generic, nationally recognized Memorial Day, they gather on the traumatic day they lost their friend to atone and "pave over" (*kaphar*, H3722) their pain with memories of the saint's triumph over evil and death. Hagiography was born in those early soldiers of Christ coming together, alienated from society at large, to feast the memory of the saints. Dates were recorded in calendars called martyrologies to preserve and distribute the calendar order of "feast days" so that communities could celebrate a popular saint from afar. The oldest existing of these martyrologies, the *Martyrologium Hieronymanium*, is attributed to none other than our hagiographical-inclined friend Jerome.

Every year, these feasts would remind participants that death had lost its sting, that a life lived well could overcome death. Stories of a martyr's last moments were preserved not for historical accuracy but to encourage survivors that perseverance would be rewarded. The popularity of the practice grew, and graves became the locations of chapels or churches dedicated to a saint as Roman oppression eased. By the fourth century, interest in the stories once restricted to oral transmission had bubbled over, leading priests and bishops to collect what they could for the *vitae* and *passiones* we know today.

The Bollandists, a Jesuit community in Belgium, are dedicated to compiling hagiographic material in order to sort local legend from historical fact. They publish the *Acta Sanctorum*, a multivolume encyclopedic work arranged like a martyrology, as well as three volumes of the *Bibliotheca Hagiographica*.[16] For many entries, only fragments of text survive, making the *vitae* of Antony, Paul, and Martin unique for having survived intact. The fragmentary nature of the earliest hagiographies, coupled with the hyper-localized, grassroots way they originated, has led some to pooh-pooh hagiography as "the artless nature of popular genius."[17]

These stories circulated widely among the middle and lower classes, who could not afford written material and who had little patience for the highbrow literature elitists thought of as classics. Hagiography connected with less-educated Christians, who inherited most of the faith not by being given tracts on the street corner but through narratives passed from person to person. The Gospels survived in the same way, shared in hushed tones under threat of exposure before Mark said fuck it and put pen to paper to create the first Gospel. Matthew and Luke followed before John took the stories and really ran with them.[18] To look down our noses at stories preserved on the margins of society puts us at odds with the pillars of Christianity. But that's not the only way we lose sight of the earthy, grassroots foundation of our faith.

As Christianity gained prominence, the cult of the saints was politicized and relics were put in service to the powers that be rather than the people of God. Graves were exhumed for the bones of holy men and women, which were thought to have magic powers. These relics could be the bones of saints or things they came in contact with, and they were credited with everything from healing the sick to prevailing in battle. One of the earliest relics brings us back to Martin.

Severus published *Vita Sancti Martini* a few years before Martin's death. The saint's popularity exploded in his final years, leading to a confrontation between the country pagans in Candes where he died, and the big-city folk of Tours, who had forced him into being their bishop. Martin died on November 8, 397, at a small church he founded a few miles downriver of Tours, in Candes. His disciples' plan for a simple funeral in an unmarked grave was foiled when city slickers stole his body under the cover of night and snuck the corpse back to the cathedral in Tours where he was buried on November 11, Martin's feast day.[19] His bones remained at the massive and influential cathedral of Tours until eighteenth-century French revolutionaries tore it apart to use lead from the roof as ammunition.

The center of Martin's cult, however, was the half of his cape he retained from that encounter in Amiens in the 330s. There is record of the *cappa Sancti Martini* in a royal inventory taken of a church in northern France as early as the seventh century.[20] Oaths would be sworn on the cape and kings would carry it before them on the field of battle, ground that Martin refused to tread upon himself. The cultic transition of relics from revered objects to magic talismans was common across the continent, and it was ushered into popularity the same way hagiography was, by way of the Constantinian shift. The emperor's mother, Helena, promoted relic-hunting by example, claiming to have found pieces of wood from Jesus' cross and the spear used to pierce Jesus' side (see John 19:34).

From *cappa* and bones to cross and spear, saintliness was co-opted from local communities for political gain. More people came to know of the subversive stories of soldiers and other saints, but with that popularity came corruption, another bitter paradox.

10.

"FOLLOW ME!"

FRANCIS AND PILGRIMAGE

WHEN FRANCIS OF ASSISI FIRST SOUGHT RECOGNITION FOR HIS Order of Friars Minor, he sent Pope Innocent III just three verses of Scripture that would constitute their rule. Luke 9:3, in which Jesus tells his disciples to take nothing on their journey; and Matthew 16:24 and 19:21, each of which ends with a simple invitation, "Follow me." This is the invitation of Christ to the cross. It is the same invitation that welcomes grunts to the Army Infantry School at Fort Benning, Georgia. Whose cross are we to pick up, and into what kind of battle does it lead?

Jesus' journey on Good Friday, from his arrest at Gethsemane to his death at Golgotha, completes his mission here on earth. Known as his passion, it culminates in his condemnation when he is given the cross upon which he will be executed. The earliest Gospels all agree that the cross is given to Simon of Cyrene to carry (see Matt. 27:32; Mark 15:21; Luke 23:26).[1] This is odd because standard operating procedure in Rome was for criminals to carry their own cross as they undertook a death march to their execution. It's also odd because this makes Jesus look like a POG.

COME, HUMP

John's passion account differs from the others by insisting Jesus carried "the cross by himself" (19:17). It is a callback to the two Matthean passages Francis sent to the pope. The first is unique in Christ telling his followers to "take up their cross" (Matt. 16:24); and in the second he instructs a rich young ruler to adopt poverty, to "sell your possessions, and give the money to the poor…then come, follow me" (19:21). The fourth gospel doesn't want God to lose his grunt bona fides; how can Jesus not take up his own cross after literally telling his followers to do so? In each of these instances, he invites believers to join him in the death road march to salvation. In the military we call that humping, because that's what it looks like your rucksack is doing to you, even though when we talk about it the grunt is the one doing the humping. When you look back on that cheesy Hallmark beach and there's only one set of footprints in the sand, that's because Jesus is humping you.

The author of John's gospel is more concerned with historical *meaning* than historical *accuracy*; what earlier accounts pass over as unimportant, John revises to make the story morally and theologically consistent. Jesus' death march is integral to salvation history; far be it from God to need some random bystander to do the work entrusted to the Son! If Jesus is a grunt, then he would never ask his friends to do something he would not do himself. That's why it's so important to John to revise the passion narrative, to show us that Jesus can take every punishment he might ask us to endure.

As a grunt, Jesus carries his own shit and then some, not just his own load but everyone else's baggage as well. The wonderful paradox is that this is his "mission accomplished" moment, this death march from Holy Land to wilderness. The paradox of Jesus' invitation to follow him should not be overlooked, since it has been (ab)used so often to promote violence rather than undermine it.

Luke's gospel also has an invitation to take up our cross and hump with Jesus in characteristically pragmatic fashion: "take up [our] cross *daily* and follow [him]" (9:23, emphasis added). Jesus' death march is a pilgrimage, something to which Christians are called— not just as an occasional practice, but as an everyday endeavor and fundamental principle of our faith. More than just religious tourism, pilgrimage is about enacting holiness rather than being a passive witness. Like liturgical dance, pilgrimage is a form of kinetic meditation in which movement deepens a person's experience of the divine. Abrahamic pilgrims are expected to get up and get out, with our forebears, to "go from your country and your kindred and your... house" (Gen. 12:1).

By leaving behind what is familiar to us, pilgrimage offers the opportunity to experience the world with fresh eyes and open minds. The act of getting out of our routine is the foundation upon which devotion is built, but it's only the beginning. For pilgrims, the destination is no more important than the journey itself, and many routes are circuitous rather than linear. Labyrinths, for example, are considered by many Christians to be a miniature form of pilgrimage.

Circularity is also reflected in the three Jewish pilgrimage holidays of Passover, Weeks, and Booths (see Deut. 16:16). The Hebrew word for "feast or festival" (*hag*, H2282) derives from the verb *chagag* (H2287), "to circle or reel." They often appear side by side, such that circling is written into how a feast is kept, as with the instructions for keeping Passover in Exodus 12:14: "You shall celebrate [*chagag*] it as a festival [*hag*] to the LORD" (emphasis added). The verb used to describe the liturgical parade that Joshua leads around the walls of Jericho to bring its walls down is *cabab* (H5437), which is repeated six times in one chapter (Josh. 6:3, 4, 7, 11, 14, 15). The Semitic root of *hag* is reflected in the Arabic word *hajj*, the Islamic pilgrimage to Mecca that involves devotees circling the *Ka'aba* several times while wearing seamless white robes. Circling reminds us that the purpose of the pilgrimage is not necessarily the destination. Sometimes the lack of a destination can be jarring, even fear-inducing.

When Abram was commanded to leave his hometown of Ur, it would have felt like a death sentence. In ancient cultures like those that birthed the Bible, banishment was a common form of capital punishment. As soon as the Israelites were freed of Egyptian oppression, they cried out to Moses, "Was it because there were no graves in Egypt that you have taken us away to die in the wilderness? What have you done to us, bringing us out of Egypt?" (Exod. 14:11). That's kind of the point: just as seeds must die to become fruitful, the faithful must die to the world to "bear fruits worthy of repentance" (Luke 3:8) if they are to follow "the way of the LORD" that Isaiah, whom John the Baptizer is quoting, calls "a highway for our God" (Isa. 40:3). If you want to be Jesus' disciple, put your best boots on and get ready to hump.

By taking us out of our comfort zone, pilgrimage makes us foreigners. It is a reminder that we may reside in a world in which evil forces exist and exert power over us, but that world is fading. As a pilgrim, you are reminded you do not belong, you become "a stranger and an alien"; that's how Abraham described himself (Gen. 23:4). The Hebrew word for "alien" is *gar* (H1616), "to be without rights, stateless." To be on pilgrimage is to be on your way to belonging.

As a pilgrim you belong nowhere.

CRUSADES

Pope Urban II was asked by the Byzantine emperor to help repel attacks from the East by the Seljuk Turks, a Muslim dynasty. Urban answered the request not by preaching the Crusades, as we may have been taught, but by calling for a pilgrimage. The word "crusade" is anachronistic; it did not exist until after the Crusades ended. The first time it appeared was in the early 1700s as a translation of the French word *croisade*, which itself grew from *cruciata*, a Latin verb meaning "to mark with the sign of the cross." The earliest published account of what we call a crusade is *Gesta Francorum et aliorum Hierosolimitanorum*, which translates to *The Deeds of the Franks and the Other Pilgrims to Jerusalem*. The author of the *Gesta* was an unidentified veteran of the First Crusade, which Urban "preached" in Clermont, France, in November 1095.

What set Urban's vision apart was a promise that pilgrims "who die by the way, whether by land or by sea, or in battle against the pagans, shall have immediate remission of sins."[2] According to the author of the *Gesta*, the papal appeal was so enticing that its hearers "caused crosses to be sewed on their right shoulders, saying that they followed with one accord the footsteps of Christ, by which they had been redeemed from the hand of hell."[3] This was such a compelling ritual that kings and nobles all participated in "taking up the cross" in this way before leaving on pilgrimage.

Following the footsteps of Christ had been popularized when Constantine the Great legalized Christianity and began building, expanding, and renovating holy sites all around Jerusalem. By 333 CE, documentary evidence suggests a robust economy had emerged to provide pilgrims with travel itineraries, guides, and souvenirs.[4] Constantine's mother, Saint Helena, even claimed to have found the cross upon which Jesus was crucified.

The symbol of the cross had always enjoyed central importance in Christianity, but the symbol of pilgrimage had been a scallop shell. There are several reasons for this. Practically, the rounded shells could be used to scoop up water to drink just like grunts are expected to carry their trusty green canteens on every road march. Ecclesiastically, pilgrimage may be prescribed by priests as penance, and the shell could be brought back as proof. There was also an aesthetic reason: the lines of a scallop shell all converge at a central point on the hinge in the same way that all pilgrim paths converge at God.

What set this First Crusade apart from established tradition was *cruciata*, the practice of using the sign of the cross rather than a simple scallop. This may be due in part to the meaning of Jesus' passion for pilgrims, to which the author of the *Gesta* attests. The opening line of his account includes a verbatim quote cherry-picked from Jerome's Latin translation of Matthew 16:24: *Si quis vult post me venire abneget semet ipsum et tollat crucem suam et sequitur me* ("If any want to become my followers, let them deny themselves and take up their cross and follow me"). These "cross-marked" pilgrimages would forever be different, distinct from others in justifying violence. The church had entered a dark new age that conflated war with salvation.

ENTER FRANCIS

Giovanni di Pietro di Bernardone, the man known as Francis of Assisi, was born in 1181 to French nobility on his mother's side. The name Francesco, meaning "the Frenchman," was given to him at an early age. That was shortened to Francis, and "Assisi" was the Italian commune loyal to the Holy Roman Empire in which he grew up.

Before Francis was born, Christians had been controlling the Holy Land under the auspices of protecting pilgrims traveling to Jerusalem to visit the lands described in the Bible. The significance of the Crusades in Francis's life cannot be understated. He was just six years old when leaders of the Western world embarked upon the Third Crusade. As tradition dictated, Kings Frederick, Richard (the Lionheart), and Philip all "took up the cross" by sewing it onto their clothes and receiving other symbols of pilgrimage like a walking staff and a satchel.

At the pinnacle of the Crusades, people likely waited with bated breath to hear news of how their heroes were faring against the faithless. The Third Crusade raged until 1192, just as Francis was coming of age, when, under canon law, he could begin receiving the sacraments of confirmation, Communion, and confession. Although it would be ten years until the next Crusade, Francis was prepared to do anything he could to attain the glory promised by the myth of salvific violence.

Had he not been drawn into a local skirmish against a nearby commune, Francis would have joined the Fourth Crusade. As fate would have it, the skirmish ended in utter defeat, leaving him a prisoner of war for a year. The experience was deeply traumatic but his desire for battlefield pilgrim-glory remained, so he set out once more in 1205. Hoping to enlist in the army of French nobles, a prophetic dream and ill health prevented him from doing so, and he was finally willing to try something new.

His next pilgrimage would be north, to Rome, rather than east to Jerusalem. Upon praying at the tomb of St. Peter, he decided to trade glory for humility by adopting the rags of poverty rather than the increasingly regal symbols of a pilgrim. It was on this journey that Francis finally seemed to find his calling not just to occasional faith, but to fundamentally reinvent faith as he knew it. The year was 1208, and Francis's conversion was fully underway.

The medieval promise of salvation was irretrievably violent. Papal decree stipulated that dying "in battle against the pagans" absolved one's sins and thereby assured pilgrim-warriors of their spot in heaven.[5] This created a problem for Christians unwilling to engage in or tolerate violence. No Christian could witness the scenes and scenery described in the Bible without at least an armed escort, a compromise of which the newly nonviolent Francis was keenly aware. He made his first post-conversion attempt in 1212 but shipwrecked on the coast of modern Croatia and was forced to return home.

The closest Francis seems to have gotten to the Holy Land was during his 1219 trip to Egypt to preach penance among Christian and Muslim soldiers near the besieged city of Damietta. This journey is best known as Francis's attempt to convert the Sultan, but it may also have been an attempt to negotiate access to Jerusalem, since it was under Muslim control at the time. Tragically, Francis would never get to behold the Temple Mount or to step foot upon its sacred ground. But that did not prevent him from improvising, adapting, and overcoming obstacles on the way to the Holy Land. During Advent in 1223, he had a revolutionary idea that would undermine the ideological force behind redemptive violence.

CIRCLING STATIONS

Crusaders called themselves pilgrims and the Holy Land represented heaven, the destination at the end of the journey of faith. The pursuit of salvation justified the violence needed to get there. Using only thinly veiled symbolism, the menacing message of mainstream Christianity was clear: a holy end justifies any evil means.

Francis wanted to literally walk the path of Jesus, but he would not endorse violence. We know this because he consistently preached against it, even amid the crusaders in Damietta while he waited for his audience with the Sultan, "crying out warnings to save [the crusaders], forbidding war and threatening disaster. But they took the truth as a joke. They hardened their hearts and refused to turn back."[6] Despite all this, Francis refused to condemn Christian soldiers, even those corrupting the practice of pilgrimage by making it dependent upon violence. The truth is, he attracted a great number of veterans to his order.

One veteran attracted to the principles Francis preached was John Vellita, a nobleman who had left armed service to mature as a Christian. John owned land in the central Italian town of Greccio and often invited Francis to spend time meditating there. In the fall of 1223, Francis first divulged to John his desire to "make memorial of that Child who was born in Bethlehem, and in some sort behold with bodily eyes His infant hardships."[7] Who needs to go to the Holy Land if we can bring holiness to us?

According to Thomas Celano's biography, the first nativity scene was created within a cliffside cave on Christmas Day in 1223. John arranged for an ox, a donkey, and a small manger of hay. A priest celebrated the Mass after Francis, who was never ordained, preached the sermon. We do not have any real clue as to how Francis came up with the idea of creating life-sized nativity scenes, but Celano does record his motivation, which was "the longing of [Francis's] mind and all the fervor of his heart perfectly to follow the teaching of our Lord Jesus Christ *and tread in His footsteps*."[8] You can take a Christian soldier out of the Crusades, but you can't take the Crusade out of Christian soldiers. According to the *Gesta*, Francis was motivated to create nativity scenes for the same reason "crusaders" were motivated to pilgrimage.

For Francis, the longtime pilgrim, faith was never just something that resided in one's heart, though it could be found there. The

Franciscans were the first mendicant order, wandering beggar monks who stood in contrast to the wealthy, landholding Benedictines and Cistercians. Francis's innovation was to make faith an activity; movement and experience were integral to living in the kingdom of God. It certainly troubled Francis that the experience of faith was, in his age, so intimately linked to violence and war. If he could not get to the Holy Land without allying himself with crusaders, then he would bring the Holy Land home.

Francis had been chugging the cultural Kool-Aid in believing that piety required violence. His attempt to reenlist in 1205 reflects an early, cautioned approach to conversion, but his final commitment to Christ was a hard break from his prior beliefs. In freeing Christians from the illusion of redemptive violence, he sparked nothing less than a nonviolent revolution. The simple, innocent act of dressing up in a cave to travel to the Holy Land in their hearts and minds was a subtle, snarky rejection of violent pilgrimages and the papal decrees justifying them. And it was only the beginning of Francis's influence in the long, slow rejection of crusader theology.

Francis was not a grunt in the modern military sense, since he had money and status that lower enlisted soldiers typically lack, but he loved rubbing elbows with other veterans, like John of Greccio, who "trampled on the nobility of the flesh."[9] It is no coincidence that nativity scenes emerged at a time when pilgrimage was exploited by aristocrats to justify violent conquest with religiosity. By innovating as he did, Francis laid the foundation for his order to do even more, to go even further in undermining the appeal that the apologists for the crusades depended upon to raise their so-called Christian armies.

Chances are, if you visit a mainline church, you will see a series of images lining the walls of the building, called stations of the cross. Since the fourth century, pilgrims have marked significant moments along the *Via Dolorosa*, the "road of suffering" that winds its way through the Old City of Jerusalem marking the path Jesus took on the way to his crucifixion. Most modern versions include fourteen stops to mark important moments along Jesus' death road march. Several mark events that do not happen to Jesus in the Bible, including three falls, having his face wiped by Veronica, and being received into his mother's arms after he dies. During his passion Jesus became a pilgrim himself, stripped of stature and dignity as he journeyed to God on a Friday that Christians call good. It was this journey within a journey that has been the focal point of pilgrims from the fourth century through today.

Across seven centuries of pilgrimage, the official station count has varied from as few as seven to as many as thirty.[10] Many of the extrabiblical stations emerged during the medieval period, suggesting the keen interest pilgrim-warriors had in local legends along the Via Dolorosa. In 1991, Pope John Paul II introduced the "Scriptural Way of the Cross," which restricts stations to only those with a basis in the Gospels. Only three traditional stations have survived the test of time to appear in some way in every form they have taken: when Jesus takes up his cross (see John 19:17); when he is nailed to it (see John 20:25); and when he dies upon it (see Matt. 27:50; Mark 15:37; Luke 23:46; John 19:30).

Very little is known with any certainty about how the stations evolved over time, but we know that the Franciscan order gave them their ultimate form. Because of Francis's friendly encounter with the Sultan, it was his order that was entrusted with custody of the Holy Land when Muslims controlled Jerusalem. They have hosted and led pilgrims along the Via Dolorosa without interruption since 1347, after a fifty-year exile while hostile Muslim forces occupied the city.

When their exile began in the 1290s, they had to reimagine liturgical practices to keep them from disappearing. As custodians of the holy places, they would have had to adapt pilgrimages to their new exilic reality. Just as their founder had innovated pilgrimage to undercut the association with violence it gained in 1095, it was probably at this time that the friars first began experimenting with the Via Dolorosa. They could not have sandals on the ground in Jerusalem, but they could journey within the walls of their own churches, marking significant points using artistic expressions like painting or statuary. The circular motion, bittersweet in its inescapability, served as a reminder that their destination was ultimately a state of mind, not the cold hard ground.

In 1686 Pope Innocent IX approved a request by the friars to install stations in their churches around the world. The letter also stipulated that the stations would bestow the same spiritual benefit as visiting the actual locations themselves. In other words, pilgrims-in-place benefited the same as those who traveled in body to the Holy Land. By then crusading had effectively disappeared, but the letter suggests the stations were already in high demand. In 1731, the Vatican allowed the stations and their spiritual benefits to be expanded to all Catholic churches, not just Franciscans. By now, it is rare to enter any mainline church without seeing this testament to nonviolent victory over bad theology, invented and popularized by a combat veteran.

DESTINED NATION

The power of Francis's life in the lives of Christian soldiers is to remind the church that combat trauma does not define what we are, even if it may shape who we are to become. Civilian bias is the only thing that stops any High Church lowlife from becoming another Francis. The way toward being "redeemed from the hand of hell" is obstructed by antiquated caricatures of Christian soldiers being crusaders.[11] One modern scholar, in an academic biography of Francis, habitually qualifies the saint's veteran status with words like "broken,"[12] "erratic,"[13] and "troubled."[14]

As with most lies, there exists a grain of truth in these harmful stereotypes. Combat stress does leave scars, but Francis is a testament for, and to, grunts today. The glory of God cannot shine forth in them until the church allows combat stress to recede into the background of the stories told by their lives. We don't think of Francis as damaged goods, and we shouldn't think of contemporary Christian soldiers and veterans any differently. If he could transform his spiritual baggage into spiritual gifts, then so can anyone who has been affected by war, poverty, and violence.[15]

We should not overlook Francis's brilliance in subverting the myth of redemptive violence. He never confronted the pope directly, but he effectively undermined the papal bait used to entice crusaders. Wars will continue to rage, make no doubt. But Francis fought and won a lesser battle against bad theology by taking up his cross, in the spirit not of violence and conquest, but of humility and perseverance.

"Follow me!" This is the cross to which Christ beckons. Some Christians take this invitation as a call to arms, plastering crosses everywhere they can to show the world their devotion and the assurance they think they have in heaven. The pilgrimage we call faith is not just about where we are going, but who we become along the way. Christians are a journeying people; we *are* the destined nation. Francis took the invitation to take up the cross and follow the Way just as seriously as crusaders, but it led him in a very different direction. May we "Go and do likewise" (Luke 10:37).

11.
WELL-BEHAVED VETERANS SELDOM MAKE HISTORY:
JOAN AND GENDER

GOOD BEHAVIOR IS NOT ALWAYS CLEAR IN THE MILITARY; SHOULD you do what you have to do to stay alive, or should you do the right thing regardless of the consequences? There's a pithy saying that gets around in activist circles: "Well-behaved women seldom make history." For a while it was attributed to feminist icon Eleanor Roosevelt, a figure on the periphery of power who had an outsized impact on history for her position. Don't behave, the quote implies; make history instead. The phrase was actually coined by a more obscure figure and it meant something very different. It was penned in 1976 by Laurel Ulrich, a Mormon historian from Idaho, in the abstract of an academic paper. What she meant was that well-behaved women *should* make history, not just the boisterous ones. History, she knew, is rarely determined by the good people. It's written by the ones that came out on top.

Combat, both spiritual and physical, is pragmatic rather than patriarchal. God does not care what kind, or whether, grunts have genitals, only that soldiers complete the mission with as few souls lost as possible. Any gender-based restriction in the military or the ministry is a product of human interests, not divine intent. God cares far less about what's between your legs than what's in your heart. Few saints prove this point more than Joan of Arc, an illiterate farmer who followed her heart to a battlefield commission and ushered an end to the Hundred Years' War between France and England.

GOD AND GENDER

It was integral to Roman gods that they be gendered; it allowed them to fuck with humans (literally and figuratively). And they could be as petty and vindictive as people. The only substantive difference, it seems, was that gods were immortal and got to live in the clouds. However, the Abrahamic deity is identified in the first line of Genesis as *elohim* (H430), a proper noun in plural form, literally God(s). Elohim's creative power is so great that entire galaxies are born with a breath. As the active agent in creation, we typically think of God as the pitcher rather than the catcher, but this is as far as that analogy goes. The seed that carries life to "Mother" Earth is God's breath, *neshamah* (H5397; see Gen. 2:7), a feminine noun. So, either God the Father has lady-sperm, or there's something else going on that undermines the stereotype in our heads of an old white guy with a long beard. Here's a hint: It's the second thing. We know because the Bible continues with this pattern.

When God(s), with the lady-sperm, tell themselves they will make *adam* (H120) in their own likeness, it is an abbreviation of the word *adamah* (H127), meaning "ground or dirt." The word *adam* is not used as a personal name and, although it *is* masculine, it's a generic noun. *Adam* does not refer to a man so much as to a person, Mankind, like the pro wrestler. At least that would interest more people in reading their Bibles.

Speaking of Genesis and creation, sex and gender do not exist in isolation; there is no man (*'ish*, H376) until there is also woman (*isha*, H802), a full chapter after Mankind debuts. (see Gen. 1:27; 2:23, 24). The Abrahamic God is gendered only allegorically, not actually. Jesus and his apostles spoke Aramaic and called God *abba* (from *ab*, H1; see Mark 14:36), a more intimate reference than the Greek *pater* (G3962) and the source of words like "abbot" and "abbey." The difference is akin to saying "dad" rather than the more formal "father." If Jesus resides in our own hearts, as Christians believe, then people cannot be any closer to God. When the Church uses gendered language like *abba*, it is a comfort for weary souls, not a declaration that God has a penis or facial hair. Calling God our Father is for our own benefit, to *feel* closer when we forget that God is already within each of us. God is not a man any more than God is a woman.

I imagine that God gained a penis the same way history gets written by the victors, through arrogance, or the way Joshua's name became Jesus, through ignorance or laziness (or both). Jesus instructed his followers to pray to "our Father in heaven" (Matt.

6:9) because Mary, his mother, was not in heaven. She also is not all humanity's mom, whereas Elohim *is* the Creator of all humanity. What makes the first person of the Trinity unique is that they are the creative source of *all* being, a characteristic that transcends sex and gender by preceding them.

As Creator, God(s) has no sex or gender because she/he *created* sex and gender. That means it is just as right (and just as wrong) to call him Father as it is to call her Mother. The impulse to assign masculinity is a human instinct, one that has disproportionately served the interests of insecure dicks like kings and generals. It is this same forced idea that God is a guy that has kept women out of places of power, from the ministry to the military.

GI JAEL AND BIBLICAL WOMEN

When you start looking closely, you find that leadership has never been exclusive to cisgendered men. If we haven't noticed their stories, it is because we've allowed someone else to read the Bible for us. If Jesus is a grunt, then we need to start at the bottom to find those hidden figures and unsung heroes God uses in the Bible.

Joshua may have been God's lieutenant in the military campaign to take the Promised Land, but it would not have been possible without the alleged sex worker of Jericho. Rahab was the only inhabitant who heard of the Israelites' victories and yielded to their God rather than resist (see Josh. 2; 6). While most in Jericho thought they could beat Israel, Rahab decided she would join them instead. This pragmatic but faithful calculation did more than simply save her life; it also earned her a place in Jesus' family line (see Matt. 1:15).

But women are not just grafted onto military campaigns; sometimes they are in command. As an Israelite judge, Deborah was the primary leader of the twelve tribes and the equivalent of commander in chief. When she issued orders to Barak to march on Mount Tabor against the Canaanite general Sisera, he insisted that *she* lead *him* into battle (see Judg. 4:8).[1] Deborah was also a prophet, and she told Barak that, because he had wavered, the medals and recognition would go to a woman rather than to him. On Deborah's command, Barak overpowered Sisera's forces and threw them into a panicked retreat. Hoping to find shelter among allies in the tent of Jael and Heber, Sisera got a stake through his head instead. GI Jael (whose name means "mountain goat") was hailed a hero in the Song of Deborah (see Judg. 5) and foreshadows Mary, who, like Jael, is "most blessed among women" (see Judg. 5:24; Luke 1:42, 48).

It isn't that "all women are great, so let's just put them in command," but that female leadership is nothing new or special. Any grunt knows that commanders are sometimes maybe good, sometimes maybe shit; and the same is true in the Bible. Queen Athalia was sole monarch of Judah in the ninth century BCE, and she was horrible (see 2 Kings 8–11; 2 Chron. 22–23). When her son, King Ahaziah, was murdered in Israel, she declared herself ruler and had other claimants to the throne, including members of her own family, killed to secure her power. She lasted six years, during which time she promoted idol worship and general debauchery, before being deposed and executed.

The New Testament has its own examples of women in leadership as well. The first church Saul planted on the European continent was thanks to Lydia of Thyatira. As a *porphyropōlis*, or "seller of purple" (G4211; see Acts 16:14), she would have rubbed elbows with the imperial court frequently and been quite wealthy. Upon hearing Saul and Silas preach, she convinced them to baptize her household and make her home their headquarters whenever they visited Philippi. Although some suggest she inherited her status from a deceased husband, that was not necessarily the case. As a citizen in far-off Philippi, Lydia's status as a Roman would have overshadowed her being a woman and she would have been encouraged to spread imperial culture, even if it meant violating typical gender roles. It's just as likely that she inherited the trade from a veteran father who used his imperial connections to create a business selling purple as he transitioned out of the military. She would have inherited her citizenship from him as well, so it is not inconceivable that her house once belonged to one of the thousands of soldiers retired in Philippi. That same house became the foundation for the first church in Europe, with Lydia as its host.

Then there is Priscilla, who with her husband, Aquila, met Saul in Corinth. They became devout followers of his teachings. The couple was deported with other Jews from Rome by Claudias, the same emperor whose wife sold the tribune Lysias of Acts 22 his costly citizenship. Saul treated Priscilla and Aquila as his equals, calling them *synergos* (G4904), "co-workers in Christ Jesus" (Rom. 16:3). The church in Corinth began in and continued to meet in their house, just as the Philippian church met in Lydia's. The three of them are together in Ephesus when Saul writes back to the Christians in Corinth meeting in Priscilla and Aquilas's home, which probably came off as a "Don't mess up the house while Mom and Dad are away" reminder (see 1 Cor. 16:19). Priscilla and Aquila also instruct Apollos, a former follower of John the Baptist, how to preach the Way of God "more accurately" (Acts 18:26). Because Paul mentions a woman before her husband, it is thought that Priscilla was the more charismatic and learned of the two. She was so steeped in Judaism that scholars once thought she wrote the epistle to the Hebrews, but now many believe it may have been her student, Apollos.

Finally, we have Phoebe, who, like Lydia and Priscilla before her, was a supporter of Saul's missionary activity. Phoebe was the bearer of his letter to the believers in Rome, whom he introduced as a *diakonos* (G1249) and *prostatis* (G4368). These titles were not mere honorifics, as Paul would not choose just anyone to take his most comprehensive work to the imperial capital. Deacons, *diakonos*, were not just helpers to priests in Saul's day. *Diakonos* means "servant," but Saul applied it to the "rulers" (*archon*, G758) of Romans 13:4, who are "God's *diakonos* for [our] good." This was the sense in which he called Phoebe a deacon, not simply a scrubber of floors or washer of linen, but a commander in the *Militia Dei*. The title *prostasis* drives this home; the only place it occurs is in describing Phoebe, a word borrowed from the verb *protasso* (G4367), "to command," the same action word attached in the Gospels to Moses (see Matt. 8:4; Mark 1:44; Luke 5:14). English Bibles lose sight of this powerful metaphor when translating *prostasis* as "benefactor" or "patron," as though all Phoebe did was pat others on the back or send them $20 on their birthday. Rather, Saul says that Phoebe "has been a *commander* of many, including me" (see Rom. 16:2; adapted with emphasis).

This emphasis on command is no accident, but as a human institution the church tends to forget that gender is not correlative to leadership; that you don't have to have a dick to lead (even if history favors those who act like one).

THE ANIMAL OF ORLEANS

You might have heard of Joan as a maid, or a maiden, but she never acted like the damsel in distress. From the outset of the Hundred Years' War in the 1330s, the English had held the upper hand while the French nobility struggled to maintain sovereignty over their lands. All appeared lost after the Battle of Agincourt in 1415, when almost half of all French nobles were killed, either in battle or by Henry V's order to kill all POWs. The chivalric code, similar but far less formal than the Geneva Conventions, was at its peak at the time, and Henry's order was an unequivocal violation of moral order. It undermined any claim at divine support that the English may have made.

Joan of Arc was three years old and just forty-five miles away, in her hometown of Domremy, when thousands of her country's nobles were slaughtered by the English monarch. Ten years later, she began to hear voices telling her she would lead the French in expelling the English to restore her country's honor and sovereignty. She was secretive about these voices, but under threat of torture she later disclosed their identities as Michael the Archangel and Saints Catherine of Alexandria and Margaret of Antioch. Just like Martin before her, she was counseled by female saints who, to modern readers, may seem obscure. What Catherine and Margaret had in

common was that the martyrs both refused the "adulterous pur-
poses" of powerful men.[2]

For three years, Joan received instructions and visions from the
saints without taking action. Then in February 1429, she finally
went to the military garrison in nearby Vaucouleurs to initiate contact with her king, Charles VII. The garrison commander, Robert
de Baudricourt, was not convinced until she predicted a French
defeat at the Battle of the Herrings. Confirmation of this sent by
a courier took several days to reach de Baudricourt, but Joan had
shared the information with him the same day it occurred, on
February 22, 1429.

Needless to say, she was granted an audience with the king, but
she would have to travel through hostile territory to see him. For
her safety, de Baudricourt dressed her as a soldier and had her hair
cut short. This would be the linchpin of the later English argument
that convicted her of heresy, but cross-dressing was neither her idea
nor her choice. Numerous witnesses would testify in her heresy trial
that she had no desire to violate gender norms, but it was a necessary
precaution against military sexual trauma. It turns out that the same
uniform meant to protect soldiers from swords and arrows was also
effective against covetousness and lust.

At this point, it's most accurate to describe Joan as a recruit,
maybe a member of the Delayed Entry Program in which potential
soldiers learn military culture, begin physical training, and so on
before formally entering the Army. She is a grunt at the bottom of
the social hierarchy with no way to go but up. Maybe she learned
about pecking orders while tending chickens on her parents' farm.

By referring to herself as *La pucelle*, from the Latin *pullus* for "a young chick or foal," she may have been calling attention to her lowly status as an inexperienced chick or her working-class dependability as a draft horse. Whether she intended to or not, she was also evoking the prophecies of one Merlin the Wizard.

Centuries before Joan was born, Geoffrey of Monmouth's *The History of the Kings of Britain* propagated a highly embellished view of Anglo-Saxons. Popular characters like Merlin and Arthur were actually based on real people, however difficult it is now to pin them down. Scholars believe Merlin was based on the Welsh prophet Myrddin Wyllt ("the Wild"), who went mad after his people were defeated in the Battle of Arfderydd. Geoffrey's work proved too appealing to remain in his native Britain, and soon all of Europe adopted Myrddin's prophecies as predictions relevant to their own lands and people. One involved a *pullus* who would come from the *nemus canutum*, or "Gray-Haired Wood," and do great deeds. The prophecy evolved over time as it crossed paths with local legends in France.

A generation before Joan, the prophet Marie Robine of Avignon told Charles VI the *nemus canutum* was actually the Bois Chesnu, a forest bordering Domremy, the village where Joan's parents lived. The Latin *pullus* was transformed into the French *pucelle*, and the maiden's great deeds would be to finally drive out the English forces from France. By the time Joan was a girl, sermons and speeches would have included this prophetic prediction in the hopes that France might one day see freedom from foreign occupation.

This legend was probably foremost in the mind of Charles VII when an illiterate teenager came to him from the farmlands promising to help him ascend to the throne of France in 1429. The Hundred Years' War looked like it was on the verge of ending in defeat for him, with little to no hope in any strategic turn of events. Even if he had zero faith in her wild claims of divine patronage, when Joan passed a clerical background check with flying colors he saw little to lose. He issued her everything she would need to lead his soldiers in battle as a knight, including a suit of armor and a battle flag, paid for out of the royal treasury.

When offered a sword, Joan refused to take the one offered by her king. Instead, she sent a messenger to a small town with a church dedicated to one of her heavenly guides. Through the messenger, she instructed the clergy of St. Catherine's of Fierbois to dig up the ground behind the altar, where they would find a rusted sword adorned with five crosses. According to legend, the sword once belonged to Charlemagne's paternal grandfather, Charles "the Hammer" Martel, making it something of a sacred relic to the French people.

Although she met her king as a lowly grunt, she left his company as a full knight, the equivalent of a battlefield commission. As a knight she was bound by the customs that the English had ignored in Agincourt, but she would exceed those expectations by never killing another soul. She carried a large guidon into battle, later telling a court, "I did so to avoid killing anyone. I have never killed a man."[3]

You don't have to be a man, or a woman, to be a Christian soldier, but you do have to avoid killing people at all costs. If this seems counterintuitive, it is because we have taken more cues from our own contemporary experience than that of the witness of the church. Godly grunts do not have to be passive or docile, but we do have to *prioritize* nonviolence, even if we fail. According to Scripture and tradition, the Christian can be combat*ive* without being a combat-*ant*. We might be pugnacious, but we avoid *pugnare*. If that's hard to imagine, let's look at the 1429–1430 Loire campaign of Charles VII, Joan's crowning military achievement.

GI JOAN'S GODLY BENDER

The term "bender" comes from nineteenth-century Britain, when pubs rebelled against rigid Victorian morality by letting customers drink all day for a tuppence ("twopence") coin. The sixpence coin was more common and worth three days of drinks, meaning you could start drinking Friday morning and go until Sunday night. Because sixpence pieces were soft, they could be bent between the teeth, so "benders" became slang for weekend drinking sprees.[4] Joan's one year of military service was greater than a three-day span, but it definitely has the hallmarks of someone having a *lot* of fun with complete disregard for their own safety, a common turn of phrase used in Medal of Honor award citations.[5] As it turns out, her term of service was framed by Easter Week, the six days following Easter Sunday. She left Vaucouleurs dressed as a soldier to meet her king on Tuesday of Easter Week in 1429, and the voices warned her of capture on an undisclosed day of Easter Week in 1430. In that one year, she had one hell of a bender that upended gendered notions about chivalry and saw her succeed where countless men had failed. I'm not sure who would have been more pissed at Joan's success, the

English enemies she defeated, or the French dudes she schooled on military prowess.

Her most famous victory was at the Siege of Orléans, which the French court meant as a test to determine her divine support. When Joan was examined by French clergy, they were sympathetic but suggested the king withhold his full endorsement until her claims could be verified by miraculous signs, like a victory at Orléans. I'm not going to say that they wanted a manly Saint Michael to possess Joan's womanly body and outsmart the English in strategic superiority or anything, but the thought definitely crossed their minds. If the priests expected the miracle to come in predictable biblical military fashion, like parting the sea or blowing trumpets until the walls came down, they had another thing coming. Joan was a grunt, and God calls up the grunts when it's time to improvise, adapt, and overcome.

What grunts lack in strategy and smarts, they more than make up for in sheer audacity and determination. Like Joshua and Caleb after their first scouting trip to the Promised Land, grunts are single-mindedly focused on mission success; just wind them up and point them in the right direction. Laying out plans, careful attention to enemy posture; that stuff exceeds their limited budget of shits to give. Grunts are there to get 'er done and go home, and Joan was a grunt. Leaving HQ in Vaucouleurs, Joan wanted to proceed directly to Orléans rather than take the safe, circuitous route. As soon as Joan laid eyes upon the city, she wanted her escort to join her in an immediate, all-out offensive on the English encampment. Grunts are used to not getting their way, and, in a way, they are idealists. Who else would sign up for a hopeless cause and expect little else than to go down fighting?

This indomitable spirit earned her zero brownie points from the standing military chain of command in the city, who shut her out of meetings despite her bearing their king's blessing. Their attitude was "This chick, this *pucelle*? She don't know shit." While the men in charge may have seen her as little more than a damsel in drag, the people of the city, bolstered by the Welsh prophecies, saw her as an animal, a warhorse, who could unfuck the cluster they were in. French forces had failed to rally Orléans' citizenry around their cause, by either complacency or hubris. For six months the military establishment had done little more than hunker down, allowing the English to maneuver almost at will. The arrival of the Animal of Orléans inspired hope in the beleaguered citizens right when they needed it the most.

If one could tease out a method to Joan's madness, it perhaps was an unceasing emphasis on spiritual and physical offense. Nowadays, soldiers say, "Take the fight to the enemy"; put them on their heels, force them to make hasty decisions by applying constant pressure. Twice a day, Joan would raise a special guidon she had made for morning and evening prayer. Knowing her, the prayers were not your typical pietistic orations. This was the chick who had written to the English, "Get out, or I'll kick you out."[6] She probably recited the psalms they don't teach you in Sunday school, the feisty, imprecatory ones like Psalm 69:25–27: "May their camp be a desolation; let no one live in their tents. For they persecute those whom you have struck down, and those whom you have wounded, they attack still more. Add guilt to their guilt; may they have no acquittal from you."

This aggressive and faith-filled approach inspired the people of the city whose cause she had taken up. When the military clique shut her out of planning meetings, militias would muster to her side and fight, drawing the professional soldiers to their ranks behind them. When the so-called commanders finished their leadership huddles they would emerge to find defensive positions abandoned, their own soldiers taking the fight across the river behind GI Joan and her army of pious peasants. When Joan was within earshot of the English captains, she would exchange insults with them, not to attack their honor but to remind them whose cause God favored.

This went on for nine days, with the French nobility in charge slowly warming up to her tactless antics. In one assault, Joan was struck by an arrow at a weak point in her armor. Soldiers rushed to her side and tried to help with magic charms, which she refused as a sinful superstition. She was taken to a protected location where the arrow had to be pulled through her trapezius muscle, which was accessible only by removing her armor. Her demeanor is noteworthy, as it suggests an advanced understanding of chastity, a chivalric virtue of which all who were present would have been fully aware.

If you think purity culture was bad in the 1990s, imagine how much stricter it was in the Middle Ages. As a pragmatist, Joan didn't see the female form as something so special and pure that it overrode the practical requirements of battle. Although Christian tradition is filled with virginal damsels who would rather die than violate a puritanical version of chastity, the transcripts of her trials reveal no objection to men seeing her naked body to clean her wounds. When left to decide between letting her soldiers down by dying or letting some wanker add to his medieval spank bank, Joan chose to live and lead. What wankers do is their own problem, not anyone else's.

After the siege was lifted, Joan would continue to lead French forces on a series of summer victories that turned the tide of the Hundred Years' War. Known as the Loire campaign to military historians, the Siege of Orléans was the first of five. The second was the Battle of Jargeau, the first French offensive in over a generation; followed by successes in Meung-sur-Loire, Beaugency, and Patay. By July 1429, the French had recovered the Loire Valley, inspiring Chalres VII to proceed to Reims Cathedral, the historic location where French monarchs ascended to the throne. The cathedral was behind enemy lines, but between Joan's misfit militia and the seasoned soldiers she commanded, he went anyway. Charles VII was crowned king of France on July 17, 1429, with Joan at his side, holding her beloved battle flag.

MISSION, CREEP(S)

When she stood beside her king as he was crowned the rightful heir to the throne of France, that was the sum total of what her voices instructed her to do. She had completed her mission and paved the road for the English to slink back, tails between their legs, across the Channel to their own land. During the summer of 1429, she secured crushing victories throughout the Loire Valley region, but her luck ran out almost immediately upon the coronation of King Charles VII in July.

A French assault on English-held Paris lasted less than a full day and left a crossbow bolt deep in Joan's thigh. Rumors flew around the camp that they had lost because Joan's sword, the same believed to belong to Charlemagne's family, had been broken. According to Joan's testimony during the heresy trial, she broke it on the back of a prostitute she was chasing out of the camp. Apparently, that was how she used her sword, not to slice and dice her enemies, but as a broad-faced paddle to whack away sex workers swarming the camp like flies. The sense of defeat was palpable, and much of its weight lay on Joan's shoulders. On September 13, 1429, she laid the armor provided by her king at the altar of St. Denis Basilica just north of the city. She could have returned home a hero, but even if you take the grunt out of the fight, there's still going to be some fight left in the grunt.

Whatever the reason, she decided to re-up and see how much more she could accomplish. Maybe it was her same indomitable spirit that compelled her to keep going, beyond the mission laid out by her angelic guides. She stole a sword from an enemy soldier and managed to collect enough armor to return to battle. Joan succeeded in taking smaller towns in autumn skirmishes, but the gains were few and far between. Perhaps to coax her home from war, Charles granted her family nobility and exempted her hometown from taxation in December 1429. But Joan was as determined as ever to drive the English out or die trying.

She heard from her voices less and less, until an undisclosed day in Easter Week, when they warned her to expect capture before midsummer. It came to pass at Compiègne on May 23, 1430, after Joan refused to retreat and remained with her rear guard until overcome by enemy forces. Because the church transcends nationalities, the English had to discredit her as a heretic rather than as a mere enemy of the Crown. Grunts may not be known for their smarts, but that doesn't mean they're stupid. Joan caught them off guard with her wit and confidence, refusing them any opportunity to accuse her of impiety or ignorance.

The day before Easter Sunday in 1431, forty male assessors creepily submitted seventy formal accusations against the Animal of Orleans. Joan calmly answered each accusation with such informed confidence that only twelve were included in her public admonition delivered a month later. The main thrust of their allegations centered on her dressing as a soldier, of doing something only men were supposed to do. With the benefit of hindsight, one might think we enlightened moderns would know better than to believe that women cannot or should not serve in battle. But superstitions have a way of digging below our otherwise quite capable rational faculties.

When I started boot camp at Fort Sill, Oklahoma, I was told all the basic training battalions were coed, except the one I would attend. I figured they put all the combat arms recruits in the last male-only unit because those specialties were closed to women. The funny thing was, either *because* or *despite* of being in an "all male" training environment, I never saw our female senior drill sergeant as novel or new. I was oblivious to why, how, or when she got there. Call it ignorance or naïveté, but I had zero context for, or interest in, gender and the military. It was only later that I realized the gift of not experiencing the trials and tribulations so many endured, to be able to take for granted that a "coed" military was normal. The truth that I would discover, and that my senior drill sergeant certainly already knew, was it was a fight and a half to overcome superstitions about gender and the military.

Every now and then I get asked by people how I would feel if my children wanted to join the military. My maternal grandfather flew supply in WWII and my dad served in the Navy in Vietnam. I was the only one of four kids to join up, and I did so for college money rather than some sense of family tradition. My partner and I have two girls, and with how much I write and speak about the military, I suspect they'll feel the sense of tradition more than I did. They will never know a time when some military specialties were off-limits to them. If they want to follow their old man into the artillery, nobody will stop them. Nothing about having a Y chromosome makes me a better grunt than someone without one, and gender identity certainly hasn't stopped people from being badass soldiers, or ministers.

The Rev. Dr. Marie-Louise Moffett was one of the first women to be ordained to the priesthood in the Scottish Episcopal Church, but you wouldn't know it without asking. That's what my partner did when working as her caretaker in 2015, after a casual remark about serving communion in All Saints' Church in St. Andrews, Scotland. Laura's ordination process was still ongoing, and we were painfully aware how contentious ordination has been for anyone other than white, heterosexual men. That awareness compelled us to join in solidarity with Rev. Esau McCaulley, a military spouse, when he led a prayer vigil at the same small church on March 13, 2015, to bear witness to Black lives being lost to police violence back in the States.[7] Marie-Louise knew about of blood, sweat, and tears shed by those who fought for women's equality, and she was grateful for being spared many of the same sacrifices. Although N. T. Wright describes Esau's *Reading While Black* as "measured, wise, friendly, and well-reasoned," it was forged in the bloody battle for human dignity.[8] Would I rather my daughters, or anyone's for that matter, burn their energy fighting for what they deserve, or inherit it from others who have? My hope is the latter, that future grunts will benefit from their predecessors in faith and in service rather than having to pave their own way.

12.

GET THE FUCK UP
AND PRAY:

IGNATIUS AND SPIRITUAL
FITNESS

ON SEPTEMBER 1, 2011, THE CHAIRMAN OF THE JOINT CHIEFS of Staff, Mike Mullen, put out an Instruction promoting a framework for Total Force Fitness (TFF).[1] The point of TFF was to improve military readiness by "understanding, assessing, and maintaining Service members' well-being" through the lens of eight domains of fitness, one of which was spiritual. According to the instruction, spiritual fitness names "the ability to adhere to beliefs, principles, or values needed to persevere and prevail in accomplishing missions."[2] A decade into the war in Afghanistan, military commanders recognized that spiritual fitness was integral to human well-being. Some may see the church as behind the times, but Ignatius of Loyola had already discovered this simple truth about 460 years earlier.

FIRST FORMATION

Grunts are trained to act first and think later, something that can help increase our odds of surviving combat. Initial training for enlisted soldiers is built around operant conditioning, a process by which soldiers are formed to act reflexively on habit, through daily, even hourly reminders that they will be punished if they fail and rewarded if they succeed. This training occurs bright and early every morning with First Formation, in which soldiers report to duty.

"Formation" has a double meaning; one physical and another spiritual. Soldiers "form" in a rank-and-file order, which over time "forms" a deep sense of collective identity and belonging. All format*ions* are format*ive*, but the first one sets the tone for the whole day. Celebrities, CEOs, and self-help gurus are onto something when they encourage the masses to get up at the buttcrack of dawn, work out, and succeed the hell out of every day. Being deliberate in planning out your day forms habits that make you the person you tell yourself you want to be. Whether you want to survive combat, make money, or get swole, forming habits will help you accomplish those goals. Unfortunately, the vast majority of Christians have liturgical hesitancy, as though to get spiritually swole you have to *wear* a habit to keep godly habits, like morning prayer. But First Formation is spiritual exercise that any Christian soldier can handle.[3]

Monks may be known for praying every day, several times a day. But daily prayer didn't begin with them. The tradition of praying several times per day began the same time the New Testament was taking shape. A noncanonical work known as the Didache, or "teaching," prescribed reciting the Lord's Prayer (see Matt. 6:9–13; Luke

11:2–4) three times per day. Before Joshua's temple was destroyed in 70 CE, most Christians were Jewish and would have been familiar with the three daily prayer times known as *shacharit*, *mincha*, and *maariv*.

Unlike the Roman clock, which begins a calendar day at midnight, the Jewish day begins at sunset, since time itself began in darkness. The Jewish calendar day began at sunset with four night watches of three hours each, followed by daylight hours being marked from dawn; like grunts, Jews started their days at 0600 hours ("zero six hundred"). Morning prayer time, *shacharit*, spanned from dawn (*sahar*, H7837), when the temple gates were opened, to the sixth hour of the day, or noon. Evening prayers, *maariv*, ushered in the night (*erev*, H6150) near the twelfth hour, at 1800 or sunset.

The Jewish day centered on *mincha* (H4503), the afternoon prayers, because that was when the daily meal offering occurred, an edible arrangement between God and humanity. Every afternoon between the sixth (1200) and the ninth hours (1500) of the Jewish day, grain or sacrificial animals were brought to the temple as an offering, *mincha*, to God. In Genesis, the "offerings" brought by both Cain and Abel are *mincha* (4:3–5). On Good Friday, "when it was noon, darkness came over the whole land until three in the afternoon" (Mark 15:33). Jesus died on the cross at the ninth hour, just as the prescribed time for prayer was ending, because Jesus is God's *mincha* to us (that's why we eat him for Communion). The ninth hour of the day is the same time that Peter and John observe "the hour of prayer" (*proseuche*, G4335) in Acts 3:1, and when Cornelius the centurion has his vision (see Acts 10:3, 30).

What *mincha* teaches us is that prayer is not some sedentary activity, like writing or podcasting. These things *can* be prayerful, but prayers are active rather than passive. Too often, Christians think of prayer as little more than conversing with or simply thinking of God. This is where the military has something to teach the church; in their proclivity for action, grunts help Christians move from folded hands and bended knee to boots on the ground and mission success. Verbal prayer has its place, but "Amen" is supposed to be the beginning rather than the end. When we are done talking to God, it is time to get up and pray, to live like we mean what we just said.

PRAY WITHOUT CEASING

Saul is not exaggerating when he encourages the church in Thessaloniki to "pray without ceasing" (1 Thess. 5:17); he is reminding us that praying should never be reduced to mere words. The ancient understanding of prayer was much more active; prayer was a 24-7 affair because everything you did was an offering to God. Your very life was a sacrifice, a *mincha*, to God. To the ancient world, there was no distinction between religious rituals and mundane routines; the afternoon prayer time was an important liturgical event that also served a very simple function: the grain and meat was their lunch. Before the invention of microwave ovens and monoculture farming, eating was a more ritualized social occasion. Prayer was just as routine but no less important.

Praying should permeate everything we do in the same way that everything we do should glorify God. After accompanying Martin Luther King Jr. on the Selma to Montgomery march, Abraham

Heschel was asked whether he found time to pray in Alabama. His daughter remembers his response: "Legs are not lips, and walking is not kneeling. And yet our legs uttered songs. Even without words, our march was worship. I felt my legs were praying."[4] Recovering a more comprehensive sense of prayer requires work; it means we must relearn ancient habits, whether we wear habits or not.

Daily prayer in the Christian tradition was popularized by monastics, but it has never been restricted to cloistered religious communities. The practice of thrice-daily prayers mentioned in the New Testament was informal and arose out of the practical needs of regular people who did not separate religion from daily life. But the word "liturgy" (*leitourgia*, G3009) meant any "public service," from the military to the ministry. Liturgy may be thought of as the "smells and bells" of special religious services, but Luke's gospel uses *leitourgia* to describe Zechariah's daily prayer duties as a "service" (1:23). Unfortunately, people sometimes benefit from *appearing*, rather than *being*, faithful.

In Matthew's gospel, before Jesus left his followers a blueprint for prayer, he gave them a warning: Don't be like all these other *hupokrites* (G5273), the fakers who like to make a big deal about (their version of) religion. In other words, he told them to be careful not to keep their faith on their sleeves because doing so made it easier to hide in the folds of their jackets when push came to shove. Jesus may have cautioned them about wolves in sheep's clothing, but as a grunt he'd have had plenty to say about Blue Falcons, too, the Buddy Fuckers who get gone as soon as the going gets tough.

Praying at meals or in church may make us feel pious, but faith doesn't evaporate when things get heated. True faith demands not just humility, but also hardiness. That's why I think grunts make especially admirable Christians; they know that pain and suffering pale in comparison to the reward of a hard job done well. It's too easy to slip into complacency by going through the motions and putting our faith on autopilot. That's the double-edged sword of rituals like daily prayer: on the one hand we need them to remind us who, whose, and why we are; but on the other hand those same practices can be so routine that they make us spiritually *numb* rather than spiritually *mature*.

By the late medieval period, the Roman Catholic Church had become so all-encompassing that complacency paved the road for rampant corruption. The last holy war to conquer the Holy Land ended in the 1270s, and the facade had already begun to crumble. In the past, Christian soldiers had been convinced of the legitimacy of fighting against Muslims for control of Jerusalem. But using violence against other Christians was a harder sell. A new name for these so-called pilgrimages arose out of the Spanish kingdom of Navarre, *cro-zada*.[5] With the cat out of the bag, rather than abandon the endeavor of rubber-stamping God's approval of military conquest, the Papal States doubled down and the Crusades continued unabated for another two hundred years.[6]

If the elites could lie about redemptive violence, then who is to say they would not also lie about other roads to salvation? Was all this ritual, the smells and bells, just another way for the clerical class to pull the wool over everyone's eyes?

MY NAME IS IÑIGO LOPEZ

This was the age into which Iñigo López de Oñaz y Loyola was born on October 29, 1491. Distrust in long-standing institutions was high and the totality of the Roman Catholic Church was fracturing. In the Middle Ages, chivalry had provided the upper classes a pseudo-Christian narrative structure, but knighthood was becoming a caricature of itself. *Don Quixote*, a comedic novel published in 1605, was like the "okay, boomer" of the late medieval period; a Spanish nobleman is seen as crazy for trying to relive the good old days by assuming the identity of a knight. The book's author, Miguel de Cervantes, wrote it to criticize the chivalrous romances of the prior century, and one in particular, *Amadís de Gaula*.

Young Iñigo aspired to be a knight in shining armor like he read about in *Amadís de Gaula* and its many sequels, pulpy as they may have been. "Pulp" is fiction that leans heavily on drama and sex appeal, named for the paper it is usually printed on, so cheap it is little more than wood pulp. Pages feel almost like sandpaper, brittle and coarse. You might know the feeling from the pages of war novels like *First Blood*, drenched in troop tropes and carnography.[7] What makes pulp fiction so appealing is the same thing that makes it so dangerous: the line between reality and fantasy is so blurred as to be believable to the uninitiated. Things get really weird when Amadís and Rambo are normalized; when fantasy becomes reality.

Iñigo, whose Latinized name is Ignatius, was obsessed with Amadís and became a novice knight as soon as he could, rising through the ranks as a member of the prestigious Loyola family in northern Spain. He is cagey about his early life in an autobiography he dictated to Luís Gonçalves da Câmara between 1553 and 1555.[8] It's noteworthy that he begins his testimony with the encounter that ended his military career because he saw combat as his ticket to earthly glory. Crusader theology may have been outdated, but it held the attention of nobles like Iñigo.

On May 20, 1521, Ignatius was seriously injured in the Battle of Pamplona, in the kingdom of Navarre, the birthplace of *crozada*, and recovered at his family's estate under the care of his sister-in-law, Magdalena de Araoz. Although he asked for the pulpy novels that had inspired his youth, Magdalena had only two books at her disposal. One was a first-edition 1503 Castilian translation of Ludolph of Saxony's *Life of Jesus Christ*, a gift from Queen Isabella, copatron of Christopher Columbus. The other was a 1511 Castilian translation of Jacob de Voragine's *Flos Sanctorum*, or Flower of the Saints, known today as *The Golden Legend*.

Reading these books challenged his understanding of virtue and whether it could be sustained by the popular understanding of knightly chivalry. One thing he seems to have felt with certainty was that he could no longer remain in military service. In February 1522, he returned to Navarre to collect his salary and resign as an earthly knight. From there he continued to the Benedictine Abbey of Saint Mary in the "serrated mountains" of Montserrat. On the way there, he met and traveled awhile with a Muslim who would unwittingly test Iñigo's old way of thinking about chivalry. His companion showed great respect for Mary, but would not be convinced of the Catholic belief in her perpetual virginity. The conversation grew heated, and the Muslim hurried off ahead of an aggravated Ignatius.

Muslims were the Enemy in a crusader worldview, the old way of knighthood and nobility. Under the traditional chivalric code, Iñigo was "obliged to restore [Mary's] honor"[9] by striking the man down, the same way another Spaniard named Iñigo was obliged to avenge his father in the comedic romance *The Princess Bride*.[10] I can almost see Ignatius catching up to the offending foreigner and stating in a loud voice, "My name is Iñigo ~~Montoya~~ Lopez, you ~~killed~~ insulted ~~my father~~ the Virgin, prepare to die!"

Just like *Don Quixote*, *The Princess Bride* pokes fun at knightly chivalry without going so far as to throw the baby out with the bathwater. Ignatius had not figured out the baby from the bathwater, but he knew there was something valuable in military service that was worth preserving. Ignatius affirms Martin's distinction between *miles Christi* and worldly *pugnare*; the essential quality of knights had more to do with dying than with killing. I know plenty of Christians who might laugh at that idea, but that's the power of satire; who does the laughing is kind of the point. How you interpret the main characters of *First Blood* or *The Hurt Locker* depends on your experience, but popularity is not necessarily a reflection of credibility. Veterans mostly roll their eyes at war-pulp, but civilians seem like they can't get enough of it.

As for Ignatius, he decided to leave the matter in God's hands by dropping the reins at a fork in the road, one path leading to the supposed infidel and the other to Montserrat. God's knights do not intentionally shed blood, which explains why Ignatius proceeded on his pilgrimage without a detour to duel.

We are often tempted to fight in the earthly ways to which we are accustomed. But God knows weapons of flesh and bone are effective only against, well, flesh and bone. Using swords and guns is playing the short game of petty squabbles and worldly interests. Godly grunts know that the real fight is against the enemy within each of us, against the vanity and insecurity that pit us against our neighbors. This was the first lesson Ignatius learned as a reborn Christian soldier, that the real struggle is "against the *spiritual* forces of evil" (Eph. 6:12, emphasis added). So he did what every knight did as they prepared to take up the good fight of the faith: he laid down his sword at the altar and kept vigil.

A (K)NIGHT'S VIGIL

Ignatius's visit to Montserrat was not a "retreat." Grunts never retreat; they break contact. When an infantry unit breaks contact, it is not running away from the fight. Breaking contact is a strategic attempt to reset conditions on the battlefield to their advantage by altering conditions in a way they can control. For example, a well-trained infantry unit might establish heavy weapons in the rear before ordering forward elements to break contact in order to lure the enemy into a hasty ambush. A tactical "retreat" is one in name only, and that goes for the church too.

The retreat at Montserrat was Ignatius breaking contact with his old ways. The word for this in the New Testament is *metanoia* (G3341), a new realization that causes someone to change direction. English Bibles often translate it as "repentance," but this gives too much weight to a Latin word, *patior*, which means "to experience suffering or regret." Repenting is not about *feeling* anything; it is about *doing* something. Ignatius, and the rest of us for that matter, might feel regret for sins we have committed, but that means nothing without action. We are not really sorry for something unless it causes us to behave differently.

Done properly, repenting is not about your old ways at all. Retreats are about "The Way" you have turned *toward*; they are the first step you take to alter conditions on the spiritual battlefield of your life.[11] While Ignatius was at Montserrat, he did what may appear to some as leaving behind his old soldierly ways by laying down his sword before a statue of Mary. But he was imitating *Amadís de Gaula*'s version of the knight's vigil, kept the evening before a novice is made a full knight.

Although often attributed authorship of the whole, Garci Rodriguez de Montalvo likely only revised *Amadís de Gaula* from an existing three-volume work. The fourth volume was entirely his own, and he engineered it to set the stage for countless sequels. In the final chapters of book 4, Montalvo turns the reader's attention from Amads to his son Esplandian. He seems familiar with knights of old, "who usually began their knighthood wearing white," but has his squire receive a coat of mail, helmet, and shield "blacker and darker than anything else could be" to symbolize "sorrow and sadness." In a small chapel, Esplandian and four battle buddies "knelt before the altar of the Virgin Mary and kept vigil over their weapons." Their vigil included prayers for "Mary to intervene with Her glorious Son to help him and direct him in such a way that in His service he could fulfill everything required by the great honor [Esplandian] was undertaking."[12]

In recalling his own "night's vigil over his arms," Ignatius cites *Amadís de Gaula* explicitly, suggesting he understood his visit to Montserrat not as the end of his military service, but the beginning.[13] He was revising his ways to better reflect the ways of a Christian soldier and chivalrous knight. Just as Esplandian's vigil included no sword, Ignatius would leave his weapon at the altar, which at Montserrat was home to a "black and beautiful" statue of the Virgin Mary and child that some Christians wouldn't be accustomed to.[14]

Montserrat was a brief but significant moment in Ignatius's life. He did not abandon chivalrous military service; rather, he reimagined it in a way commensurate with biblical faith. Soldiering was the baby, and the bathwater he left behind was violence, symbolized by leaving his sword at the foot of Mary and Jesus. The experience was sacramental, a spiritual rebirth. By keeping silent on his life before Pamplona, we may never know if Ignatius underwent the customary vigil as a novice knight. If he had, then his experience at Montserrat takes on added weight as a rebaptism that implicitly rejected his original vigil.

As the beginning of his new life as a Christian soldier, his "retreat" at Montserrat was profoundly formative. Ignatius spent most of his time in prayer, preparing for a devout life of *leitourgia*. To guide him in this effort, a resident priest offered Ignatius the prayer book used by monks. *Ejercitatorio de la vida espiritual,* or Exercises for the Spiritual Life, was composed by abbot García de Cisneros and published by the Abbey of Montserrat in 1500. If his sister-in-law's books had been his spiritual wake-up call, a First Formation, Cisneros's *Exercises* would be his PT, a way to maintain his spiritual fitness through daily (prayerful) exercise.

GET THE FUCK UP AND PRAY

Ignatius may have been tight-lipped about his life prior to Pamplona because he knew that the point of vigils is the morning after, not the night before. The abbey was the beginning of a military service he could be proud of as a spiritually maturing Christian. His next stop was a yearlong stay in Manresa to learn humility, the cardinal virtue of grunts. He divested himself of everything of value and begged for everything he needed. A cave provided shelter and served as a grotto for daily, sometimes hourly, prayer. His hopes for living in the Holy Land were dashed when the Franciscans expelled most pilgrims, so he decided to study theology in Barcelona and Paris. Like most student veterans today, Ignatius was much older than his peers.[15]

The war veteran also had the equivalent of an arrest record; the ecclesiastical courts were on high alert against Protestant influence, but Ignatius was cleared every time. What landed him in hot water was his passion for instructing others in piety, which was prohibited without the proper academic/ecclesiastical training. He had been adapting what he learned at Montserrat from Cisneros's prayer book, creating a curriculum he could share with others seeking spiritual improvement. Faith is a muscle that can weaken without the proper care and maintenance. As Ignatius put it, "For as strolling, walking and running are bodily exercises, so every way of preparing and disposing the soul to rid itself of all the disordered tendencies…is called a Spiritual Exercise."[16] Just like so-called fitness "boot camps" lean heavily on military imagery to help others get in physical shape, Ignatius was spreading the gospel of spiritual exercise based on his own experience as a Christian combat veteran.

He had been tweaking and perfecting his take on Cisneros's *Ejercitatorio de la vida espiritual* from the moment he left Montserrat. By 1524, he had completed the first draft of *Exercitia spiritualia,* or *Spiritual Exercises.* It had taken shape as he begged in Manresa, long before he had any formal theological training. In Paris, he began giving his exercises to fellow students and his professors, several of whom tried to adopt asceticism before being dragged back to the university by students eager to complete their coursework. Trouble seemed to follow Ignatius, but the same people he upset often came around after taking the time to hear him out or see his exercises for themselves.

In the simplest terms, Ignatius's *Spiritual Exercises* is a guided, silent "retreat" made up of four themed segments called "weeks." The book is for an experienced spiritual director to draw from in guiding others through the exercises, allowing for some variation between individual trainees. And that is the point, to train and strengthen our souls, to eventually no longer require a director, and perhaps become one for someone else. This wasn't a spiritual pyramid scheme, since no money ever changed hands; it was the first spiritual fitness program.

Pope Paul III praised the 1548 print edition of Ignatius's *Exercises* as "extremely useful and salutary for the spiritual profit of the faithful."[17] By then, he had completed his studies and was ordained a priest, but he completed his *Exercises* as a grunt with little more than a prayer book and a twinkle in his eye. His spiritual exercise program attracted a devoted following among the students at Paris. Among them was Francis Xavier, whose family had opposed Ignatius's forces at Pamplona. In 1534, the spiritual fitness junkies decided together that they wanted to adopt a life of poverty, commit to chastity, and visit Jerusalem. Just for funsies, they decided to name themselves Compañía de Jesús.

By calling their friend-group the "Company of Jesus," Ignatius's devotees were referencing 2 Timothy 2:4: "No one serving in the army gets entangled in everyday affairs; the soldier's aim is to please the enlisting officer." The Reina-Valera Bible uses *campaña militar* to translate *strateuomai* (G4754), a body of soldiers or an army. Rather than refer to Jesuits as companions, it would be more reflective of their martial foundation to call them *sysstratiotes* (G4961), "fellow soldiers," the same title Saul gives Epaphroditus (see Phil. 2:25) and Archippus (see Philem. 1:2). Five years after joining one another by vows, the fellow soldiers of Jesus prepared to become a formal religious order. In 1539, Ignatius drafted five "chapters" that eventually become the founding documents of the order. He began by addressing "all who desire to serve as a soldier of God beneath the banner of the Cross in our Society."[18] Ignatius would have drafted it in his native Spanish, without the Latin *societas*. The word he used would have been *compaña*, as in the one Saul popularized for soldiers of God, *campaña militar*.

Christian soldiers exceed the standard. They do not just pray with their eyes closed and their hands pressed together. Everything they do is steeped in prayer, from first light to nautical twilight. Ignatius taught the church universal what soldiers already know, that every waking moment must be oriented toward mission success. Salvation is our objective, but without constant exercise in bodily prayer, our souls become weak and our hearts become hard. When they get beaten down, grunts do not "shut the fuck up and drive on"; ritual without soul is meaningless. Just like when you first get out of bed, when you're knocked on your ass, you *get* the fuck up and *pray*. Not just with your words, but with your feet and hands.

Prayer is like exercise because it changes you rather than others. You can't pray away the faults of your neighbor; all you can do is pray away your own, in hopes the change in yourself might inspire change in others. Although Ignatius may have asked God that the *stranger* be guided to the truth, God instead led Ignatius there. As the Muslim traveler hurried off after their awkward exchange, I can imagine him praying, "*In sha'Allah*, don't let this whack job come after me!" Sometimes we are God's answer to the prayers of others. Thanks be to God.

13.
AIN'T I AMERICAN?
RALPH AND GI JUSTICE

D EMOCRACY IS LIKE A MUSCLE: IT NEEDS EXERCISE TO KEEP IT IN working order. The ancient Greeks formed democracies as a means of power or rule (*kratias*) that derives authority from the people (*demos*) themselves. While it sounds great, groups unable to rally 51 percent of popular support would be at the mercy of those groups that could. At worst, democracies create a tyranny of the majority. Republics, on the other hand, made all national matters a thing (*res*) of public interest (*publica*) as opposed to private interests, like kings or despots. While the people were still the source of authority for republics, electors would represent (*repræsentare*) them in legislative bodies. The founders combined these two forms of government in the hopes that each system's strengths would act as a check upon the other's weaknesses. As a product of human hands, however, our union reflects human frailties. Like the people who make it up, our country is imperfect, but good.

In the midst of charged debates about who got which rights, Sojourner Truth made her famous plea for human equality known as "Ain't I a Woman?"[1] By insisting Eve was no less than Adam, she was connecting freedom with the very origins of humanity. The same method had seen some success in Britain, where posters and broadsides featured a Black man kneeling above a banner that read "Am I Not a Man and a Brother?" By the 1960s it was no longer a question, with activists sporting picket signs demanding "I AM A MAN." In America, power (*kratias*) and representation (*repræsentare*) belong with all people, or they're supposed to at least. The history of civil rights is a military history as well as a religious history; without Christian soldiers coming home from war to demand proper treatment, there would be no civil rights movement. Society mistreated them because they were Black, but a combination of their faith and service compelled them to demand not just their civil rights, but human dignity as well.

WANT JUSTICE? JOIN THE MILITARY

Black Americans served in every battle in both the Army and the Navy until 1820, when John Calhoun, Secretary of War to President James Monroe, barred them from service. Although many were conscripted against their will, many volunteered to serve. Christopher Parker, a political scientist and Navy veteran, explains their desire to serve as fitting within "the rights-obligation trade-off that is part of the American conception of citizenship."[2] Military service, which many had willingly fulfilled, was supposed to create a duty upon *society* to extend the benefits of membership to its members. Enlisting represented a way that Black communities, vicariously through their service-eligible men, might force the system to bend toward justice.

Despite the institution of slavery and their susceptibility to it, enough Black Americans felt they were, or were supposed to be, on equal footing with Whites if they had put their lives on the line for the liberties promised by the Constitution. As governor of Virginia from 1781 to 1784, Benjamin Harrison impelled the state legislature to extend to Black veterans "that liberty which they [had] been in some measure instrumental in securing to us" during the Revolutionary War.[3] Sure enough, Black soldiers who served in Virginia's regiments received the freedom they had helped secure, regardless of their rank, specialty, or character of service.

The rights-obligation trade-off wasn't forceful enough to work all the time, and it proved pretty useful *against* Black citizenship in the infamous *Dred Scott v. Sandford* Supreme Court decision of 1857. The opinion of seven justices was that Black people were not required to serve and therefore could not be citizens and were not owed the rights enshrined by the Constitution. Chief Justice Roger Taney based his reasoning upon the Militia Act of 1792, pointing out that the law "directs that every 'free able-bodied white male citizen' shall be enrolled in the militia." The language, he concluded, explicitly excluded "the African race," because Black Americans formed "no part of the sovereignty, owing it no allegiance and therefore no obligation to defend it."[4]

As Parker sees it, "Scott's petition for citizenship was denied in part because he had never performed even a day of military service."[5] You know who else never performed a day of military service? Chief Justice Taney.

The reasoning is also a bit of a strawman argument because the Militia Act of 1792 set *federal* standards for military organization. In the interest of colonial unity, the word Taney's logic hung upon, "white," was included to appease slaveholding states. The decision ignored the interests of free territories, but so much for states' rights, huh?

The Civil War was fought to protect the "rights" of eleven Confederate states against twenty-five Union free and border states. As a war to end the institution of slavery, many Black men enlisted enthusiastically, hoping the rights-obligation trade-off might finally pay off. Recognizing Black military service, Frederick Douglass argued for the "all important right of suffrage" by asking the Massachusetts Anti-Slavery Society, "Shall we be citizens in war, and aliens in peace? Would that be just?"[6]

It certainly looked promising, with several civil rights acts passed in the years following the Union's victory. Arguing in favor of what would become the 1875 Civil Rights Act, Massachusetts congressman Benjamin Butler recalled his service commanding Black soldiers during the Civil War. On January 7, 1874, he spoke on the floor of the House of his "colored comrades, slain in the defense of their country...whose flag had only been to them a flag of stripes on which no star of glory had ever shone for them."[7] It was at that moment, looking upon the bodies of 534 Black soldiers, *his* soldiers, that he swore "a solemn oath, 'May my right hand forget its cunning and my tongue cleave to the roof of my mouth if I ever fail to defend the rights of these men who have given their blood for me and my country this day and for their race forever.'"

The first verse of Psalm 137 is well known as a Bob Marley song: "By the rivers of Babylon—there we sat down and there we wept when we remembered Zion." Israel is in mourning, exiled far from their home in Jerusalem, which the ancient composer worries the people might forget: "If I forget you, O Jerusalem, let my right hand wither! Let my tongue cling to the roof of my mouth, if I do not remember you" (vv. 5–6).

Every officer I've ever heard from has said their greatest responsibility is bringing each of their subordinates home safely. A retired Union general, Butler was making a promise to more than five hundred soldiers that he failed to bring home safely. By promising to never forget them in his oath, his unuttered prayer was that they *were* home, they were (in) Jerusalem, full members of that eternal city where justice flows like a river and righteousness like an everflowing stream.

FIGHT, RESIST; REPEAT

The rights-obligation trade-off was not universally accepted in the Black community, however. In wake of the First World War, editors of *The Crisis*, the publication of the NAACP, encouraged men to join up, writing, "Come, fellow black man, fight for your rights."[8] The *Boston Guardian*, *Cleveland Gazette*, and *Baltimore Afro-American* all took another tack, pointing out the duplicity of bringing freedom to Europe when there was none at home in the United States.[9] Civil rights have always been a contested topic even within communities they are supposed to support.

Civil rights are not compulsive; just because you *have* a right does not mean you are required to *exercise* it. Protections are there so that if and when we cry out for justice, the nation has an obligation to turn its ear to our cry. The hope is justice, but that cannot always be guaranteed. That's why scholar and activist W. E. B. Du Bois, whose ancestor Tom Burghardt was freed for his Revolutionary War service, wrote, "We return. We return from fighting. We return fighting."[10] With these words, Du Bois was cautioning returning WWI Black soldiers not to expect our nation to uphold its moral and legal obligations. Military service *should* trump hate, but optimism could get Black veterans killed.

As the Second World War began to rear its ugly face, Black men again volunteered to fight for freedoms they rarely received. That was the case for eighteen-year-old Felix Hall, who volunteered for service before Pearl Harbor inspired others to do the same.[11] Felix was assigned to the all-Black Twenty-Fourth Infantry Regiment at Fort Benning where, on February 13, 1941, he failed to appear for First Formation. His battle buddies were told he deserted, but when his body was discovered with a rope tied around his neck, they were told he hanged himself. Few believed it, and several submitted statements accusing a White defense contractor of threatening to kill Private Hall the day before he disappeared for failing to call him "Sir." As a civilian, he would not have been entitled to be referred to as a commissioned officer.

Felix's is the only recorded murder of an active-duty soldier on a federal military base, but it was probably more common than most realize. Record of his murder survives because it was reported by a White-owned paper in Alabama, which did not indicate whether his death was by "suicide or homicide."[12] The Black press (newspapers owned, operated, and read by African Americans), would have certainly carried the news throughout the South, but archives of these papers have not been well preserved. Some, like the *Carolina Times* of Durham, North Carolina, have lost parts of their archives to arson, bankruptcy, and other preventable tragedies. Had the Black press been treated with the same value and worth as White-owned papers, we would recognize how Felix's murder was an unfortunately common marker of Black life in America.

Booker T. Spicely of Blackstone, Virginia, was thirty-four when he was drafted in December 1943 and assigned to Camp Butner, North Carolina.[13] During his first few months in service, secret integrated basketball games were being played in Durham at YMCA "pray and play" meetings between the North Carolina College for Negroes (now NC Central University[14]) and a team of Duke medical ROTC cadets preparing to deploy. Between these games and the success of D-Day a month prior, Booker's spirits were probably especially high the weekend after Independence Day in 1944.

On Saturday, July 8, 1944, Private Spicely was in uniform on a weekend pass traveling to Durham with other (White) soldiers on a city bus when an argument broke out about the segregated seating. Before exiting the bus near the Black neighborhood of Walltown, Booker apologized for any offense he caused. The driver followed him off the bus, shot the American soldier in the chest and back, reboarded his bus, and completed the route before surrendering himself to police. Booker was not treated at the Whites-only Watts Hospital because military service does not trump skin color.[15] His murderer was out on bail before the sun came up thanks to the owner of Durham's city buses, Duke Power.[16]

As a theology student at Duke University, I worked at a coffee shop around the corner from where Booker was killed. I served smoothies to teenagers from the School of Science and Math, formerly Watts Hospital, which had put racial prejudice above patriotism and the Hippocratic oath. I didn't learn about Booker from the university or from talk around town. I was trying to learn about Alex Ney, the soldier I served with in the Eighty-Second Airborne Division who had taken his own life off campus two years before I started at Duke. Crawling the internet for "soldier death certificate Durham NC," I came across Booker's story. Suddenly my anxiety about a fellow White veteran paled in comparison to the maddening anonymity to which Booker T. Spicely was consigned.

If Americans really cared about the military, their deaths, whether by "suicide or homicide," would not be tolerated. Dead soldiers and veterans would be more important to the masses than our petty insecurities about race. The truth is that military personnel have never resided atop the lofty pedestals we pretend they occupy. Black soldiers believed those patriotic pedestals would protect them from at least some racial prejudice upon their return, but it was not to be. As they came home from WWII, Black soldiers were not going to return fighting "against enemies of blood and flesh, but against the rulers, against the authorities," the laws and customs of Jim Crow

(Eph. 6:12). The cohort of Black WWII veterans who made modern civil rights possible would put the Avengers to shame, and not just notable civilians like Rosa Parks, Martin Luther King Jr., and Jesse Jackson. Grunts are conditioned against self-interest and to shun the spotlight, which may be why we overlook veteran workhorses like Sergeant First Class Ralph Abernathy.[17]

BRING THE WALLS DOWN

Ralph Abernathy served in Europe during WWII before being involuntarily discharged for medical reasons. He recounts his service in *And the Walls Came Tumbling Down: An Autobiography*.[18] As a child his sights were set on the ministry, but his plans would be delayed by the outbreak of war. He was just fifteen when Pearl Harbor was bombed, but the war was still raging by the time he would register for the draft. In August 1944, Ralph was one of about three hundred Black inductees from Alabama who began training at Fort Benning, Georgia, the same military base where Felix Hall had been murdered in 1941. Booker Spicely had been shot in the back just a month prior in North Carolina.

Those who know Ralph for his commitment to nonviolence might question his decision to serve, pointing out alternatives available to him. James Farmer, for example, registered as a conscientious objector and cofounded the Congress of Racial Equality shortly after the war began. But Ralph was inspired to patriotism by Black athletes Jesse Owens and Joe Louis when they triumphed over their German counterparts, hailed by Hitler as champions of Aryan superiority.[19]

Others may have joined for similar reasons, only to complete their military service obligation and start fighting at home for social and legal equality. Command Sergeant Major Charles Evers, field director of the NAACP in Mississippi from 1963 to 1969, entered military service at Camp Shelby, Mississippi, in February 1942 and remained on reserve status until sometime in 1949. First Lieutenant Jack R. "Jackie" Robinson joined the same month as Charles. The future baseball legend and devout Methodist would later be arrested and court-martialed for violating Jim Crow in Texas' Camp Hood on July 6, 1944. Charles's younger brother, Technician Fifth Grade Medgar Evers, who regularly attended New Hope Baptist Church in Jackson and preceded him as field secretary until he was assassinated, entered service in October 1943.[20]

Women joined up as well. Captain Dovey Johnson was among the first Black women commissioned as officers in the Women's Army Auxiliary Corps on August 29, 1942. At a Miami bus terminal in the early months of 1943, Dovey experienced "that comforting sense of oneness I always felt when in the company of others in uniform."[21] That sense faded when she was forced to give up her seat to a White enlisted soldier who apparently felt no such sense of camaraderie. It was no accident that bus terminals and interstate travel became central to the later strategy of civil rights organizations. Dovey went on to become one of the first women to be fully ordained in the African Methodist Episcopal Church, but her experience as a veteran was the rule rather than the exception, and despite expectations, military service offered no protection from racial hatred.

Staff Sergeant Hosea Williams entered the Army a week after

VE Day but he, too, faced violence on his way home, presumably after his discharge.[22] He talked about when he "came out of the army" and was traveling home to Bainbridge, Georgia, from New York City.[23] Two hours from his destination, at a stop in Americus, Hosea attempted to fill a coffee cup with water from a fountain while leaning through the doorway of the Whites-only terminal. He was beaten so badly by offended Whites that he was left for dead. A Black undertaker found a pulse and had him taken to a hospital in Thomasville.

As he tells it, Hosea was in uniform "with all these medals and everything," which would have included his noncommissioned officer rank. If he was still active duty, he would have been taken to Finney General Hospital, which the Army established in June 1943 to treat convalescing soldiers. As a "selectee," his compulsory service would have ended in early 1946, when Hosea was under the Veterans Administration and transitioning to a domiciliary.[24] Either way, he spent eight weeks laid up, "crying, hating, and wishing that [he] had fought on the side of Adolf Hitler." However horrible it may be to imagine a uniformed soldier being beaten to within an inch of his life, what the White residents of Americus did was culturally acceptable. Even if it's obvious that criminal assault occurred, charges were usually leveraged against *victims* for violating Jim Crow laws. That would change, with the help of the very heroes listed above, and a few more.

Hosea, who worked with Ralph and Martin extensively, called himself "a general in the war for human rights and personal dignity."[25] The NAACP, which led the legal fight against Jim Crow, picked up on the martial enthusiasm by actively recruiting Black veterans, "who were very militant and who didn't scare easy."[26] Bus routes that crossed state lines were vulnerable to federal jurisdiction, so companies with routes to or from destinations in the North could be dragged before the Supreme Court. And that is precisely what the NAACP did.

The first legal victory was thanks to Irene Morgan, a Black "Rosie" employed by Glenn L. Martin, the precursor to Lockheed Martin, in Baltimore, Maryland, where she supported the war effort building B-26 Marauders. Just three hours away and one week after Booker Spicely was shot in cold blood in 1944, Irene refused the driver's demand to forfeit her seat to a White passenger. The first deputy arrived with an arrest warrant, which Irene promptly tore up and threw out the window before kicking the officer right in the testicles. Irene's "We Can Do It!" attitude persisted as the next deputy approached, but this time she only clawed his face and tore his shirt. She was finally arrested and charged with one count of resisting and another count of violating state segregation laws. She apologized and paid a fine for the first charge but refused to plead for the second. Her lawyers argued all the way to the Supreme Court that Virginia's Jim Crow laws violated interstate commerce. On June 3, 1946, the court ruled in her favor, chalking up the first major legal victory for civil rights.

Morgan v. Virginia may have outlawed segregation in interstate travel, but there were loopholes that other cases, with closer ties to the military, would have to close. The wording in *Morgan* was legally lazy and could be interpreted in such a way as to apply only to direct routes to and from integrated stations in the North. Terminals in the segregated South, like in Americus, could be legally exempt from the Morgan decision. Not only did Hosea Williams find himself in this position, but it was also the situation for soldiers and veterans during the war in Korea, like Private First Class Sarah Keys.

Sarah grew up Catholic in Washington, North Carolina, the daughter of Navy WWI veteran David Keys.[27] On July 31, 1952, Ignatius of Loyola's feast day, PFC Keys boarded a Carolina Coach at Fort Dix, New Jersey, to head home on leave. The bus was just two hours away when it made a stop in Roanoke Rapids. When the new driver arrived, he demanded that the Black Soldier give up her seat to a White Marine from Camp Lejeune. She refused and was arrested. At the encouragement of her Black Catholic Navy WWI veteran father, she agreed to take Carolina Coach to court. Dovey Johnson, who had recently begun practicing law, took her case all the way to the Interstate Commerce Commission (ICC), which found in Keys's favor on November 1, 1955.

A year and a half before, on May 17, 1954, the Supreme Court had handed down its landmark decision in *Brown v. Board of Education*. The namesake plaintiff was Rev. Oliver Leon Brown, a WWII veteran and pastor of St. Mark's AME in Topeka, Kansas. What *Brown* did for education, *Keys* did for interstate travel. Something I've never seen reported is that neither case would have happened were it not for supportive Black fathers. Or, for that matter, Black veterans of faith.

Although she preferred anonymity, Sarah Keys's case emboldened another young woman to stand up publicly and demand that the earlier successes be recognized and enforced. Rosa Parks made her fateful decision to follow in the footsteps of CPT Johnson, 1LT Robinson, PVT Spicely, and "Rosie" Irene Morgan less than one month after PFC Keys's success with the ICC. It was not the *start* of the civil rights movement, but it *was* just the beginning.

MONTGOMERY TO RESURRECTION CITY

Although *Brown* ended segregated education, the justices failed to overturn or even address *Plessy v. Ferguson*, the 1896 decision that established states' rights to keep races "separate but equal" as law. What made the *Keys* ruling significant was that the ICC used the logic of *Brown* to reject *Plessy* in writing, the closest any juridical body has ever come. The law was set, now the states just had to enforce the rights of all Americans within their borders.

When Rosa Parks made her stand on the shoulders of Black soldiers who went before her, she had no way of knowing the consequences. Back in 1944, three Black defense employees had faced three very different results within a ten-day span following Independence Day. At Fort Hood in Texas on July 6, 1LT Robinson had been forcibly removed but later acquitted at court-martial, ending his military career. Two days later in North Carolina, PVT Spicely was murdered despite removing himself and apologizing for any offense. And in Virginia on July 16, defense contractor Irene Morgan put up a fight that Rosie the Riveter herself could be proud of and walked away with a ticket. Eleven years later, there was still no telling what might happen to a Black woman who took up the fight Black soldiers had begun.

Without *Morgan* and *Keys* prohibiting segregation in transportation, there would have been no Freedom Riders or Montgomery Bus Boycott. Montgomery, Alabama, was home to Ralph and his young friend and Atlanta transplant Martin Luther King Jr. Rosa's arrest the evening of Thursday, December 1, 1955, sent shock waves through the city and she was bailed out quickly by the local NAACP. By the following Monday, plans were already underway for a one-day boycott, the success of which inspired local leaders like Ralph and Martin to extend the boycott indefinitely as a means of forcing change. They decided to create a new entity because Ralph and Martin thought the local NAACP "was moribund."[28] The final name, the Montgomery Improvement Association, or MIA, was Ralph's idea. MIA would have been especially resonant the month after our nation's second Veterans Day, when Black veterans' civil rights were "Missing in Action."[29] Intended or not, the timing of Rosa's action would have evoked the fact that some veterans were recognized not for their service, but for their skin color. The burning question in the minds of Black soldiers and veterans would have been "Ain't I American?"

The bus boycott in Montgomery was the first of many struggles Ralph engaged in with Martin, who was too young to fight during WWII. MIA was considered a success and was absorbed into a broader campaigning organization, the Southern Christian Leadership Conference, or SCLC, in 1957. Martin was elected president and Ralph became his second in command. Their close relationship cannot be overstated; Martin was Jonathan to Ralph's David.[30] Montgomery was followed by campaigns in Albany, Georgia, in

1962; Birmingham in 1963; and St. Augustine, Florida, in 1964, with their influence peaking during the Selma to Montgomery voting marches of 1965.

Following a disappointing campaign in Chicago through 1966, Ralph and Martin decided to reassess. The success of the civil rights movement meant they had worked themselves out of a job: "We had eliminated virtually all of the statutory barriers to our own advancement and equality."[31] Seeing the need to pivot, Ralph and Martin started focusing on the underlying issue of poverty and its causes. The Sanitation Workers' Strike in Memphis was part of this pivot, and it returned to the tried-and-true human appeal. It was in Memphis that the movement turned Sojourner Truth's appeal to humanity into a demand for human equality. No longer *Ain't I?*, but the great *I AM!*

Ralph and Martin had already begun to plan for a Poor People's Campaign to advocate not just for racial equality, but for economic justice as well. The idea of a large march to advocate for economic justice was not new. Father James Cox was a Catholic hospital chaplain in France during WWI who became a labor activist inspired by Pope Leo XIII's social justice encyclical *Rerum Novarum*.[32] In January 1932, Father Cox, known as the Pastor to the Poor, led twenty thousand Pennsylvanians to Washington, DC, to demand antipoverty and employment legislation. Cox's Army, as it became known, was the largest and most orderly demonstration the capital had ever seen.[33] They were moderately successful and formed the Jobless Party to continue advocating for their demands.

Five months later, Father Cox was a legitimate contender for the

Democratic presidential nomination as another twenty thousand marchers descended upon the capital. This time it was the Bonus Army, made up of mostly poor Black and White veterans accompanied by their families. Rather than march there and back, as Cox's Army had, Bonus marchers set up a shantytown called Camp Marks, after a supportive DC police chief. They were there to demand payment of service compensation withheld by Congress because of the Great Depression. Veterans had given life and limb to end the Great War and in return were given $500 and a ticket home. Camp Marks was a living city for about a month before inhabitants were forcibly removed on July 28, 1932, by units of the Third Cavalry under the command of George "Slap-the-PTSD-Outta-You" Patton.[34] When active-duty soldiers began forming up, the Bonus marchers applauded, assuming they were there to support the veterans seeking payment of their military wages. After six tanks leveled Camp Marks, Patton sent in the infantry armed with fixed bayonets and chemical agents that induced vomiting. Two veterans were killed, one of their wives miscarried, fifty-five were injured, and 135 were arrested under the pretense that the Bonus marchers were attempting to overthrow the government. The debacle contributed to Herbert Hoover's unpopularity and electoral defeat to Franklin D. Roosevelt, who would reluctantly sign the Servicemen's Readjustment Act of 1944, the "GI Bill," into law.

Ralph and Martin's 1968 Poor People's Campaign was a direct spiritual descendant of the Cox and Bonus armies. Not only were they both clergy, but like Father Cox, they also wanted to build upon the idea of an Economic Bill of Rights for the poor and used an election year to bolster public attention. The campaign was also originally supposed to start in Marks, Mississippi, where Martin wept at the sight of malnourished Black schoolchildren, and the name would have evoked Camp Marks and the Black and White military families who lived beside one another in tents to demand economic justice.

The poor people's encampment was called Resurrection City and, like Camp Marks, its residents ultimately failed to secure their demands. Nonetheless, it would be resurrected fifty years later by Rev. Dr. William Barber II, Rev. Dr. Liz Theoharis, and Jonathan Wilson-Hartgrove. Their recent campaign, however, does not share the same connection or commitment to our military that either "army" had in 1932.

I met Jonathan at a summer festival in rural Tennessee shortly after I applied to be a noncombatant conscientious objector. He gave me an autographed copy of his first book, *Born Again in Babylon*, about his time in Iraq as a civilian protesting the invasion of Iraq. Before the bombs began to fall over Baghdad, Jonathan traveled there with Shane Claiborne and the Iraq Peace Team. Alex Ney and my battle buddies in the Eighty-Second Airborne were there at the same time, doing the initial invading. Shane and Jonathan had made a space for me in the "New Monastic" movement as I transitioned reluctantly from soldier to veteran.

But as the years went by and I continued to mature spiritually and intellectually, we grew apart. I fit easily in the pacifist box at first; there was room to breathe, to explore. When CBS broke the news about military suicide, I was shook. It was like survivor's guilt, getting out only to learn the military was in crisis. Folks in my circles at the time used the data as prooftexts for pacifism; *Soldiers are killing themselves faster than they can be killed in combat; it must be PTSD!*[35] "Why do we still need evidence? You have seen the data!" It reminds me of Caiaphas's own dramatic display of confirmation bias after he questioned Jesus (see Matt. 26:65; Mark 14:63–64; Luke 22:71). It's not that I believe killing is free of moral pain or psychological stress; I'm just not convinced that the problem is exclusively about mental health. I think military suicide has a lot to do with the human dignity that soldiers and veterans are denied, with how they get put in boxes, or on top of them, to serve the interests of others while their own interests continue to be ignored.

On Veterans Day in 2017, William Barber tweeted to more than 330,000 followers: "We're building a #PoorPeoplesCampaign, led by veterans like Matthew [Hoh], to challenge America's dangerous addiction to the war economy. #VeteransDay."[36] William and Jonathan's campaign was *not* led by veterans; they were just paraded about at strategic moments and expected to amplify *others'* interests. I knew Matthew, and I was not confident his interests were being represented. I replied, "As long as Veterans like Matthew are denied basic civil rights, the campaign Martin called for remains out of reach; Injustice anywhere threatens justice everywhere." I attached a link to an article I wrote for *The Hill* just three days prior: "Veterans Deserve Civil Rights Protections Too," to which no reply ever appeared.[37]

I also knew that Jonathan was aware that military personnel were denied their rights because I spoke with him about it a year and a half prior. On June 30, 2016, I spoke with my influential friend about organizing around soldiers' and veterans' civil rights. I emailed him later that day, offering resources in the event that "organizing leadership is curious and wants to pursue including veterans in their messaging," pointing out "the biggest employer in Durham County (Duke) makes no mention of their support of veterans."[38]

The fourth principle of William and Jonathan's Poor People's Campaign reads "We believe that equal protection under the law is non-negotiable."[39] Apparently principles are more like guides than rules, because equal protection under the law is still being negotiated, not through the lens of race, color, religion, sex, or gender, but through military rank and veteran status. Matthew and I returned from fighting and returned fighting. Not for ourselves, as Du Bois had inspired countless Black veterans to do, but for others. Dovey, Jackie, Charles, Medgar, Ralph, Hosea, and Sarah knew they had a stake in their own rights. Would they have kept the fight going if they knew that they could be attacked on account of their military service? I think so. Ralph acknowledges that he thought the fight had to change, that the statutory protections achieved for civil rights, voting, and fair housing signaled victory. What he could not have predicted, and what Matthew, William, Jonathan, and I took for granted, was that the fight was not over; it had only changed shape. The enemy of dehumanizing injustice had evolved, but our thinking had not.

SPIT SHINING
A MIRROR, DIMLY

MEMBERS OF GROUPS THAT ARE UNDER THREAT FORGE A DEEPER, lasting bond with one another. That's what happens in boot camp; the drill instructors create stress to teach recruits to look past their petty differences and work together to avoid as many smoke sessions as possible. It's no coincidence that the military could and did integrate sooner than the rest of society. Camaraderie results when you realize your fight is the same as the fight of the person beside you. Veterans like Ralph Abernathy, the Evers brothers, Dovey Johnson, Jackie Robinson, and so many others learned this from their time in service. When they got out, the fight didn't change; it only moved from one area of operations to another.

In Saul's first letter to the Christians of Corinth, he tells them, "For now we see in a mirror, dimly" (1 Cor. 13:12). From the grand scheme of human history, we can only hope to glimpse what's really going on. After this world passes away, we'll see clearly, face-to-face. Like Saul, I'm not convinced we see ourselves and our story very clearly. Filling out the history of military service in our country requires a little spit shine, a closer look at what happened to soldiers and veterans around the same time the civil rights movement was in decline.

CIVIL(IAN) RIGHTS

The difference between camaraderie and solidarity is *membership*; comrades share an interest in combating injustice because they suffer together, but allies in solidarity do not. Being an ally means you *make* the fight yours, even if you might escape the consequences of failing. I am fascinated by soldiers in church history because I identify with them; I imagine they share a certain set of experiences like mine. When I read the Bible, I get drawn in and want to know more about the grunts, centurions, and tribunes who helped make our faith what it is. I want to learn from their mistakes and help the church not make the same mistakes again. Because when the church gets soldiers wrong, I feel the effects. I'm not an ally to veterans; I *am* a veteran.

Before Vietnam and the end of the draft, military service was not as unique an aspect of American identity as it is now. The outliers were those who avoided (or dodged) the draft. Identifying as a soldier or veteran for Black Americans was often a place of pride, something that might displace the stigma White Americans attached to their race and color. The hope was that they were veterans who happened to be Black, that military service was enough to earn the respect of the dominant (White) culture.

If anyone deserves the benefits of citizenship, it is those who fight to defend them. This is the basic maxim underwriting the inverted logic behind the 1857 *Dred Scott* decision; the obligation to defend America secures a part in its sovereignty. Black veterans were not asking for special treatment for their families and communities; they were asking our nation to uphold its standing obligation. Depriving soldiers and veterans of the same rights they fought for is the epitome of duplicity. Exposing the particular hypocrisy of denying a soldier or veteran the rights they fought for was a cornerstone of the civil rights movement. Without civil rights for military families, they're just civilian rights. Imperfect, but not exactly good either—justice for some, not all.

Thanks to the advocacy of the civil rights movement of the 1960s, legislative protections guarantee equal opportunities in employment as well as access to education, fair housing, and public accommodation. The earliest laws created protections based on race, color, religion, sex, and national origin. As advocacy continued, federal protection was extended to groups disadvantaged due to age, sexual orientation, gender expression, citizenship, family size and status, disability, and genetic information.

Ralph and other Black veterans never had to assert their rights *as veterans* because their race and color were the primary site of prejudice, not military service. Vietnam changed that, though its effects would not be clear until after the civil rights movement had already accomplished most of their goals. Until 1967 the war was only marginally unpopular, and a high number of African American men were enlisting for the same reasons earlier generations had: food, clothing, shelter, salary, and veterans' benefits promised a path to the middle class. It was not until the 1968 Tet Offensive and news of the My Lai Massacre that public sentiment swung heavily against the war.

Martin was a comparatively early convert to the antiwar movement. His famous 1967 speech "A Time to Break the Silence" put him at odds with most civil rights organizations, which remained supportive of military policy. Ralph, who used his veterans' benefits to great effect, must have heard from young men and women hoping to do the same: "So you got a steady paycheck, the GI Bill, mortgage assistance, and now I ain't supposed to do the same?" Within a year, the war would lose any semblance of popular support, and veterans returning from Vietnam would bear the brunt of (un)popular opinion.

Vietnam changed the way we looked at our soldiers and veterans, and while veterans were never debased or assaulted to the same extent as African Americans were, the fact remained that the veil had been torn open and America could no longer pretend it cared for its military as it claimed to. In the fall of 1967, the *New York Times* ran two separate stories that revealed a problem the military had not widely encountered before: spitting on soldiers. On August 27, Neil Sheehan reported that, as part of military training in the National Guard, soldiers were being spit on, abuse to which they were instructed not to respond.[1] This "New Control Technique" was employed just two months later by units of the Eighty-Second Airborne Division when protesters "spat on some of the soldiers in the front line of the Pentagon and goaded them with the most vicious personal slander."[2]

When spitting occurred, those on duty typically adhered to military protocol including "very strict orders…just to stand in dignified silence."[3] Veterans, on the other hand, were free to respond as they saw fit, with one WWII Medal of Honor recipient punching a civilian who had assaulted him and called him a "killer."[4] Spitting on soldiers and veterans became more commonplace, peaking in 1971 as stories appeared in the *Washington Post*,[5] *Reno Gazette Journal*,[6] *Associated Press*,[7] and on *CBS Evening News*.[8] The incidents continued to occur through the 1980s, documented by articles in *Time* magazine,[9] reports on *ABC Evening News*,[10] and a string of columns in the *Chicago Tribune*.[11] Spitting on someone was not made a criminal assault until recently, so soldiers and veterans had no reason to call the police because no crime had occurred.

The most noteworthy case came toward the end of 1972 when the activist Ron Kovic was spit upon in Miami Beach, Florida, at the Republican National Convention.[12] Two months later Congress passed what would become the Vietnam Era Veterans' Readjustment Assistance Act (VEVRAA), guaranteeing equal opportunity in employment for some veterans.[13] The last draft call was made in December of that year, and the authority to conscript men into military service expired June 30, 1973, making the distinction between soldier and civilian hard and fast. Since then, we have been a nation in which *nobody* is obligated to enroll in the military, and everybody is supposed to be protected by the laws secured by those who do. So much for Justice Taney's racist inversion of the rights-obligation trade-off, huh?

In 1974, VEVRAA was amended for the first time, bringing it

into the emerging legal concept of affirmative action.[14] Affirmative action began in the military, with President Harry Truman, an artillery officer during WWI. Truman had instructed his attorney general to investigate, and subsequently indict, a South Carolina sheriff for the blinding of Sergeant Isaac Woodard on February 12, 1946.[15] The US attorney argued that federal jurisdiction applied because Isaac was still a soldier; his honorable discharge did not take effect until midnight. In response to the all-White jury returning an acquittal, Truman issued Executive Order No. 9808, creating a presidential commission on civil rights.

The commission's report the following year, *To Serve these Rights: Indifference (f)or Hate?*, called for the postwar military to begin integration July 26, 1948, which Truman directed in his Executive Order No. 9981.[16] As the first president to address the NAACP, Truman had called for "equality of opportunity,"[17] a phrase borrowed later by President Kennedy's Executive Order No. 10925 in 1961 and codified into law by Title VII of the same Civil Rights Act of 1964 that Martin and Ralph helped get passed.

Currently, federal law prohibits harassment and discrimination based on certain protected characteristics: race, color, religion, nationality, age, sexual orientation, gender expression, citizenship, family size and status, disability, and genetic information. Legislative protections guarantee equal employment opportunity, access to education and fair housing, prevention of hate crimes, and reasonable public accommodation. Despite the epidemic of homelessness, depression, and suicide in our military communities, soldiers and veterans receive only limited federal protections compared to other groups. Some of the federal laws that create these protections are not only unenforced, federal agencies don't seem to know they exist.

Section 4712 of the Matthew Shepard and James Byrd Jr. Hate Crimes Prevention Act (HCPA) of 2009 extends hate crimes protections to soldiers and their immediate families for up to five years after discharge.[18] The resulting federal law, 18 US Code section 1389, could have protected Lieutenant Colonel Ira Phillips when he received a voice mail threatening, "We're gonna blow your fucking brains out" because "you are taking orders from" the president[19]; or a military family in Ohio "targeted for murder at home solely on account of service to our country."[20] However, the Department of Justice shows nothing about these specific protections on any affiliated website and provides no means for military families to report hate crimes. The United States Commission on Civil Rights (USCCR), in their decennial report on HCPA, made no mention of Section 4712 or 18 US Code section 1389.[21] Staff at the USCCR, including the commission chair, spokesperson, and general counsel, whose spouse is a veteran, didn't like it when I started asking why military families were being left out of the conversation.[22] Representatives at the Department of Justice and subordinate agencies had no knowledge of Section 1389 or how it would be enforced when I made multiple calls to various regional offices.

Most people don't *see* this treatment or the lack of protection because it doesn't *affect* most people. Even combining Total Force members and dependents with veterans, the military community represents just 8 percent of the population.[23] By comparison, about 26 percent of Americans live with a disability,[24] 13.4 percent indicate their race as Black or African American,[25] and 5.6 percent identify as LGBT (a number that is increasing every year).[26] The need for civil rights for some groups is being met at a pace that has eclipsed the need by military families, a group that continues to shrink in size.

BACK TO THE FUTURE

After I filed my bias and discrimination complaint internally with the Duke University Office of Institutional Equity, it became clear it was a check-the-box situation. Part of my concern was disclosing activity that was supposed to be protected, thereby exposing me to retaliation. I learned that meant exactly squat on August 29, 2016, when the senior vice president (SVP) for Institutional Equity stood up in front of fifty of my peers and used my complaint to try to embarrass me. During a Q&A session, I raised my hand and asked him to discuss the university's Affirmative Action Plan for Veterans and People With Disabilities, noting that teaching assistants in attendance would encounter both.[27] One witness noticed that he "disclosed that Isaac was asking about something they'd discussed privately, on a different occasion. It seemed unprofessional for [SVP] to disclose to the whole group that he and Isaac had spoken about the matter."[28] A month later I filed a federal complaint with the Department of Labor (DOL) with hopes that getting outside the institutional bubble might help me. Long story short: nope.

I was supposed to be protected by VEVRAA, but as it turns out, it's so poorly worded that it amounts to basically nothing. In *Greer v. Chao*, retired justice Sandra Day O'Connor dismissed a Vietnam veteran's lawsuit asking the Department of Labor to enforce the law because the statutory language "leaves us with no law to apply."[29] After years of bias and prejudice, I was calling foul: "It isn't fair!" But all that people heard was "I didn't get what I want." Before I elevated my complaint to the federal level, I was warned that I could effectively be blacklisted if I went ahead with my complaint. At that 2012 Society of Christian Ethics conference on war, the veteran I chatted with had warned me to just keep my head down until tenure. It sounded more like combat than a career field, not exactly a bright future.

The details of what happened next are complicated, just like social justice and military service. My complaint was dismissed almost a year later.[30] It didn't matter how much evidence I supplied, nor did it matter that Duke University violated federal law by altering policies while under investigation.[31] When VEVRAA is "no law at all," a real investigation would have been little more than a favor to me, like a TYFYS hire by a registrar who never read my résumé. When investigations are pencil-drilled, the weakest link in the social justice chain will always suffer the most.

I started to look into the enforcement procedures and data for VEVRAA, and it turns out the Department of Labor hasn't been reporting enforcement data to Congress in accordance with the law.[32] That may be because they turn away VEVRAA complaints as many as four times as often as they do other types of statutory complaints. That kind of information isn't publicly known, in part because the subagency at DOL that prepares and sends the reports, the Veterans'

Employment and Training Service (VETS), fails to include data that is mandated by federal law.[33] When I pointed this out to the director of compliance at VETS, he thanked me for my service, because of course he did, and kindly asked me to fuck off. Even in the places where VEVRAA *is* worded properly, it doesn't matter if public officials simply refuse to do their jobs.

The privilege I have, that anybody in America has, is affected by many factors at once. I can be subject to antimilitary bias and still benefit from my race. When I dug deeper into the enforcement data I also found that VEVRAA complaints were ten times more likely to return a finding of merit if they were filed on the basis of being White rather than being Black.[34] When I was asked by DOL investigators whether I thought I was being mistreated because I was a veteran or because I was disabled, I didn't know how to answer them. My disabilities are irrevocably linked with my service; how was I supposed to stop being one and start being the other? When millions of Christians saw me as "War-Torn," was that messed up because it was ableism, or because it was antimilitary?

When I remember Martin saying, "Injustice anywhere is a threat to justice everywhere," this is where my head goes. I may have plenty of privileges as a White, cisgender dude, but not so much as a veteran. And I say this knowing that there are still people joining the military hoping to earn their citizenship, figuratively and literally. Do I tell them it's a fool's errand, that it's all a ruse? Or do I get the fuck up and pray with my feet, my legs, with whatever dwindling strength I have left and help make our country the kind of place it claims to be? What kind of patriot, what kind of *Christian* would

I be if I didn't? If the future is up to us, that includes me as well as you. Human dignity for soldiers and veterans is up to all of us, and we each have a stake in how the universe bends back toward justice.

I grew up helping my mom grade math papers and cleaning shit out of animal cages in my dad's science classroom. I'm an educator through and through; I love teaching almost as much as I love learning. As a stubborn grunt, I fought because it was the right thing to do. Friends questioned my sanity, churches asked my family not to attend, and a federal investigation fell apart because veterans' laws are about mental health and material wealth, not civil rights and human dignity. I don't want veterans' benefits and service entitlements; I want justice. It's not fair that those who serve are denied the rights they help secure for everyone else. What's worse is when veterans return fighting for everyone but themselves. Anger is perfectly appropriate, and, if we're being honest, so are sadness, depression, and self-isolation.

I'm reminded of Ryan Martin, the anger psychologist. He insists that anger is a natural reaction to unfairness, and it's equally natural to feel sad when we don't get what we want. Sometimes the things we want are things we deserve, like human dignity. We *should* be mad when we see people treated unfairly; it is right to see injustice and get pissed. The bad news is that veterans are treated unfairly, but the good news is that you can get smad and do something about it. The question is: Will you?

SAFETY BRIEF
(AN EPILOGUE)

EVERY FRIDAY BEFORE SOLDIERS GET RELEASED FOR THE WEEK-end, the commander or other duly appointed representative must give something called a safety brief or liberty brief for Sailors and Marines. Part pep talk, part disclaimer of liability, every single one from time immemorial can be summed up as "Don't do stupid shit." Don't drink and drive. Don't do drugs. Don't get yourself or anyone else pregnant. Don't get in a bar fight. Don't get anyone pregnant in a bar fight. Officers and NCOs wouldn't find out what kind of creative stupidity grunts had dreamed up until Monday. The safety brief is their last chance to impart some wisdom to their *familia* and hopefully spare them a night in jail or, worse, a lifetime of regret.

Every time I give a presentation somewhere or have a Q&A after a sermon or talk, someone always asks me what I would tell soldiers and veterans. It's usually a loved one or family member unsure of how to connect with grunts in their lives. Every so often it's a soldier or veteran themselves, wondering what my bottom line is: What do I believe about Christians doing violence? What do I do with the regret I feel, or that (I think) my loved one feels?

261

We are left with simplistic questions because churches and communities are not doing a sufficient job of educating their members. The questions in our minds are vague and amorphous because the intermediate questions (who does the killing, why, when, under what authority, and what system of accountability?) aren't even being examined. Any direct answer I give will be as unsatisfying as the questions I'm asked until there is better conversation between a uniform and a dead body.

Because those are the stakes, aren't they? Either our so-called enemies have a bullet in their heads or our "war-torn" loved ones have a garden hose around their necks, right? Sometimes I wish it were that black-and-white, that there was a road map I could hand out to battle buddies and their families and say, "This is how you navigate the road from military discharge to natural death." The truth is that there isn't one answer that works for everyone. Not that morality is relative, but time and reality are. At least, that's what Einstein said, and he's smarter than me.

What I mean is that we need to get away from looking for tidy solutions in a messy world. Just because I applied to be a noncombatant conscientious objector does not mean I think every Christian soldier must. If Christians want to serve in combat specialties, they must be prepared for the moral weight of their actions, whatever they are. There are two soldier-saints that help illustrate my point, and they may light the way for others too.

After a rough start to life in rural Tennessee, Alvin York got that old-time religion and became a Bible-thumpin' mo'fucker. When news of WWI reached his little town, the draft was right behind it.

Alvin was a hoss, and the Army wanted him bad, but his church was pacifist and he wasn't one to challenge his tradition. He applied to be a conscientious objector, writing on his draft card, "Don't want to fight," but he was denied. He reapplied twice and got rejected twice.

He didn't complain or resist, but he didn't hide his beliefs from anyone either. After a heart-to-heart, Alvin's commander told him he would release him if he sincerely felt his faith was incompatible with military service. On a weekend pass, Alvin prayed for forty-eight hours straight on a mountaintop near his home. When he came down, he reported to his unit and deployed with them to France. It was there, in October 1918, that he accomplished what he came to be known for by single-handedly capturing nearly 130 German prisoners.

York was awarded the Medal of Honor as well as French and Italian medals for bravery. After the war ended, he came home a national hero and was given property, a pension, the whole nine yards. He refused opportunities to profit off his fame but he did leverage his notoriety to make the lives of others better. By all accounts, he was a virtuous man loved by all and unblemished by vanity, greed, or pride. But he carried something with him from that French battlefield in 1918 that would haunt him his entire life. Near his death, he asked one of his sons, "Do you think God will forgive me for those six Germans I killed?"[1]

For forty-six years, more than half his life, Alvin carried the moral weight of six human lives upon his shoulders. He never talked about philanthropy as atonement or gave any hint that he was trying to earn his salvation. He lived with it, with the burden of six lives. At the end he had nothing comforting or wise to share with his children; rather, he humbled himself, asking his own offspring what *God* must think of *him*.

Desmond Doss's story has a few similarities with Alvin's. Both came from rural Appalachia, from families of little to no means, and had misgivings about fighting in a war. A few months after Pearl Harbor, Desmond volunteered to serve even though he had a deferment because he worked at a shipyard supporting the war. He, too, was a conscientious objector, though he preferred the term "conscientious participant." Desmond was willing and ready to serve in uniform, but it had to be without the standard-issue firearm.

He was trained as a medic while members of his unit beat, intimidated, and harassed Desmond for his nonviolent beliefs. Thick-skinned *as fuck*, Desmond deployed with them to the Pacific combat theater and saw action in Guam and the Philippines, where he earned not one, but two Bronze Stars with V devices for Valor. As if that weren't enough, he single-handedly saved more than seventy lives in one day during the Battle of Okinawa in April 1945, earning him the Medal of Honor.

Shot four times and riddled with shrapnel, Desmond nonetheless gave up his own stretcher so another soldier could be carried to medical care. He reluctantly agreed to carry the soldier's weapon, the only time he touched a firearm, but not before emptying the chamber of rounds. Shortly thereafter he was shot a fifth time by an unseen sniper, so he used the stock of the rifle as a splint and kept walking.

Just like Alvin, Desmond came home to boisterous fanfare. The same soldiers who had harassed him recanted, barely able to sing his praises loud enough. He received the Medal of Honor from President Truman at a White House ceremony after the war. Everyone knew him from his smile and warm personality, even though his experience of postservice care with the VA was, well, it was normal for the VA: overlapping prescriptions, botched care, you know—the usual. Desmond just didn't let it get him down. When his death neared, he greeted the end with the same characteristic sunny disposition. No hushed tones or questions of God's forgiveness. He may not have had anything profound to say either, but he left the world the same way he inhabited it, with clear eyes and a big smile.

Forget all the philosophizing and smarty-pants bullshit about killing being justified or not. Given the choice, which would you prefer? Who in their right mind would choose a lifetime of doubt?

But let's pretend that's the hand you've been dealt, that you or someone you love struggles with the things they've done in uniform. The problem is far more often that people *think* someone has done something regrettable and expect that person to act a certain way: "You have done something I think is wrong; you must feel how I would feel if I did that thing." It makes sense if you think about it. But most soldiers haven't done much of anything, and still get treated as though they have.

John 9 includes this story about how sin does (or does not) manifest. A man has been born blind and everybody thinks it is because his parents, or his parents' parents, or his parents' parents' parents, did something wrong. Even Jesus' disciples ask, "Who sinned, this man or his parents, that he was born blind?" (v. 2). We want to believe that bad people get punished, and blindness sure feels like punishment! When he is miraculously healed, everyone gets their panties in a knot trying to hold on to that equation—shitty circumstances come from shitty behavior, right?

The equation works in reverse too: if a veteran looks like they're having a hard time, they must have PTSD or moral injury. It feels right; it feels like that's how things are *supposed* to be. If my loved one won't talk to me, or if I don't hear what I expect to hear, then it must be because *they* have all this spiritual baggage from all the horrible shit (I think) they've done.

The religious elites try to get to the bottom of it, asking the man, his parents, and then the man again what happened. The guy is like, "I have told you already," WTF do you want from me? (see John 9:27). He seems to have the same karmic equation in his own head: "We know that God does not listen to sinners, but he does listen to one who worships him and obeys his will" (9:31). Whereas the man has experienced unearned grace, the holier-than-thous apparently have not.

What the man is saying is, "Jesus clearly obeys and worships God; otherwise, how could he have healed me?" The implication is too much for the experts to handle, not because the equation is wrong (it might be), but because *they* are wrong. The priestly caste, with their self-righteousness, can't appreciate God's grace. They need to feel in control, to have their hand on the steering wheel. At the end, rather than letting go of their myopic, formulaic prejudices, they are right back at square one: "You were born entirely in sin, and you are trying to teach us?" Well, actually, yeah.

The clue to unlocking the rigid pseudo-morality of the masses is right at the beginning. As soon as his disciples ask who sinned that the man was born blind, Jesus redirects the whole conversation: "He was born blind so that God's works might be revealed in him" (John 9:3). The man was an agent of God's glory, a walking testament to what God can do. So yeah, he *was* teaching them. Just like the trolls they are, the religious purists throw their hands up, repeat the same line they started with, and storm off in a huff.

The unnamed man was the work of God revealed. Who said anything about sin? We are supposed to leave sorting everyone's sins to God; that's why the tree we are forbidden to eat from is "the tree of the knowledge of good and evil" (Gen. 2:17). Religious purists like to throw around the line "If all you have is a hammer, all you see is nails." Well, if you've fetishized salvation, all you'll see is sinners.

Everybody has done shit they regret, soldiers and civilians alike. Sin is of one kind, even if it comes in different densities. Murder is worse than adultery, but the moral substance is the same. Christians should not be talking about military service, even if it *does* include killing in combat, any differently than they do other professions. Yes, some soldiers kill. And, I believe, that takes a significant toll on any human being. But that toll, that weight, belongs between God and that person. If you want to help carry it, don't bring your own baggage to throw on their shoulders as well.

And if you are that person carrying a heavy load, don't carry it alone. The church is God's hands and feet; share it with someone you trust. And when you do, don't expect to feel the same burden. Don't feel guilty when God, through the body of Christ, helps you on your march by lightening your load. There's no shame in being helped, so don't let people put you in a box you don't belong in; you might find yourself in a coffin if you try to help *others* feel better without making sure you do too. And that would be a terrible waste of God's glory being revealed through you. Because you *are* the good news.

Semper Familia

ACKNOWLEDGMENTS

This book would never have been possible without those courageous souls who heard me out, put up with me, and finally saw this book through. I am especially grateful to my agent, Kathleen Neindorff; and the editorial team at Hachette Nashville, including Kate Hartson, Sean McGowan, Alex Pappas, and publisher Daisy Hutton for believing in me and in what I am setting out to do.

I am also indebted to the scholars who did their best to check my work, offered suggestions for improving it, and helped me locate relevant research, including Christian Barthel, Chris Haw, Russell Johnson, David Moffitt, Jeff Porter, William Portier, Joshua Smith, Warren Smith, Vivian Taylor, Brandon Williams, and Christopher Zeichman. I could never have crossed the finish line without friends offering encouragement and support, including Jessica Andrews, Rachel Beard, Hillary Bylund, Carrie and Scott Hilmuth, Chris Lombardi, James McSavaney, Brian Meagher, Amber Noel, Titus Peachey, and Naaman Wood.

Of course, I cannot express with words how grateful I am for the loving support of my partner, Rev. Laura Isaac, and our family for lifting me up when I felt down and bringing me back to earth when I'd get lost in the clouds. As hard as I tried to be coherent in an incoherent time, I fear I have been only partially successful. Alas, the truth belongs to God. The mistakes are mine.

NOTES

WHISKEY TANGO FOXTROT
(A PROLOGUE)

1. "The Fascinating Beginning of the Term 'Grunt,'" We Are the Mighty, March 5, 2021, https://www.wearethemighty.com/mighty-history/the-fascinating-beginning -of-the-term-grunt/. The quote is credited to Major H. G. Duncan, likely in his hard-to-find self-published book *Green Side Out* (1997).

2. For the most up-to-date Veterans Affairs statistics, visit www.mentalhealth.va.gov /suicide_prevention/index.asp. The Defense Department equivalent shares data through the Defense Suicide Prevention Office at www.dspo.mil.

3. Office of Suicide Prevention, "Suicide among Veterans and Other Americans," August 3, 2016, 4.

4. Office of Suicide Prevention, 22.

5. Before Margaret Atwood's *The Handmaids Tale* popularized another, equally improper, version (*nolite te bastardes carborundorum*), General Joe Stillwell kept *illegitimi non carborundum* on his desk during and after WWI.

6. Watch her segment online at https://www.youtube.com/watch?v=ELo6VBDdfJ8.

7. Armen Keteyian, "Suicide Epidemic among Veterans," *CBS News*, November 13, 2007, www.cbsnews.com/news/suicide-epidemic-among-veterans-13-11-2007.

8. Some people prefer "died by suicide," but this takes away the person's agency. Depression can make someone feel powerless, and the tragic appeal of suicide includes the promise of control.

9. This is from a TikTok video I found while doom-scrolling, so getting lost in social media can't be all bad. He has a book, podcast, and Ted Talk, all of which can be found at www.AllTheRageScience.com.

10. Martin said this at a sermon given at the Temple Israel of Hollywood on February 26, 1965.

11. A student veteran I taught in the spring of 2016 remarked privately to me that he felt like other students in our section thought he "had STUPID stamped across [his] forehead."

12. One student veteran informed me that in a course on the Crusades, the professor associated modern soldiers with medieval pilgrim-warriors (see chapter 10 for more). Sensing that some might take offense, the professor implied it was okay to make the analogy because she had family in the military.

13. The alumni were General Walter Boomer, class of 1960; Admiral Frank Bowman, class of 1966; and Lieutenant General Emerson Gardner, class of 1970.

14. According to his LinkedIn profile, he's still there as of September 2021.

15. Lily Levin, "This is Duke," *Chronicle*, October 11, 2019, https://www.dukechronicle
    .com/article/2019/10/duke-this-is-duke.
16. Duke Today Staff, "Memorial Service for Alexander Ney on Monday," *Duke Today*,
    April 20, 2008, today.duke.edu/2008/04/ney.html. Who wants to bet that it
    disappears shortly after this book goes to press…?
17. To read more, see dukevets.wordpress.com/2017/11/20/ofccp-interview-relations
    -dean.
18. From email on April 21, 2016, at 8:21a.m. All quotes in the paragraph are from the
    same email.
19. Emailed to the professor's personal assistant, March 21, 2016.
20. Fannie gave this speech beside Malcolm X at the Williams Institutional CME Church
    in Harlem, New York, on December 20, 1964.

INTRO

1. All of this and more is covered in my free "Intro to the Military" course at www
   .PewPewSchool.com.
2. I explain all the various pronouns that servicemembers go by according to branch in
   my essay "What Is a Soldier: Pro(per) Nouns and Military Service" at https://pewpew
   .substack.com/p/soldier.
3. Title 38 US Code, Section 101(2).
4. Scott Gebicke and Samuel Magid, "Lessons from Around the World: Benchmarking
   Performance in Defense," *McKinsey on Government*, no. 5 (Spring 2010). Learn more
   about the so-called "tooth to tail ratio" at PewPewSchool.com.
5. Abraham Kaplan coined the "Law of the Instrument" in a February 1962 speech at
   UCLA, summarized by his quip, "Give a boy a hammer and everything he meets has
   to be pounded."

CHAPTER 1.
WHAT HAVE WE DONE?

1. Fred Wellman, a twenty-two-year Army retired officer and longtime veteran's
   advocate.
2. The May 2015 Instagram post, which originally tagged me, was subsequently deleted.
3. You must be a paying subscriber to view his Letter to the Editor at https://www
   .christianitytoday.com/ct/2015/september/reply-all.html.
4. Hilde Lindemann Nelson, *Damaged Identities, Narrative Repair* (Ithaca, NY: Cornell
   University Press, 2001).
5. My second book, *For God and Country (in That Order)* (Harrisonburg, VA: Herald,
   2013), profiled more than forty soldier-saints and patriot pacifists. I try to maintain a
   more comprehensive list of Pew Pew People at PewPewHQ.com/saints.
6. Check out the award-winning series in one place at PewPewHQ.com/ponder-ct.
7. Check out the mock-ups at https://twitter.com/i/events/1087051228884987904.
8. Scott Gebicke and Samuel Magid, "Lessons from Around the World: Benchmarking
   Performance in Defense," *McKinsey on Government*, no. 5 (Spring 2010): 4. The

report used different terminology of "Combat," "Support," and "Other." It also did not include Reserve or Guard forces. The average of thirty developed nations was 26 percent Combat, 11 percent Support, and 63 percent Other. For the US, the study found 16 percent Combat, 7 percent Support, and 77 percent Other. See "Intro to the Military" at PewPewSchool.com for more details.

9. "Fobbit" is military slang for a soldier who spends most of their time on Forward Operating Bases (FOBs) rather than outside the wire.

10. Tertullian, *Patience*, 5.15, https://ccel.org/ccel/tertullian/patience/anf03.vi.vii.v.html.

11. Saint Basil, *Collected Letters*, Letter 260, trans. Roy Joseph Deferrari (Loeb Classical Library), vol. 4, pp. 49–73.

12. Karin Orvis, *Quarterly Suicide Report (QSR) 1st Quarter, CY 2021*, DSPO. For the latest numbers, see www.dspo.mil/qsr.

13. *2020 National Veteran Suicide Prevention Annual Report* is accessible at www .mentalhealth.va.gov/mentalhealth/suicide_prevention/data.asp.

14. W. H. Auden, "As I Walked Out One Evening," https://poets.org/poem/i-walked -out-one-evening.

CHAPTER 2.
TYFYS

1. For example, military communities on Reddit regularly use TYFYS rather than Thank You For Your Service, and the entry for "TYFYS" on Urban Dictionary has more reactions than the one for "Thank You For Your Service."

2. Veterans Day Survey 2019, Cohen Veterans Network, https://www .cohenveteransnetwork.org/wp-content/uploads/2019/11/Press-Release-Veterans -Day-2019_Final-1.pdf.

3. You can read more at pewpew.substack.com/p/tyfys-performative.

4. Diana Rau, "What I Really Mean When I say Thank You For Your Service," *Forbes*, November 11, 2020, https://www.forbes.com/sites/dianatsai/2020/11/11/what-i -really-mean-when-i-say-thank-you-for-your-service.

5. Jan Bremmer, "Scapegoat Rituals in Ancient Greece," *Harvard Studies in Classical Philology* 87 (1983): 302.

6. Bremmer, "Scapegoat," 304.

7. The whole phrase in Exodus 12:5 is *seh tamiym zakar*. *Seh*, H7716, is not specifically a lamb, but rather any young herd animal, as distinguished from a bovine animal.

8. Augustine, Tractate IV-10, https://www.ccel.org/ccel/schaff/npnf107/npnf107 .iii.v.html.

9. Some English translations of Exodus 12:21 have "Passover lamb," but the Hebrew word is simply *pesach*, H6453, the same as 12:11, 27, 43, and 48.

10. The official title of rank-and-file imperial Roman soldiers was Miles Gregarious, from *grex*, meaning "herd or flock."

11. Jared Keller, "The Top Five Reasons Soldiers Really Join the Army, According to Junior Enlisted," *Task & Purpose*, May 14, 2018, https://taskandpurpose.com/joining -the-military/5-reasons-soldiers-join-army.

12. Meghann Myers, "Studies Tackle Who Joins the Military and Why, but Their Findings Aren't What Many Assume," *Military Times*, April 27, 2020, https://www.militarytimes.com/news/your-military/2020/04/27/studies-tackle-who-joins-the-military-and-why-but-their-findings-arent-what-many-assume.

13. According to the organization's website, www.veterati.com.

14. A 2018 sponsored post paid for by Forevermark, a jewelry retailer, https://www.theatlantic.com/sponsored/forevermark-2018/diana-rau-her-supporting-cast/1898/.

CHAPTER 3.
TO PROTECT AND SERVE

1. Carlson left the Army in 1916, going from an E-1 to an E-8, before reenlisting for WWI and receiving a battlefield commission to O-3. In 1922, he joined the Marines as an E-1 but was commissioned again and eventually retired as an O-7 in 1946.

2. Don Burke, "Carlson of the Raiders," *Life* 15 no. 12, September 20, 1943, 58.

3. James Clark, "Marine NCO Delivers the Most 'Moto' Speech of All Time," *Task & Purpose*, September 16, 2016, askandpurpose.com/humor/marine-nco-delivers-moto-speech-time.

4. In Hebrew, he is *sar* (captain) *tsaba* (assembly). The Greek has *archistrátigos*, a complex combination of *arche* (top, example); *stratos* (army); and *agos* (leader).

5. See chapter 1 on Cain for more on *arche* and types.

6. Regina Varolli, "My Mom Wrote the Motto 'To Protect and To Serve," *Culinary Epicenter*, June 2, 2020, https://www.culinaryepicenter.com/my-mom-wrote-the-motto-to-protect-and-to-serve.

7. Genesis 2:15 uses verbs: *abad* and *shamar* in Hebrew, and *ergazomai* and *phylasso* in Greek. The noun form of *phylasso* is *phylax* (G5441).

8. The same is true for the Greek word *stratiotes* (G4757), which appears in the New Testament as "soldier." It comes from the primitive root *stratos*, meaning "arrangement or layered" (i.e., the stratosphere), which epic poetry used to describe commoners who could be called upon to serve.

9. 10 USC § 7062 records three preceding capabilities: "(1) preserving the peace and security… (2) supporting the national policies; (3) implementing the national objectives."

10. In Genesis 2:1, the NRSV translates *tsaba* as "multitude."

11. In Exodus 6:26, the NRSV translates *tsaba* as "companies."

12. "Blue Falcon" is military slang for Buddy Fucker, also known as Bravo Fox; someone who betrays their battle buddies. Ironically, it is also the mascot for the infantry battalion I was attached to as a paratrooper, the 3-325 Parachute Infantry Regiment. The first and second battalions were red and white falcons.

CHAPTER 4.
IF JESUS IS GOD, THEN GOD IS A GRUNT

1. Zerubbabel is mentioned as Jesus' ancestor in the genealogies of Matthew and Luke, and became the first governor of *Yehud Medinata*, the Persian province that included the historic Promised Land.
2. According to Josephus, the Zealots had "an inviolable attachment to liberty" and represented a fourth political party, after the Sadducees, Pharisees, and Essenes. They were founded by Judas of Galilee, an insurrectionist who opposed the census of Quirinius that forced the holy family to Bethlehem, Joseph's ancestral home.
3. Matthew 10:3 identifies the apostle as a tax collector, but it may not be the same individual who composed the gospel bearing that same name.
4. To learn more, read my essay "Roman Military Structure" at pewpew.substack.com /p/roman-military-structure.
5. In Genesis 32:28 and 35:10 Jacob is renamed Israel, meaning "wrestles with God."
6. Numbers 2 lays out the procedure for marching and encampment.
7. A combination of H7626 (wand or staff) and H5608 (scribe or accountant).
8. David Grove, "Why the term 'every Marine is a rifleman first' needs to stop," *We Are the Mighty*, May 18, 2019.
9. Vernon Loeb, "Army Plans Steps to Heighten 'Warrior Ethos,'" *Washington Post*, September 8, 2003.
10. FM 3-21.75 (originally published January 2008), page 1-1. Title 10 USC § 7062 lists three organizational capabilities that precede "overcoming any nations responsible for aggressive acts."
11. Tremper Longman III and Daniel G. Reid, *God Is a Warrior* (Grand Rapids, MI: Zondervan, 1995).
12. This motif is scattered through a few chapters of Isaiah, but the most popular for Christians is chapter 53.
13. Read more about Saul's letter to military communities at pewpew.substack.com/p /philippians.
14. Read my essay about the armor of God at pewpew.substack.com/p/armor. An academic resource I found helpful is Tom Neufeld's *Put on the Armour of God: The Divine Warrior from Isaiah to Ephesians* (Sheffield: Sheffield Academic Press, 1997).

CHAPTER 5:
EARLY ATTITUDES, OR *THE EARLIEST* ATTITUDES?

1. "Great President…or Greatest President?" *The Colbert Report*, season 4, Comedy Central, 2008, cc.com/video/d5rh5f/the-colbert-report-great-president-or-greatest -president.
2. Richard B. Hays, *The Moral Vision of the New Testament: A Contemporary Introduction to New Testament Ethics* (San Francisco: HarperSanFrancisco, 1996), 335.
3. "Stephen Colbert, For Real." *CBS News*, CBS, September 6, 2015, cbsnews.com /news/stephen-colbert-for-real.
4. Andy Alexis-Baker, "What about the Centurion?" in *A Faith Not Worth Fighting For*,

ed. Tripp York and Justin Bronson Barringer (Eugene, OR: Wipf and Stock, 2012), 174.

5. Hays, *Moral Vision*, 337 (emphasis added).

6. Richard B. Hays, "Narrate and Embody: A Response to Nigel Biggar," *Studies in Christian Ethics* 22, no. 2 (May 2009): 187.

7. Hays, *Moral Vision*, 335.

8. George Kalantzis, *Caesar and the Lamb: Early Christian Attitudes on War and Military Service* (Eugene, OR: Wipf and Stock, 2012), 8.

9. I have more in my essay at pewpew.substack.com/p/roman-military-structure. I owe much in this chapter to Christopher Zeichmann's *The Roman Army and the New Testament* (Lanham, MD: Fortress, 2018).

10. Zeichmann, *Roman Army and the New Testament*, 6. He is also the editor of *Essential Essays for the Study of the Military in First-Century Palestine* (Eugene, OR: Wipf and Stock, 2019), which highlights two underappreciated essays on GI Jews. The first is "Jewish Military Forces in the Roman Service," written by Jonathan Roth in 2004; and "Sons of Israel in Caesar's Service: Jewish Soldiers in the Roman Military," written by Andrew Schoenfield in 2006.

11. Zerubbabel is listed as Jesus' ancestor in Matthew 1:12–13 and Luke 3:27, meaning John's and Jesus' families had been collaborating for five hundred years before they were even born.

12. Zeichmann, *Roman Army and the New Testament*, 76–78.

13. Alex Kyrychenko agrees in his PhD dissertation, *The Roman Army and the Expansion of the Gospel: The Role of the Centurion in Luke-Acts* (Boston: De Gruyter, 2014), 147n7.

14. The nobleman described in Luke 9:11–27 is Archelaus. Don't let Dave Ramsey bullshit you; the parable of the pounds is not about saving money. The "wicked" servant who buried the cash is a satirical device to expose the evilness of the nobleman, like the main "character" of the *Colbert Report*. Everyone in Jesus' audience knows he is poking fun at the recently deposed Archelaus because it happened *in their lifetime*.

15. Zeichmann, Kyrychenko, and Laurie Brink (2014, see note 17 below) all agree it is the second cohort of two stationed in Syria at the time the story takes place. The only disagreement is the precise name of the unit. See also Nikko Huttunen, "Brothers in Arms: Soldiers in Early Christianity," chapter 4 of his *Early Christians Adapting to the Roman Empire* (Brill, 2020), 138–228.

16. Kyrychenko, *Roman Army and the Expansion*, 164n84.

17. Laurie Brink gives the most detail of this possibility, pointing out that rather than trying to locate a unit within a certain time and place, it may simply be a historical fact, rather than current status. *Soldiers in Luke-Acts: Engaging, Contradicting, and Transcending the Stereotypes* (Tübingen: Mohr Siebeck, 2014), 151.

18. See Acts 3:1, where Peter and John go to the temple to pray. As for Cornelius, Acts 10:2 mentions that he prays immediately before noting the time of day. The implication is that he was praying when the vision occurred.

19. Aristotle's *Politics* is the most relevant example.

20. Brink, *Soldiers*, 152.

21. *Lictores*, the Latin equivalent, were men who carried the *fasces*, the symbol of Roman power and an instrument that represented the death penalty.

22. Some English Bibles have "Sirs," but the Greek is *kyrioi*, the plural form of *kyrios* (G2962), "Lord."

23. For more on this, see my essay "Saul's Letter to Veterans" in *Mennonite World Review*, December 7, 2016, anabaptistworld.org/pauls-letter-to-veterans. For an updated version, see pewpew.substack.com/p/philippians.

CHAPTER 6.
FREEDOM ISN'T FREE

1. Joseph's brother Benjamin was the youngest of Jacob's sons. The boy may have been denied special status because his birth was connected to Rachel's death.

2. Unlike most genealogies in the Bible, Genesis 11:26–27 does not list the birth order for Terah's three sons, Abram, Nahor, and Haran.

3. God addresses Cain without prompting in Genesis 4:6–7, whereas Abel never speaks or is spoken to, even by his own parents.

4. This word was used by a veteran friend who moved to another country after serving in combat. Fully aware that expatriate was a thing, he preferred "ex-patriot" because it did not hide its meaning behind fancy linguistics.

5. Carl Forsling has two really good pieces that explore military entitlement at *Task & Purpose*, "Unpacking the Veteran Entitlement Spectrum" (October 6, 2014); and "Military Families Need to Get Over Their Sense of Entitlement" (March 25, 2015).

6. Zeichmann sees no evidence, but Brink supplies the example provided here.

7. Laurie Brink, *Soldiers in Luke-Acts: Engaging, Contradicting, and Transcending the Stereotypes* (Tübingen: Mohr Siebeck, 2014), 115.

8. King Saul is identified as "a Benjaminite" in 1 Samuel 9:2; and the apostle Saul says he is "a member of the tribe of Benjamin" in Romans 11:1.

9. Saul will later point out, in Romans 4, that the agreement preceded circumcision; that covenant and circumcision were not one and the same.

10. For more information on what it means to be a Christian, listen to the "What Is a Christian" episode on PonderXchange.com.

11. Jerome in his *Commentary on Philemon*; and Photios in question 116 of his *Amphilochia*.

12. Peggy McIntosh, "White Privilege: Unpacking the Invisible Knapsack," *Peace and Freedom* (July/August 1989), https://nationalseedproject.org/Key-SEED-Texts/white-privilege-unpacking-the-invisible-knapsack.

13. Editors usually title essays and articles, even books if an author isn't very creative, but not in this case. Two years after *Reborn on the Fourth of July* was published, *Faith and Leadership* just slapped that title onto my June 2015 article, https://faithandleadership.com/logan-mehl-laituri-isaac-reborn-fourth-july.

CHAPTER 7.
DEATH BEFORE IDOLATRY

1. The Imperial Rescript on Education was memorized by schoolchildren from 1890 until it was abolished by Allied occupation authorities in 1948. It included the imperative that all citizens "should emergency arise, offer yourselves courageously to the State; and thus guard and maintain the prosperity of Our Imperial Throne coeval with heaven and earth." During the war, "kamikaze" was used in the press for the informal pronunciation of *shinpu*, or "divine wind."

2. To learn more about martial virtues, check out "The Virtues of War" at PewPewSchool.com.

3. Nancy Sherman, *Stoic Warriors: The Ancient Philosophy behind the Military Mind* (Oxford: Oxford University Press, 2005), ix.

4. Sherman, *Stoic Warriors*, ix. The abbreviated description of hers I've quoted here does not necessarily represent the scholarly consensus, but few philosophers have had as much of an impact on the American military apparatus as Sherman.

5. *Forrest Gump*, directed by Robert Zemeckis (Universal, 1994).

6. *Odes*, bk. 3, poem 2.

7. Adapted from Plutarch, "Sayings of Spartan Women," *Moralia* 241F. A Spartan mother to her child: "Either this or upon this."

8. See Plutarch's *Moralia*, section 235A, in which a family welcomes their dead son upon his shield.

9. Owen, *Dulce et Decorum Est*, https://poets.org/poem/dulce-et-decorum-est.

10. Owen, *The Parable of the Old Man and the Young*, https://poets.org/poem/parable -old-man-and-young.

11. Owen's poems were published posthumously by friends sometime in 1920. The amphitheater was dedicated in May of that year.

12. *Odes*, bk. 2, poem 7.

13. The Septuagint, a Greek version of the Hebrew Scriptures, uses *martys* for *ed* (H5707), meaning "witness."

14. Luke 22:71 uses *martyria* (G3141), "testimony," and substitutes "the Sanhedrin" for Caiaphas.

15. Josephus, *Antiquities of the Jews*, 9.1.

16. Tacitus, *Annals*, 15.44.

17. See "Pliny, *Letters*, 10.96–97," https://faculty.georgetown.edu/jod/texts/pliny.html.

18. Eusebius, *Ecclesiastical History*, bk. 5, chap. 1, https://ccel.org/ccel/schaff/npnf201 /npnf201.iii.x.ii.html.

19. Eusebius, *Ecclesiastical History*, bk. 5, chap. 5, https://ccel.org/ccel/schaff/npnf201 /npnf201.iii.x.vi.html.

20. *Roman History*, bk. 72, chap. 8, https://penelope.uchicago.edu/Thayer/E/Roman /Texts/Cassius_Dio/72*.html.

21. Tacitus, *Annals*, 15.44, https://penelope.uchicago.edu/Thayer/E/Roman/Texts /Tacitus/Annals/15B*.html.

22. Lactantius, *On the Deaths of the Persecutors*, chap. 10. The rituals involved human or animal sacrifice, and it isn't clear if the Christians were crossing themselves out of disgust or participation. The Roman imagination was inclusive of gods, and they may well have seen themselves as participants. On the other hand, the Jerusalem Council made sacrifices one of two primary prohibitions for Gentile Christians.

23. Eusebius, *Ecclesiastical History*, bk. 8, chap. 1.8, https://ccel.org/ccel/schaff/npnf201 /npnf201.iii.xiii.ii.html.

24. Tertullian, *Apology*, chap. 50, https://www.ccel.org/ccel/schaff/anf03.iv.iii.l.html.

25. Lactantius, *On the Deaths of the Persecutors*, chap. 13, https://ccel.org/ccel/lactantius /persecutors/anf07.iii.v.xiii.html.

26. Eusebius, *Ecclesiastical History*, bk. 8, chap. 5, https://ccel.org/ccel/schaff/npnf201 /npnf201.iii.xiii.vi.html.

27. Author unknown, "Quintus the Apostate," *Martyrdom of Polycarp*, chap. 4, https: //ccel.org/ccel/polycarp/martyrdom_of_polycarp/anf01.iv.iv.iv.html.

28. Jonathan Merritt, "In the Middle East, Not America, Christians Are Actually Persecuted," *Religion News Service*, April 3, 2013.

29. Lactantius, *On the Deaths*, chap. 13.

30. Samantha Riches, *St. George: Hero, Martyr, and Myth* (Gloucestershire: Sutton, 2000). See Table 2, p. 219.

CHAPTER 8.
LIFE, LITURGY, AND THE PURSUIT OF HOLINESS

1. CFR Editors, "Demographics of the US Military," Backgrounder, *Council on Foreign Relations*, July 13, 2020, cfr.org/backgrounder/demographics-us-military.

2. "2010 Census Results, Population Density by County or County Equivalent," Census Bureau, https://www2.census.gov/geo/pdfs/maps-data/maps/thematic /us_popdensity_2010map.pdf.

3. National Center for Veterans Analysis and Statistics, "Age/Gender" table, https: //www.va.gov/vetdata/veteran_population.asp.

4. Virginia sends a high ratio of enlistees, is relatively dense, *and* maintains a high veteran concentration.

5. Ruth Igielnik and Kim Parker, "Majorities of U.S. Veterans, Public Say the Wars in Iraq and Afghanistan Were Not Worth Fighting," Pew Research Center, July 10, 2019, pewresearch.org/fact-tank/2019/07/10/majorities-of-u-s-veterans-public-say -the-wars-in-iraq-and-afghanistan-were-not-worth-fighting.

6. Stephen Goranson, "Others and Intra-Jewish Polemic as Reflected in Qumran Texts," in *The Dead Sea Scrolls after Fifty Years: A Comprehensive Assessment*, vol. 2, ed. Peter W. Flint and James C. Vanderkam (Leiden: Brill, 1999), 539 (emphasis added).

7. Theodoret of Cyrrhus, *A History of the Monks of Syria*, trans. Richard Price (Kalamazoo, MI: Cistercian, 1985), xx.

8. Daniel Caner, *Wandering, Begging Monks: Spiritual Authority and the Promotion of Monasticism in Late Antiquity* (Berkeley: University of California Press, 2002), 56.

9. Athanasius did not title his treatise on Antony, but he states in the prologue that he has been asked to describe *tes politeia tou makarios Antoniou*. Some translators render the phrase "the way of life of blessed Antony," but *politeia* literally means "politics," as in, *The Politics of Blessed Antony*. Read it for yourself at ccel.org/ccel/schaff/npnf204 .xvi.ii.i.html.

10. Athanasius, *Vita Antonii*, chap. 1, https://ccel.org/ccel/schaff/npnf204/npnf204.xvi .ii.iii.html.

11. Ibid.

12. . The Latin title is *Vita Pauli primi eremitae*, accessible in English at ccel.org/ccel /schaff/npnf206.vi.i.html.

13. Jerome, *Vita Pauli*, chap. 2.

14. Jerome, *Vita Pauli*, chap. 5.

15. Jerome, *Vita Pauli*, chap. 13.

16. Eusebius, *Ecclesiastical History*, I.7.11, 13, 14.

17. Compare ναζιραῖον (Judges) and Ναζωραῖος (Matthew). The difference is grammatical; it is the same word and essentially the same pronunciation.

18. Eusebius borrows from a fragment of Hegesippus's *Hypomnemata*, Memoirs, written no later than 180 CE. See *Ecclesiastical History*, bk. 2, chap. 23.5, https://www.ccel .org/ccel/schaff/npnf201.iii.vii.xxiv.html.

19. A klick is one kilometer in military slang.

20. *De Re Militari*, an English version is available to read at digitalattic.org/home/war /vegetius.

21. A rubber duckie is the name given in the Army to heavy plastic or rubber model M16s. Just like betters warm up by using weights, rubber duckies are heavier than the real thing.

22. This is the title of chapter 2 of Paul Dilley's *Monasteries and the Care of Souls in Late Antique Christianity: Cognition and Discipline* (Cambridge 2017), quoted in Barthel, "In Militia Dei?," 8n32.

23. Christian Barthel, "In Militia Dei? A Sociohistorical Perspective on the Pachomian Koinonia," *Zeitschrift für Antikes Christentum* 25, no. 3 (Dec. 2021), 19–20 pre-publication pagination.

24. The Monastery of St Antony is still there, though probably not at the exact site.

25. Jerome, *Vita Pauli*, chap. 8, describing Anthony's journey to see Paul.

26. Barthel, "In Militia Dei?," 7 pre-publication pagination.

CHAPTER 9.
"I AM A SOLDIER OF CHRIST"

1. *De Corona Milites*, bk. 11, ccel.org/ccel/tertullian/corona/anf03.iv.vi.xi.html.

2. *Against Praxeas*, ccel.org/ccel/tertullian/against_praxeas/anf03.v.ix.i.html.

3. The year of Martin's birth is disputed, and scholars do not agree if it was 316 or 336. Tours, the city in France where he served as bishop for thirty-six years, maintains his birth was the former. That's good enough for me.

4. Sulpicius Severus, *Vita Martini*, chap. 2, https://www.hospstmartin.org/vita/#ch2.

5. Sulpicius claims Martin served under both Constantine and Julian, without providing details by which to verify either claim. Assuming the 316 timeline, the episode with the cape would have occurred before Constantine's death in 337.

6. If he was inducted at fifteen, his military service began in 331, placing him at Worms in the final year of a twenty-five-year requirement.

7. Sulpicius, *Vita Martini*, chap. 4; https://www.hospstmartin.org/vita/#ch4.

8. You can also check out my course "Intro to the Military" at PewPewSchool.com.

9. John Chrysostom, "On Saints Juventinus and Maximinus," in *The Cult of the Saints*, trans. Wendy Mayer (Crestwood, NY: St. Vladimir's Seminary Press, 2006), 89–99.

10. Quoted in James Wm. McClendon Jr., *Biography as Theology: How Life Stories Can Remake Today's Theology* (Eugene, OR: Wipf and Stock, 2002), 84.

11. Sulpicius, *Vita Martini*, chap. 4, https://www.hospstmartin.org/vita/#ch4.

12. Alan Jacobs, *Looking Before and After: Testimony and the Christian Life* (Grand Rapids, MI: Eerdmans, 2008), 78.

13. Sulpicius claims in chapter 6 of his second Dialogue that the emperor Maximus's wife, whose name is not recorded, was a devoted follower of Martin's and was catechized by him.

14. *Vita Martini*, chap. 9, www.hospstmartin.org/vita/ch9.

15. Severus mentions this in passing in his *Sacred History* in bk. 2, chap. 51, ccel.org/ccel /schaff/npnf211/npnf211.ii.vi.ii.li.html. Ambrose admits to it himself in Letter 24.12, https://www.gutenberg.org/files/58783/58783-h/58783-h.htm#b176.

16. The *Bibliotheca Hagiographica* is in three language groups: *Latina* (Latin); *Graeca* (Greek); and *Orientalis* (Middle/Eastern languages).

17. Hippolyte Delehaye, trans. V. M. Crawford, *The Legends of the Saints: An Introduction to Hagiography,* (London: Longmans, Green, 1907), 17.

18. John's gospel is not one of the three "Synoptics" and stands out for its highly developed theological agenda.

19. The townsfolk continue to celebrate the theft of Martin's corpse. Or at least they did when I was there on pilgrimage for the seventeen hundredth anniversary of his birth, in November 2016.

20. Jean-Pierre Brunterch, *Un Village au temps de Charlemagne: Moines et paysans de l'abbaye de Saint-Denis, du VIIe siècle à l'an mil* (Musée national des arts et traditions, 1988), 90–93.

CHAPTER 10.
"FOLLOW ME!"

1. Although the precise order is disputed, the scholarly consensus is that John's gospel was composed last.

2. Although the *Gesta* was the first eyewitness account to be published, its version of Pope Urban II's sermon is seen as less reliable than Fulcher of Chartes' 1106 account, which I've used here, https://sourcebooks.fordham.edu/source/urban2-5vers.asp#Fulcher.

3. Rosalind M. Hill's *Gesta* translation (Oxford, 1962) is featured on Fordham's Medieval Sourcebook, https://sourcebooks.fordham.edu/source/gesta-cde.asp#urban.
4. The anonymous "Bordeaux Itinerary" was written just twenty-one years after Christianity was legalized. An 1887 English translation by Aubrey Stewart is in the public domain and can be found at https://archive.org/details/cu31924028534158.
5. See Fulcher of Chartes' account of Pope Urban II's speech at the Council of Clermont, from note 2, above.
6. Bonaventure, *The Life of Blessed Francis*, chap. 11. See Regis J. Armstrong (ed), *Francis of Assisi, Early Documents, Vol.2: The Founder* (Hyde Park, NY: New City Press, 2002), 614, https://www.franciscantradition.org/francis-of-assisi-early-documents/the-founder/the-legends-and-sermons-about-saint-francis-by-bonaventure-of-bagnoregio/the-major-legend-of-saint-francis/the-life-of-blessed-francis/1703-fa-ed-2-page-614.
7. Celano, *First Life of Saint Francis*, Part 1, chap. 30, part 84, https://dmdhist.sitehost.iu.edu/francis.htm#1.30.
8. Ibid. (emphasis added).
9. Ibid.
10. The best resource on the history of the stations is Herbert Thurston, *The Stations of the Cross: An Account of Their History and Devotional Purpose* (London: Burns & Oats, 1914), https://archive.org/details/stationsofcrossa00thuruoft.
11. From Hill's translation. See note 3, above.
12. Augustine Thompson, *Francis of Assisi: A New Biography* (Ithaca, NY: Cornell, 2012), 10.
13. Thompson, *Francis*, 11, 178.
14. Thompson, *Francis*, 13.
15. These are the distinct chrisms of the Hospitallers of Saint Martin. Learn more at https://www.hospstmartin.org.

CHAPTER 11.
WELL-BEHAVED VETERANS SELDOM MAKE HISTORY

1. Technically, Barak insists she go "with" him in Judges 4:8, maybe as equals. But verse 14 makes it *very* clear that she is in command; it is she who issues the order to engage.
2. Margaret's life is hard to pin down, but Eusebius may be speaking of Catherine in his *Ecclesiastical History*, bk. 8, chap. 4, sec. 15–16, which I have quoted here. Accessible online at https://ccel.org/ccel/schaff/npnf201/npnf201.iii.xiii.xv.html.
3. Fourth public examination, held February 27, 1430, https://www.jeanne-darc.info/trial-of-condemnation-index/trial-condemnation-fourth-public-examination.
4. It must be said that the same word eventually was used by Victorian types to dehumanize men who violated gender norms by liking other men. By failing to be "straight," gender variant people are seen as abominations by self-righteous pricks who haven't read their Bible. The fact is that none of us are "straight," we're all just as crooked as the next.

5. See as examples First Lieutenant Daniel K. Inouye (WWII); Airman First Class William H. Pitsenbarger (Vietnam); or Lance Corporal W. Kyle Carpenter (OEF).
6. Joan made open threats against the English every month she was at Orléans. My favorite was delivered to the English forces by a French archer on May 5, 1429, http://archive.joan-of-arc.org/joanofarc_letter_May_5_1429.html.
7. The Rev. Dr. Esau McCaulley was working on his PhD while I was in the Master of Letters program at the University of St. Andrews. Because he had not defended his PhD thesis at the time of the vigil, I omitted "Dr." from this specific reference.
8. Esau McCaulley, *Reading While Black: African American Biblical Interpretation as an Exercise in Hope* (Downers Grove, IL: InterVarsity Press, 2020).

CHAPTER 12.
GET THE FUCK UP AND PRAY

1. Chairman of the Joint Chiefs of Staff Instruction (CJCSI) 3405.01, updated September 23, 2013, https://www.jcs.mil/Portals/36/Documents/Library/Instructions/3405_01.pdf.
2. CJCSI 3405.01, page A-2. A 2021 planned reboot of the TFF framework, still being unveiled, has revised the domain to "Ideological and Spiritual Fitness." Not all Defense assets reflect this change, but updates will likely be posted to https://www.health.mil/Military-Health-Topics/Total-Force-Fitness/Ideological-and-Spiritual-Fitness.
3. *First Formation* is also the name of a morning prayer podcast I have hosted for several years. Check it out wherever you listen to podcasts!
4. John Merkle, ed., *Abraham Joshua Heschel: Exploring His Life and Thought* (New York: Macmillan, 1985), 17.
5. The epic poem *Canso de la crozada*, or Song of the (Albigensian) Crusade, was first published in 1213 by William of Tudela.
6. The last was the Portuguese Crusade in 1481.
7. John Skow, "Carnography," review of *Rambo: First Blood*, by David Morrell, *Time*, May 29, 1972. Skow coined the term "carnography," which means an excessive and indulgent display of violence in literature.
8. Ignatius did not dictate a title for his testimony, but the English edition I prefer is *A Pilgrim's Journey*, trans. Joseph Tylenda (Ignatius Press, 1985).
9. Ignatius, *Pilgrim's Journey*, 58.
10. William Goldman, *The Princess Bride: S. Morgenstern's Classic Tale of True Love and High Adventure* (London: Bloomsbury, 1973)
11. The New Testament does not contain the word "Christianity," but does refer to *hodos* (G3598), a path or journey, as a proper noun that named the whole community of Jewish and Gentile Christians.
12. Quotations all come from Sue Burke, *Amadis of Gaul*, bk. 4 (BurglarHouse Books, 2018), https://amadisofgaul.blogspot.com/2017/05/chapter-133-part-3-of-3.html.
13. Ignatius, *Pilgrim's Journey*, 60.

14. The Virgin of Montserrat's dark color is attributed to its great age and the effects of candle and incense smoke. It once bore an inscription in Latin: "Nigra Sum Sed Formosa" (I am Black and beautiful).

15. According to the VA, "Only 15% of student Veterans are the traditional age of college students. Most student Veterans are ages 24–40," https://www.mentalhealth.va.gov /student-veteran/docs/VAM-061-VITAL-Characteristics-of-Student-Veterans-1-0 -508.pdf.

16. Ignatius of Loyola, *The Spiritual Exercises of St Ignatius of Loyola*, trans. Elder Mullan (P. J. Kenedy & Sons, 1914), 11, https://ccel.org/ccel/ignatius/exercises/exercises .ix.html.

17. Ignatius of Loyola, *Spiritual Exercises*, 4, https://ccel.org/ccel/ignatius/exercises /exercises.iii.html.

18. Boston College's Institute for Advanced Jesuit Studies provides the English version online at https://jesuitportal.bc.edu/research/documents/1539_fivechapters/.

CHAPTER 13.
"AIN'T I AMERICAN?"

1. The titular line does not appear in an 1851 version published months after the speech, only in an 1863 version.

2. Christopher S. Parker, *Fighting for Democracy: Black Veterans and the Struggle against White Supremacy in the Postwar South* (Princeton, NJ: Princeton University Press, 2009), 18.

3. Benjamin Quarles, *The Negro in the American Revolution* (Chapel Hill, NC: University of North Carolina Press, 1961), 183.

4. U.S. Reports: *Dred Scott v. Sandford*, 60 U.S. (19 How.) 393 (1856), 420; https: //www.loc.gov/item/usrep060393a.

5. Parker, *Fighting*, 24.

6. Frederick Douglass, "What the Black Man Wants," given at the 1865 Annual Meeting of the Massachusetts Anti-Slavery Society; www.blackpast.org/african -american-history/1865-frederick-douglass-what-black-man-wants.

7. Lucia K. Knoles, "Civil Rights: Speech of Hon. Benjamin F. Butler, of Massachusetts, in the House of Representatives, January 7, 1874," *American Antiquarian Society*; www .americanantiquarian.org/Freedmen/Manuscripts/Broadsides/butlercivilrights.html.

8. Editorial, *The Crisis* 16, no. 5 (September 1918): 217, https://modjourn.org/issue /bdr511442.

9. William Jordan, "'The Damnable Dilemma': African-American Accommodation and Protest during WWI," *Journal of American History* 81, no. 4 (March 1995).

10. National Association for the Advancement of Colored People, "Opinion of W.E.B. Du Bois: Returning Soldiers," *The Crisis* 18, no. 1 (May 1919): 24.

11. Alex Mills, "A Lynching Kept Out of Sight," *Washington Post*, September 2, 2016, https://www.washingtonpost.com/sf/national/2016/09/02/the-story-of-the-only -known-lynching-on-a-u-s-military-base/.

12. "Dead Soldier Revealed as Montgomery Youth," *Huntsville Times*, April 8, 1941.
13. His draft card cites his birthdate as December 1, 1909. That puts him a couple of months shy of his thirtieth birthday when he was registered for the draft on October 16, 1940. He was inducted a few weeks after his thirty-fourth birthday, on December 31, 1943.
14. Scott Ellsworth, "Jim Crow Loses: The Secret Game," *New York Times Magazine*, March 31, 1996. Ellsworth states, "That same year, a black G.I. had been killed," but the wording is misleading. Booker was killed four months *after* the game, on July 8, 1944. Reprinted by NCCU at https://nccueaglepride.com/sports/2011/3/8 /MBB_0308110905.aspx.
15. The attending physician at Duke Hospital indicated "homicide" on Booker's death certificate and marked "yes" in answer to a question of whether the killing of a uniformed servicemember occurred "While at work."
16. News of Council's acquittal was carried by the *Dothan Eagle* and the *Selma Times-Journal* on September 17, 1944. Durham's own Black paper, the *Carolina Times*, probably reported on the murder of Spicely. It cannot be known for certain because much of its archive was lost to arson in 1979.
17. Where possible, I have adapted references to military rank to reflect current structure. Ralph was a platoon sergeant, the equivalent of a sergeant first class.
18. Ralph Abernathy, *And the Walls Came Tumbling Down* (New York: Harper & Row, 1989).
19. Abernathy, *And the Walls*, 33.
20. Before 1948, soldiers could continue to increase their rank and pay without the burden of command authority as Technicians, later referred to as Specialists. Contrary to popular belief, Medgar was not discharged as a noncommissioned officer, but rather as a Technician Fifth Grade. That is the rank recorded both on his military records and on his gravesite at Arlington National Cemetary.
21. Dovey Johnson Roundtree and Katie McCabe, *Mighty Justice: My Life in Civil Rights* (Chapel Hill, NC: Algonquin, 2019), 65.
22. Military records indicate an enlistment date of May 16, 1945.
23. University of West Georgia, "Oral Interview with Hosea Williams," May 15, 1998, https://ohms.libs.uga.edu/viewer.php?cachefile=dlg/phc/williams19980515.xml. Hosea claims to have lied about his age to enlist in 1944, but if his birthday was January 6, 1926, then he would have been nineteen years old. He also claims to have been injured by the Germans in the same interview, but only the Pacific theater would have still seen combat by the time he completed basic training.
24. Selectees were drafted "for the duration of the war...plus six months." WWII ended in August 1945, so conscripts would have to be mustered out before the end of February 1946. On a few occasions, Hosea claims he volunteered for service, but his records do not appear to reflect this. Pvt. Felix Hall, for example, is identified as "Regular Army" rather than "Selectees (Enlisted Man)," but that does not confirm whether he entered service voluntarily or not.

25. Ibid.

26. Robert F. Williams, *Negroes with Guns* (Detroit, MI: Wayne State University Press, 1998), 14.

27. Some stories identify her hometown as Keysville, North Carolina, but the Army site would have access to her home of record. T. Anthony Bell, "The Quietly Defiant, Unlikely Fighter: PFC Sarah Keys and the Fight for Justice and Humanity," US Army, February 25, 2014, www.army.mil/article/120456/the_quietly_defiant _unlikely_fighter_pfc_sarah_keys_and_the_fight_for_justice_and_humanity.

28. Abernathy, *And the Walls*, 143.

29. November 11 had been Armistice Day, in remembrance of the treaty, or armistice, that ended WWI in 1918. But on June 1, 1954, it was renamed "Veterans Day" by an act of Congress, making November 11, 1954, the first, and the second in 1955.

30. Ralph was born David Abernathy, but the name stuck after his sister Manerva began using it when he was twelve. Six years later he entered the military as Ralph David Abernathy, but his birth certificate was never changed. In so far as Martin was assassinated and Ralph lived a long life, the former represents Jonathan and the latter David.

31. Abernathy, *And the Walls*, 495.

32. In May 1931, Pius XI renewed interest in Catholic social justice by publishing *Quadragesimo anno* on the fortieth anniversary of *Rerum Novarum*.

33. "National Affairs: Cox's Army," *Time*, January 18, 1932, http://content.time.com /time/subscriber/article/0,33009,742927,00.html. His march came seven months after *Quadragesimo anno*.

34. On two separate occasions in August 1943, Patton slapped privates recuperating from what was then referred to as "shell shock." One had served four years and had just seen a friend killed beside him. Eisenhower forced Patton to apologize but did not relieve him of duty.

35. One Christian influencer literally asked me for the CBS link for no other reason than to use it as a footnote in a book. Like Superman, able to leap from evidence to conclusion in a single bound!

36. From @RevDrBarer, November 11, 2017, https://twitter.com/RevDrBarber/status /929370871336235008.

37. Logan Isaac, "Veterans Deserve Civil Rights Protections Too," *The Hill*, November 8, 2017, https://thehill.com/opinion/civil-rights/359398-veterans-deserve-civil-rights -protections-too.

38. Email to Jonathan Wilson-Hartgrove, June 30, 2016.

39. See https://www.poorpeoplescampaign.org/about/our-principles.

SPIT SHINING A MIRROR, DIMLY

1. Neil Sheehan, "Guardsmen Cope with Simulated Rioting to Learn New Control Techniques," *New York Times*, August 27, 1967.

2. James Reston, "Everyone Is a Loser," *New York Times*, October 23, 1967.

3. Dale Pullen, "Marines Lose Campus Battle," *Playground Daily News*, June 16, 1969, 10.
4. Tom Tiede, "Medal of Honor Winners Find Themselves Subjected to Abuse," *Sheboygan Press*, March 16, 1968, 5.
5. For the *New York Times*: Ken W. Clawson, "Veterans for a Just Peace' Formed to Offset Kerry Unit," June 2, 1971; Alfred Fitt, "The Lack of a Defined Goal... Bothered Me Most," September 15, 1971.
6. Alexander Holmes. "'Silent Majority' of Veterans Organize to Counter Publicity Given Protesters," *Reno Gazette Journal*, June 9, 1971, 4.
7. John Lang, "Girl Demonstrator Faces Loss of Job," *Associated Press*, July 19, 1971, 4.
8. Morton Dean, "Vietnam Veteran #214568," *CBS Evening News*, December 27, 1971, https://tvnews.vanderbilt.edu/broadcasts/214568.
9. Nation editors, "Heroes without Honor Face the Battle at Home," *Time*, April 23, 1979.
10. Peter Jennings, "Vietnam Veteran #95827," *ABC Evening News*, April 30, 1985, https://tvnews.vanderbilt.edu/broadcasts/95827.
11. Bob Greene had a column in the *Chicago Tribune* in July 1987 in which he solicited stories of being spit upon. He later compiled the responses in *Homecoming: When the Soldiers Returned from Vietnam* (New York: G. P. Putnam's Sons, 1989).
12. Ron Kovic, *Born on the Fourth of July: 40th Anniversary Edition* (Brooklyn, NY: Akashik, 2016), 192–93. John Kifner confirmed some details of the account in a front-page story, "War Foes Harass G.O.P. Delegates," *New York Times*, August 23, 1972.
13. Read about the history of VEVRAA at pewpew.substack.com/p/vevraa-history.
14. See section 402 of Public Law 93-508, passed December 3, 1974.
15. Michael Gardner, "Harry Truman and Civil Rights: Moral Courage and Political Risks," University of Virginia, *UVA News Makers*, September 26, 2003.
16. Harry S. Truman Presidential Library and Museum, *To Serve These Rights: The Report of the President's Committee on Civil Rights*; https://www.trumanlibrary.gov/library/to-secure-these-rights.
17. President Harry Truman, "Address before the NAACP," June 29, 1947, https://www.americanrhetoric.com/speeches/harrystrumannaacp.htm.
18. "Attacks on United States Servicemen," Public Law 111–84, Section 4712. See also Statutes at Large, vol. 123, p. 2842. It has been codified into law in Title 18 of the US Code, at Section 1389.
19. *US v. Martin*, District Court, Western District of Wisconsin case number 3.17-cr-035-jdp.
20. Sentencing Memorandum of United States, *US v. Abdulkader*, page 15. District Court, Southern District of Ohio case number 1:16-cr-019.
21. US Commission on Civil Rights, *In the Name of Hate: Examining the Federal Government's Role in Responding to Hate Crimes*, November 13, 2019, https://www.usccr.gov/files/pubs/2019/11-13-In-the-Name-of-Hate.pdf.

22. See GIJustice.com/usccr for more information.

23. There are approximately twenty million veterans and eight million soldiers and dependents in the Total Force.

24. According to CDC, https://www.cdc.gov/ncbddd/disabilityandhealth/infographic -disability-impacts-all.html.

25. According to the 2019 Census, https://www.census.gov/quickfacts/fact/table/US /PST045219.

26. Jeffrey Jones, "LGBT Identification Rises to 5.6% in Latest U.S. Estimate," *Gallup*, February 24, 2012, https://news.gallup.com/poll/329708/lgbt-identification-rises -latest-estimate.aspx.

27. Until 2017, the university maintained a few Affirmative Action Plans (AAPs), one of which covered "Veterans and People with Disabilities." When I looked more recently for annual updates, a requirement of 38 USC 2412, I could not find any listed publicly.

28. Statement emailed to me for use in the complaint, under condition of anonymity, on October 3, 2017.

29. *Greer v. Chao*, 492 F.3d 962 (8th Cir. 2007), 5.

30. I was told of the results in June, but documents from a subsequent Freedom of Information Act request revealed that the conclusion had been decided two months prior, about a week after interviews were done.

31. Title 18, USC section 1519 prohibits altering records or documents within the jurisdiction of a federal agency. The Department of Labor opened an investigation into Duke on September 13, 2016. On November 7, 2016, Duke University altered two documents, "Discrimination Grievance Procedure" and "Harassment Policy & Procedures," to include "veteran status" in compliance with VEVRAA. In other words, Duke was noncompliant when the investigation began, and they altered records while being investigated. I pointed this out to investigators before they closed the file and I pointed it out in a written Request for Reconsideration. At no point did the DOL have any fucks to give about veterans' civil rights.

32. In their annual report to Congress, the Department of Labor has repeatedly omitted critical information required by 28 USC § 4212(c). Changes were made while this book was going to print. For more information, see https://pewpew.substack.com/ p/vevraa-complaints-3.

33. 38 USC 4212(c) requires the Secretary of Labor to report on the "the number of complaints…the actions taken thereon and the resolutions thereof." That responsibility has been delegated to VETS, which introduced its 2019 report, the very first sentence, with the statement "This report is prepared in accordance with Title 38, United States Code, sections 4107(c), 4212(c)…"

34. Since 2004, 30 percent of complaints filed on the basis of being White returned a finding of merit, but only 3 percent of complaints filed on the basis of being Black managed to do the same.

SAFETY BRIEF
(AN EPILOGUE)

1. "Disc Two: Special Features," Featurette, *Sergeant York: Two Disc Special Edition,* Warner Home Video, 2006.

MANDATORY FUN:
REQUIRED READING FOR
GODLY GRUNTS

Cain/Confession

- Mellinkoff, Ruth W. *The Mark of Cain.* Berkeley: University of California Press, 1981.
- Nelson, Hilde Lindemann. *Damaged Identities, Narrative Repair.* Ithaca, NY: Cornell University Press, 2001.
- Peters, David W. *Post-Traumatic God: How the Church Cares for People Who Have Been to Hell and Back.* New York: Morehouse, 2016.

Moses/Sacrifice

- Girard, René. *The Scapegoat.* Translated by Yvonne Freccero. Baltimore, MD: Johns Hopkins University Press, 1986.
- Watts, James W. *Ritual and Rhetoric in Leviticus: From Sacrifice to Scripture.* Cambridge: Cambridge University Press, 2007.
- Wiener, Nancy H., and Jo Hirschmann. *Maps and Meaning: Levitical Models for Contemporary Care.* Minneapolis: Fortress, 2014.

Jesus/Warrior

- Josephus. *The Wars of the Jews, or History of the Destruction of Jerusalem.* Translated by William Whiston. Project Gutenberg Ebook, 2009. gutenberg.org/files/2850/2850-h/2850-h.htm.
- Longman, Tremper, III, and Daniel G. Reid. *God Is a Warrior.* Grand Rapids, MI: Zondervan, 1995.

- Yoder Neufeld, Thomas R. *Put on the Armour of God: The Divine Warrior from Isaiah to Ephesians*. Sheffield: Sheffield Academic Press, 1997.

GIs in the NT
- Brink, Laurie. *Soldiers in Luke-Acts: Engaging, Contradicting, and Transcending the Stereotypes*. Tübingen: Mohr Siebeck, 2014.
- Kyrychenko, Alexander. *The Roman Army and the Expansion of the Gospel: The Role of the Centurion in Luke-Acts*. Boston: De Gruyter, 2014.
- Zeichmann, Christopher B. *The Roman Army in the New Testament*. Lanham, MD: Fortress, 2015.

George/Martyrdom
- Eusebius. *Ecclesiastical History*. Translated by Arthur C. McGiffert. Edinburgh: T&T Clark, 1997. ccel.org/ccel/schaff/npnf201/npnf201.
- Lactantius. *On the Death of the Persecutors*. Translated by A. Cleveland Coxe. Edinburgh: T&T Clark, 1997. ccel.org/ccel/lactantius/persecutors/anf07.
- Riches, Samantha. *St. George: Hero, Martyr and Myth*. Gloucestershire: Sutton, 2000.

Pachomius/Monasticism
- Athanasius. *Life of Antony*. Translated by Archibald Robinson. Edinburgh: T&T Clark, 1997. ccel.org/ccel/schaff/npnf204/npnf204.xvi.i.html.
- Barthel, Christian. "In Militia Dei? A Sociohistorical Perspective on the Pachomian Koinonia." *Zeitschrift für Antikes Christentum* 25, no. 3 (Dec. 2021).

- Rousseau, Philip. *Pachomius: The Making of a Community in Fourth-Century Egypt*. Berkeley: University of California Press, 1999.

Martin/Hagiography

- Delehaye, Hippolyte. Translated by V. M. Crawford. *The Legends of the Saints: An Introduction to Hagiography*. London: Longmans, Green, 1907.
- McClendon, James Wm., Jr. *Biography as Theology: How Life Stories Can Remake Today's Theology*. Eugene, OR: Wipf and Stock, 2002.
- Severus, Sulpicius. *Life of Martin*. hospstmartin.org/vita.

Francis/Pilgrimage

- Hill, Rosalind M. T. *Gesta Francorum: The Deeds of the Franks and the Other Pilgrims to Jerusalem*. Oxford: Clarendon, 1967.
- Thomas of Celano. *The First Life of Saint Francis*, 1.29. dmdhist.sitehost.iu.edu/francis.htm.
- Thurston, Herbert. *The Stations of the Cross: An Account of Their History and Devotional Purpose*. London: Burns & Oats, 1914. https://archive.org/details/stationsofcrossa00thuruoft.

Joan/Gender

- Deen, Edith. *All the Women of the Bible*. New York: Harper & Row, 1955.
- Pernoud, Régine, and Marie-Véronique Clin. *Joan of Arc: Her Story*. Translated by Jeremy duQuesnay Adams. Edited by Bonnie Wheeler. New York: St. Martin's, 1999.
- Williams, Kayla. *Love My Rifle More Than You: Young and Female in the U.S. Army*. New York: W. W. Norton, 2006.

Ignatius/Fitness

- Ignatius of Loyola. *A Pilgrim's Journey*. Translated by Joseph Tylenda. Ignatius Press, 1985.
- ———. *The Spiritual Exercises of St Ignatius of Loyola.* Translated by Elder Mullan. P. J. Kenedy & Sons, 1914. ccel.org/ccel/ignatius/exercises/exercises.
- Nieuwsma, Shenandoah. "Broken Spirits: A History of Spiritual Fitness Training in the United States Army since World War II." PhD diss., University of North Carolina, 2019. https://cdr.lib.unc.edu/concern/dissertations/cn69m5159.

Ralph/GI Justice

- Abernathy, Ralph. *And the Walls Came Tumbling Down*. New York: Harper & Row, 1989.
- Marsh, Charles. *The Beloved Community: How Faith Shapes Social Justice, from the Civil Rights Movement to Today*. New York: Basic Books, 2006.
- Parker, Christopher S. *Fighting for Democracy: Black Veterans and the Struggle against White Supremacy in the Postwar South*. Princeton, NJ: Princeton University Press, 2009.

Spit Shining

- Greene, Bob. *Homecoming: When the Soldiers Returned from Vietnam*. New York: G. P. Putnam's Sons, 1987.
- Mahedy, William. *Out of the Night: The Spiritual Journey of Vietnam Vets*. Greyhound Books, 2005.
- Siemon-Netto, Uwe. *The Acquittal of God: A Theology for Vietnam Veterans*. Eugene, OR: Wipf and Stock, 2008.

ABOUT THE AUTHOR

Logan M. Isaac spent over six years in the United States Army as an artillery forward observer, including a deployment in support of Operation Iraqi Freedom in 2004. He was discharged as a noncommissioned officer in 2006 and went on to earn a BA from Hawaii Pacific University and a Master of Theological Studies from Duke University. Logan spent a year teaching at Methodist University in North Carolina before leaving to study at the University of St. Andrews in Scotland, from which he received a Master of Letters in Systematic and Historical Theology in 2015. After returning to a teaching position at Duke University, he went on to earn a Certificate in Business Administration from Georgetown University and started Pew Pew HQ, a social enterprise based in the Washington, DC, metropolitan area. Logan is the sole author, as Logan Mehl-Laituri, of *Reborn on the Fourth of July* (InterVarsity, 2012) and *For God and Country (in That Order)* (Herald, 2013). His first book received a Publishers Weekly Starred Review, and he has served as a consultant or contributing author of nearly twenty additional publications, including books such as *The Gospel of Rutba* (Orbis, 2012) and *Jesus, Bombs, & Ice Cream* (Zondervan, 2012). He has been featured on the cover of *Christianity Today* magazine and was awarded an Evangelical Press Association award for Best Article Series for "Ponder Christian Soldiers" in 2016. He lives in Maryland with his spouse, his children, and two dogs.